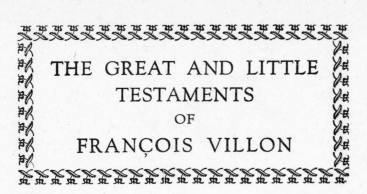

THE GREAT AND LITTLE
TESTAMENTS
OF
FRANÇOIS VILLON

THE TESTAMENTS
OF
FRANÇOIS VILLON

TRANSLATED BY
JOHN HERON LEPPER

Including the texts of
JOHN PAYNE AND OTHERS

LIVERIGHT PUBLISHING CORPORATION
NEW YORK

A BALLAD OF FRANCOIS VILLON

Prince of All Ballad-makers

By ALGERNON CHARLES SWINBURNE

Bird of the bitter bright gray golden morn
    Scarce risen upon the dusk of dolorous years,
First of us all and sweetest singer born
      Whose far shrill note the world of new men hears
      Cleave the cold shuddering shade as twilight clears;
When song new-born put off the old world's attire
And felt its tune on her changed lips expire,
    Writ foremost on the roll of them that came
Fresh girt for service of the latter lyre,
    Villon, our sad bad glad mad brother's name!

Alas the joy, the sorrow and the scorn,
    That clothed thy life with hopes and sins and fears,
And gave thee stones for bread and tares for corn
      And plume-plucked jail-birds for thy starveling peers
      Till death clipt close their flight with shameful shears;
Till shifts came short and loves were hard to hire,
When lilt of song nor twitch of twangling wire
    Could buy thee bread or kisses; when light fame
Spurned like a ball and haled through brake and briar,
    Villon, our sad bad glad mad brother's name.

Poor splendid wings so frayed and soiled and torn!
    Poor kind wild eyes so dashed with light quick tears!
Poor perfect voice, most blithe when most forlorn,
      That rings athwart the sea whence no man steers
      Like joy-bells crossed with death-bells in our ears!

v

What far delight has cooled the fierce desire
That like some ravenous bird was strong to tire
    On that frail flesh and soul consumed with flame,
But left more sweet than roses to respire,
    Villon, our sad bad glad mad brother's name.

Envoi

Prince of sweet songs made out of tears and fire,
A harlot was thy nurse, a God thy sire;
    Shame soiled thy song, and song assoiled thy shame
But from thy feet now death has washed the mire,
Love reads our first at head of all our quire,
    Villon, our sad bad glad mad brother's name.

CONTENTS

To
LOUIS J. McQUILLAND

VILLON

THE MAN AND THE POET

*T*HE SOLE OBJECT *of the following pages is
to bring together in a succinct form all that
we know, & it is not much, of the life of a man who
lived some four hundred years ago: a man of strong
passions and great genius; one whose poetry contains much levity & not a little pathos, a strange
medley where the most vulgar buffoonery cuts capers
on the stage beside the stern figures of tragedy &
regret; one whose manners appear to have been
none of the choicest even for that day of licence;
whose morals require the veil of charitable excuse;
whose whole career, as we know it, formed a chain
of discreditable escapades. Such was the scapegrace student of Paris University who has become
one of the glories of French literature, Master
Francis Villon.*

*He was born, as we learn from the Grand Testa-
ment, at Paris in the year 1431. The times were
troubled and unsettled, and the unrest was mirrored
in the lives of the people. For a long time war had
been in the land.*

The Hundred Years' War!

*The rightful king of France was exiled from his
capital. The French nation was a house divided*

against itself, suffering all the horrors of civil strife and foreign invasion.

The year that witnessed the poet's birth saw two other notable events in the history of France: the martyrdom of Jeanne d'Arc la bonne Lorraine *at Rouen from whose ashes rose the star of French unity, and the coronation of our Henry VI, then a boy of ten, as king of France in the Cathedral of Notre Dame de Paris. It is a striking coincidence that the very year which brought two such humiliations to France saw the birth of the man who leads the procession of her patriotic poets.*

Master Francis was five years old before the king of France enjoyed his own again in the city of Saint Geneviève, and many more had to pass after that before Paris recovered from the confusion of laws & manners introduced by a foreign occupation. The most susceptible years of the young poet's life were passed in a state of society that was weakened by civil war, corrupted by the vices of the camp, & surfeited with that unholy mixture of tyranny & licence which afflicts the life of a people in times of public insecurity. The administration of civil justice was in a chaotic condition: there was one law for the peasant, another for the burgess, yet another for the scholar, with different jurisdictions having authority over each class; thus a skilful criminal by playing off one magistrate against another might often ultimately escape the consequences of his misdeeds. We shall get a glimpse of what resulted in following the story of our poet.

It seems fairly certain that the name Villon is one of adoption, but by no means so certain what was his true patronymic, & scholars are divided in their opinions about his claims to be known as François de Montcorbier, de Monterbier, or de Monteclier. Possibly his signature may have favoured some latitude of doubt as in the case of Shakespere. At any rate he chose to call himself Villon, and no one had a better right to decide the name by which poſterity should know him.

This much is beyond dispute, as we have his own word for it, he ſprang from a family of the people & had no claim to rank with the noblesse. (Grand Teſtament: stanza XXXV). *In early youth the boy would seem to have been adopted by a prieſt Guillaume de Villon, who provided him with the means of ſtudying & helped him on the many occasions in after life when summer friends were not to be found though sought. Several passages in the* Grand Teſtament *witness the affeſtion the poet bore to his foſter-father; & when broken in health by the effects of riotous living & prison, the madcap appears less affeſted by his own miserable condition than the thought of the grief it will cause to his benefaſtor & also to his old mother,* la povre femme.

From his own revelations & contemporary evidence we learn only too exaſtly what the conduſt was that ruined Maſter Francis in health & reputation. It may be summed up as idleness, carelessness, a disregard for every kind of law, & a determination to seize the present moment, coſt what it might.

Villon was not a victim of self-deception. He does not search the stars for excuses, or mumble platitudes about fate. So far from being under any delusions about the cause of his sorrows, he tells us frankly that if his life has been a failure the fault was his own. In all his writings it would be hard to find a line accusing fortune or luck; he accepts what has happened without whining & speaks of the past without many glosses; nor does he deign to offer an apology to men, but carries his contrition to a place where he believes it will have a better chance of being accepted. He has the courage of his vices, but he also has the courage of his regrets; we know too little of his latter days to decide whether he had the courage of amendment.

Were nothing worse to be revealed than those sins of which Villon accuses himself in his poems, his Lehrjahre might be skimmed over with the excuse that his faults were those of his age & generation, redeemed in his case by wit & the love of merriment; but the advocatus diaboli *demands to be heard with extracts from mouldy old law papers, disinterred from the* Archives Nationales *by the industry of modern men of letters. They tell the following story.*

About nine o'clock on the evening of Corpus Christi Day, 1455, three young people were sitting together on a stone bench beneath the belfry of Saint Benoît le Bientourné in Paris. They had supped in company & were passing the fine summer evening amicably enough out of doors, chatting, gossiping or what not. One was a damsel, of whom we know nothing except her name Ysabeau, but we can picture her readily enough with her long, trailing robes, tight-fitting bodice & wide sleeves, her merry face peeping from beneath the curious steeple headdress of the times: no prude I opine. The second in that company was a priest, one Gilles, whose profession, alas, is no guarantee of his respectability. The third was a student of the university, Master Francis, called Villon from his adopted father who was one of the canons attached to the church beneath whose clock-tower they were gathered. Guillaume de Villon lived in the neighbourhood, & we may take it that his adopted son had slipped out of the house in order to spend a social hour with his two cronies or others of a more jovial kidney than were to be met with at home. The dryasdust law papers have preserved some details of his appearance: he was clad in a short mantle on account of the cold night air & at his girdle carried the dagger which was an indispensable part of the costume of the time.

The scene of peace beneath the belfry did not last long, for there entered a spark of discord in the shape of Philippe Chermoie, another priest, accompanied by a certain Jehan le Mardie, described as a Master of Arts. That the newly arrived cleric bore a grudge against one of the company soon became evident, for on Villon rising & inviting him and his companion to take a seat beside them on the bench Philippe Chermoie declared with a most unclerical

*oath: "I have found you at laſt, so you can make
up your mind to give me satisfaction!"*

*"Moſt reverend Maſter Philippe," replied Villon,
"what have I done to you? Why are you so angry?"*

*The only reply he received from the other was a
blow that ſtretched him on the pavement. Villon
picked himself up, and, without retaliating, de-
camped towards the cloiſter where his adopted
father lived. The three ſpectators of the brawl,
Mistress Ysabeau, Prieſt Gilles and Maſter Jehan
le Mardie made off at top ſpeed; they foresaw
trouble and did not wish to be drawn into it.*

*Chermoie pursued his enemy up to the doors of
the cloiſter where he overtook him. Then drawing
a long dagger from beneath his robe he ſtruck Villon
with it in the face, wounding him on the lower lip.
Villon, having by this time got out his own weapon,
ſtabbed the other in return, but the belligerent prieſt
was too carried away by rage to feel the wound.
At this ſtage in the proceedings Maſter Jehan le
Mardie reappeared and, no doubt with the idea of
doing his friend a good turn, grappled with Villon
and succeeded in disarming him; thereupon the latter
seeing himself weaponless picked up a paving-ſtone
and with it ſtruck Philippe Chermoie on the head,
so that he fell to the ground senseless.*

*With the prieſt disabled the brawl came to an
end. Villon fled to the house of a barber-surgeon in
order to get his wound dressed, & was queſtioned
by the leech as to how he came by his hurt, as the
profession was obliged by law to report such matters*

to the police, then as now, there as here, a body that
concerned itself much with names & addresses &
other folk's private affairs. Villon gave an account
of the quarrel & the true name of his antagonist,
but modestly offered a nom de guerre for himself;
the inference being that he wished to steer wide of
the forces of law & order. As for Philippe Chermoie, he was carried into a house near the scene of
the fight, & a surgeon & the mediæval equivalent of
a commissaire de police were summoned to attend
him. The officer asked him, if in the event of his
death he wished his friends & relatives to proceed
criminally against his adversary? He replied, that
he did not so desire, on account of certain causes
which had moved him to do as he had done. Evidently in the hour of death Chermoie's conscience
accused him of having been the aggressor & bring-
ing his fate upon himself. He was removed to a
hospital where he died in a few days, and Villon fled
away from Paris to escape prosecution. The exile,
however, was not to last for long. In January, 1456,
lettres d'abolition, otherwise a free pardon, was
granted him for the murder, on condition that he
conducted himself well in other matters, & had
never been convicted of any other crime or misde-
meanour.

As to the origin of the feud between Villon &
Chermoie we must fall back on conjecture. The
French commentators, typically enough, suggest a
histoire de femme, a lady in the case, & mention a
certain Katherine de Vauselles, on whose account

Villon once received a good drubbing, as he con-
fesses in one of the ballades; but there is nothing to
show that Chermoie had any interest in that affair,
or that the lady had anything to do with the quarrel
on Corpus Christi Day. So many names of fair
ladies occur in the poet's verse that it would be a
very acute critic who dared presume to saddle any
one of them with the discredit of the fatal quarrel
in the neighbourhood of Saint Benoît le Bientourné.
One of Villon's French editors remarks:

> It is probable that his love affairs were
> very varied & very transient. It is certain
> that they landed him in more than one
> scrape; that of the cloister Saint Benoît
> doubtless being the first in date.

This last conjecture seems highly improbable, but
let it pass.

So far Master Francis appears more sinned
against than sinning, but the next scrap of biography
that has come down to us, & be it noted that these
scraps are few & far between, carries the conviction
that we are not dealing with one who was a model
of all the virtues.

About Christmas, 1456, we find Villon preparing
to leave Paris once more. He was then living in
the house of his protector in the cloister Saint Benoît
where he had returned on receiving his pardon eleven
months before. By way of preparation for this
new excursion into the provinces he occupied some
time in writing a will in verse, the poem now known

as Le Petit Testament. *It was no new theme, for other versifiers had already brought this form of literary exercise into fashion, but Villon seasoned his legacies with a cynical humour & invective that were not borrowed from his predecessors. Most of the gibing allusions to his contemporaries cannot now be explained even by the commentators, & for the ordinary scholar the spice & flavour have not improved by keeping, but the poem is most valuable as affording us a glimpse at Villon's friends, their amusements & occupations, their haunts & their hobbies, their follies & their fates. The fact at once becomes disclosed, even were external evidence of another kind wanting, that the wild young man was hand in glove with all the ruffians of the University, in comparison with whom the* mauvais sujets *of our modern seats of learning would appear very miracles of innocence.*

In this connection let us hear what one of the editors has to say about student life in Paris in the fifteenth century.

The University of Paris with its privileges, which made it a state within the state, with its population gathered up from all over Europe and, for the greater part, without private resources, often concealed the most dangerous class of criminal, those whom a certain culture gave more capacity for mischief and more skill in evading the pursuit of justice. Every time that an assassin or a

robber belonging to the student class was arrested there ensued a conflict between the
ecclesiastical authorities, who claimed the
right to judge him as a clerk, and the royal
jurisdiction. The ecclesiastical authorities
almost invariably acquitted the criminals. In
order that the civil magistrate could lay
hands on them again crime had to succeed
crime, until the delinquents were considered
to have deprived themselves of the clerical
privilege, and to have fallen *in profundum
malorum;* this was the consecrated formula.

Such a favourable situation attracted to
the University a swarm of scoundrels, sons
of ruined families and rakes; to attain the
rank of scholar it was enough to enter one's
name for some course of lectures. In consequence of this, there soon developed brother-
hoods consisting of robbers, thieves, cheats
and picklocks; the lost legion of the Schools
gave most trouble to the Parisian police.

*There will be something to add later about this
brotherhood of criminals wherein Villon became an
initiate, but for the present let us return to* Le Petit
Testament, *whence an idea can be gained of the companions with whom he was hail fellow well met. His
associates are Regnier de Montigny who had fallen*
in profundum malorum *& whose privileges as a
cleric did not save his neck from the hangman's rope,
Perrcnet de la Barre who lived on what he could
make by cheating at dice, Jean le Loup and Chollet*

*who combined business with pleasure by robbing hen-
roosts, & many other youths of bad repute whose
ways of life were not such as commend themselves
to an apologist. What a commentary on the adage
that a man shall be known by his friends!*

*Alas, Villon's acquaintance with the seamy side
of life does not stop short at bad company in his
own station. He exhibits an unhealthy knowledge
of every tavern and disreputable haunt in old Paris;
he knows & is known by the police; he has even come
in contact with the whips of justice, and can judge
by experience of the view seen through the barred
windows of the Châtelet prison. Of a truth, says
one of his biographers drily, this is no novice; there
is nothing of the milksop about him!*

At the beginning of the Petit Testament *the poet
tells us that he is leaving Paris for Angers very soon,
& gives as reason for this departure the cruelty of
a lady with whom he is in love. Unfortunately for
his reputation the real reason for this journey is
now known; it was occasioned less by a woman's
frown than the jingling of an old gentleman's money-
bags & perhaps a dread of the gallows as well. To
understand the situation we must again examine the
criminal records of the time.*

*On the 9th of March, 1457, the priest & profes-
sors of the Collège de Navarre at Paris were thrown
into consternation by the discovery that during the
previous night the sacristy had been entered, the
treasure-chest broken open, & all the money in it,
amounting to five hundred golden crowns, a large*

*sum in those days, carried away. The police were
called in, & with the conservatism of their class proceeded to take notes & draw up a report. Their
investigations showed that a large iron-bound chest
had been broken open & also a smaller one chained
inside it containing merely memoranda of money
deposited at various times. They ransacked the
rooms of those supposed to be in charge of the
sacristy, but without result; they summoned a jury
of expert locksmiths, who examined the damaged
chest & declared the breaking open to be the work
of amateurs & of recent origin: that was all the
satisfaction the poor priests got for the time being.
The authorities discovered plenty of clues but not
the thieves.*

   *Some time passed & on the eve of Quasimodo
Sunday (admirers of Victor Hugo will appreciate
the date) a certain country clergyman, Messire
Pierre Marchant, rector of Paras in the diocese of
Chartres, came up to Paris on his lawful occasions.
Dining one day at a tavern he made the acquaintance of a student, a pleasant young fellow, Master
Guy de Tabarie, & aided, perhaps, by the good
cheer, the two soon became very friendly. So confidential did the younger man wax that he divulged
many things he had better have concealed, going to
the length of boasting that he was one of the most
skilful picklocks in Paris; nor did he hide the fact
that he had just escaped from the archbishop's
prison where he had been confined on account of this
fatal dexterity. Furthermore, when Messire Pierre*

mentioned the robbery at the Collège de Navarre as a matter agitating the minds of the idle, Guy de Tabarie asserted with pride that he had been one of the gang which had extracted the clerical treasures from the sacristy; and he then proceeded to describe the cracking of the crib with so much minuteness of detail that no doubt was left as to the genuine character of his story.

For reasons of his own, the country priest appeared not in the least shocked by these youthful indiscretions of his new-found friend; on the contrary, he was loud in his applause of such dexterity. Finding him such a genial old soul, Guy de Tabarie then escorted him to Notre Dame & showed him half a dozen young men lounging about the ambulatory who had sought sanctuary there after escaping from the archbishop's enforced lodgings. The fifteenth-century Parson Adams was introduced to these promising young prentice clergy & past masters in the craft of thieving, & gave himself out to be much edified by their conversation. So intimate did they become that Guy proposed Messire Pierre should join them in another robbery they contemplated. Its execution was being delayed, he said, only till the young gentlemen had provided themselves with false keys & till an Augustine monk of their acquaintance should return to Paris, he having promised to hide them in his chamber after the deed was done. Guy also gave his open-eared friend a great deal more information, which however interesting in itself as a commentary on student life of

*the day does not call for repetition here. One item,
however, throws some light on a journey undertaken
by a member of the gang.*

*One of their accomplices, said Guy de Tabarie,
was Maſter Francis Villon; and at present he was
at Angers in an abbey where he had an uncle a prieſt.
He was paying his visit there in order to find out all
about an old prieſt of the abbey who was supposed
to be worth five or six hundred crowns; & they were
only awaiting his return & report before they went
to Angers in a body to relieve the old man of the
trouble of looking after so much wealth.*

*Messire Pierre Marchant by this time thought
he had heard enough & withdrew himself from their
society. Soon after he went to the police &, in the
language of prisons,* blew the gaff. *It was quite a
year after that, however, before Guy de Tabarie was
at laſt arreſted & shut up in the Châtelet prison.
Juſtice in those days had leaden feet. Of course he
pleaded his quality as a scholar, & was at once removed to the archbishop's prison. Here in June,
1458, a sad day of reckoning came to him. The
scheme of ſpoliation devised by him & his comrades
was too much in advance of the times; the queſtion
both ordinary & extraordinary was applied, & under
the torture of the rack he gave a full account of the
robbery at the Collège de Navarre, incriminating
amongſt others Francis Villon. Be it noted in passing, Guy bitterly complained of having being cheated
by his companions in the division of the ſpoil.*

Villon was arreſted & interrogated in the same

way as his friend, that is under torture, but of a different kind. The torment consiſted in making the poet swallow large quantities of cold water, a beverage for which he ever after entertained a hearty & not unnatural aversion. We may take it that he made a full confession, for he was found guilty & sentenced to be hanged. It was while lying under sentence of death that he composed the famous couplet, to be freely & euphemiſtically translated as follows:

> Here is Francis, one of the boys,
> Born in Paris, near to Ponthoise,
> Whose neck in a noose must learn the joys
> Of weighing his body's avoirdupois.

He also wrote a ballade at the same time, one of his beſt, wherein a piĉture is drawn of the poet & his companions as they will appear to onlookers when their souls have gone to find le grand peut-être. *In those days the corpses of criminals were exposed on the gibbet where they suffered & did not receive Chriſtian burial, a vile old cuſtom, now happily abolished, that laſted till well within the laſt century; it cannot have been a grateful sight to the virtuous, & assuredly did not aĉt as a deterrent to the wicked.*

To return to our poet's fate. The rope was not easily knotted in those days to contraĉt the throat that claimed benefit of clergy. Villon appealed to the Parliament, & no doubt his adopted father brought influence to bear in high quarters: in any case, the appeal was allowed. The sentence was commuted into banishment from the kingdom, which may be interpreted as banishment to a safe distance from Paris.

Villon appears to have chosen Meung as his St. Helena, for there he turns up in 1461, having come to loggerheads with the authorities again, now personified in Thibault d'Aussigny bishop of Orleans. The cause of the disagreement so far remains unrevealed, but it resulted in Villon spending the whole summer of that year in an underground dungeon of the Castle of Meung on a diet of water and stale bread, and not too much of the bread. No doubt the bishop thought these lodgings the most suitable spot for an embryo cleric of knavish tendencies, & in laying Villon by the heels was actuated by the most worthy motives; unhappily for the prelate's good repute we possess only Villon's account of the matter, & it is hardly to be expected that he should have viewed their little difference of opinion with unprejudiced eyes. Hence, rightly or wrongly, Thibault d'Aussigny is held up to the odium of all succeeding ages as an oppressor & unjust judge. Danger dogs his footsteps who offends a poet: the fifteenth century bishop finds himself in the company of many distinguished men whose characters have suffered because they fell foul of contemporaries who had the knack of catching the ear of posterity. What Voltaire did for Frederick the Great, what Skelton did for Cardinal Wolsey, that was done for

*Thibault d'Aussigny by Villon at the first opportu-nity. That opportunity might never have come, &
the world might have been the poorer wanting* Le
Grand Testament, *had not the young king Louis
XI made a state entry into Meung on the 1st of
October, 1461. To celebrate this event the gaols
were thrown open, & among other prisoners released
was the scholar scamp.*

*His sojourn in the dungeon had ruined his health,
already impaired by the excesses of his previous life,
and he came into the open air prematurely grey, his
vitality sapped, &, as he says himself, already an old
man at thirty. What he thought about Meung, its
bishop & his officials may be read in detail in* Le
Grand Testament *itself.*

*The hardships which had broken Villon's body
had at the same time tempered & refined his spirit.
Too weakened by privation to fly back at once to
the gay, careless, wanton way of life that had been
his delight aforetime, he turned to poetry for con-solation. Helped, no doubt, by friends & his
adopted father, he withdrew to some quiet lodging,
we do not know in what city, & there composed* Le
Grand Testament, *his magnum opus, a wonderful
poem the world will not soon let die. And with this
swan song Master Francis disappears from our ken.*

*Whether his health returned & with it he betook
himself to his former courses we do not know; the
black curtain of the centuries has come down on the
stage where he acted, & no voice out of the darkness
tells us anything more of his hates or jests or sor-*

rows or loves; not even the year of his death or name of his final resting place has come down to us.

Only one other significant fact regarding his life has to be recorded. During the fifteenth century an association called the Beggars, Les Gueux, had come into existence, forming a kind of mediæval free-masonary of crime, distinguished by grades or degrees of eminence, & possessing a cant language the better to conceal its mysteries. As this brotherhood had modelled itself on the rules of the Guild of Merciers, one of the names it assumed to distinguish one of its tribes (there were at least five of these tribes paying allegiance to the Roi de Thunes, the grand master of these ragamuffins) was that of the mercerots, or mercelots. To this fraternity there is no doubt that Villon belonged. In Le Grand Testament he refers to himself as a mercerot de Rennes, & he wrote ballades in the jargon of the order, which remained a puzzle to commentators till the genius & industry of M. Vitu showed the way to their meaning. Knowing this fact helps us to a better understanding of why all his life Villon fell from one scrape into another, & it also may explain some of the obscurity met with in his poetry which may have an esoteric meaning not to be understood by the profane.

Thus far we have found nothing very worthy of examination, an idle, dissipated, unbalanced, rhyming scholar, without pride & without shame; such is the Villon revealed by contemporary records, to borrow again the words of a French biographer, a true bandit.   But to know all is to forgive all.   Quite another man discloses himself in his poetry; the sin & shame still cling to him but cannot obscure his fascination & charm.

In what does that charm consist: why does he fascinate us?   A friend to whom I put this question replied: "Because he is so modern."   Does not that criticism, however, hold good of the whole galaxy of immortals?   Your true bard, whether he lived in the centuries before Christ, or in the dark ages, or in our self-styled days of enlightenment, possesses the magic of being able to make the human heart throb in time to his music, & so far as records go the human heart does not seem to have altered much through the æons.   Since first men began to inscribe their thoughts & feelings on dead materials, from the first incised flint to the latest evening edition, the sage, the historian, the poet has been assured of a larger audience than draws breath in his own day, an audience, too, that goes on widening, if the message be worth hearing.   In the great choir of poets singing of the eternally interesting in more tongues than Babel knew we cannot deny Villon an honoured place; for he is concerned with things that will attract men's thoughts so long as humanity remains what it is; & his outlook on life is not bounded by the environment of his own generation, but transcends prejudices & reaches a standpoint whence the trifles that make up an individual existence become merged in the stream that bears all mankind forward to fulfil its destiny.   He sees & describes the very river of life whereof at the moment we form atoms; he thinks our very thoughts; he dreamt the same dreams as we in our youth; he has anticipated the philosophy of our riper years; no wonder we find him interesting.

As few writers have made a more complete confession of their feelings or faults, after studying his poems for some time we begin to know the writer very well indeed & can supplement the scanty facts of his biography by what we learn from himself. These bits of self-revelation enable us to understand him better, & this essay may fittingly be closed with a few indications to serve as general sign-posts for the student.

He was no profound scholar, & yet the width of his knowledge is surprising. Contemporary & ancient history are drawn on by him with ease when the lines of a ballade have to be filled with imagery, or an illustration found to parallel his own mishaps. The philosophy of the day is sufficiently familiar to him to be parodied in Le Petit Testament. *He can argue theology in verse with imaginary opponents. Latin is well known to him; with Greek he has an acquaintance of sorts, & has evidently read some of the* New Testament *in that tongue. He has observed operatives working at their craft, merchants plying their trades, the learned professions engaged in their occupations, & is able to borrow metaphors & similes from them all to enliven his own verses. If Villon's knowledge was merely that of an idle scholar, as he asserts, then the standard of learning*

*obtainable at a fifteenth-century university was by
no means to be despised.*

*His education as a lover appears to have been
equally extensive; but it suffered from the licence of
the times. The Hundred Years' War had had its
effect upon morals as destructively & as surely as
all wars must tend to destroy idealism & exalt brute
passion. Undoubtedly he met many facile beauties
in his years of adolescence; undoubtedly his behaviour was abominable; undoubtedly on many occasions his pleasant sins entailed painful penalties; &
these perhaps are some of the reasons why his verse
is lacking in that high respect, that tender chivalry
we are more accustomed to associate with a poet's
conception of women. Compare the work of
Chaucer writing three generations previously & no
one can hesitate to call the Englishman the better
gentleman. But before passing judgment let it not
be forgotten that the latter was writing in the
shadow of a court, in a land undevastated by invasion
& outrage, in a position of comfortable independence that always induces a man to see the best side
of things; while the Frenchman was poor, the citizen
of a country impoverished by an alien mailed fist, &
occupied that grade of society, the intellectual bour-
geoisie, most susceptible to all the moral diseases
begotten by the aftermath of war.*

*Yet Villon, as we shall see in reading his poems,
did not wholly lose his respect for womanhood.
Misfortune in waylaying him seems too often to
have worn petticoats, & he retaliates with enough*

ribald jests and sarcasms directed against the whole female sex. Katherine de Vauselles is worth a whipping to him, & he sacrifices all womankind in a ballade by way of retaliation; Rose makes a fool of him, & he has some bitter things to say about feminine cunning; another damsel deserts him, & he vents his disappointment in language gathered from the Parisian gutter. Yet no mere cynic & voluptuary could have written those marvellous pieces of delight The Complaint of the Fair Armouress *& the* Ballade of Dead Ladies. *If he wasted too much of his time with* la grosse Margot, *still he was not without his dreams of* la bonne Lorraine: *he opens a mouth soiled by the husks of the Prodigal to praise the saints in heaven with no unmelodious hymns.*

It may seem a paradox to call Villon a moral writer, for few have given us sadder pictures of human depravity or shown better acquaintance with evil things; yet no one has portrayed more exactly the unavoidable ugliness & inevitable retributions that accompany vice. If a man breaks God's commandments he must pay the price, declares our poet; & he drives home the argument much more convincingly than Defoe is able to do with all his sermonising, or Swift with all his grossness. No man who reads Villon's account of his own peccadilloes will be tempted to follow in the same path. He strips vice so completely that not even a rag of glamour is left her. The process is indecorous, but certainly not immoral.

From one inexhaustible source of delight to a

poet, the marvel & beauty of nature, Villon drew but little, & indeed seems to be lacking in a perception of it, for he weaves no magic out of woods, hills & meres in his verse. The country to him is a place of hard work & sudden dangers. Clowns till its fields, wolves & bandits lurk among its copses. Perhaps this indicates a deliberate breaking away on his part from the conventional mediæval school of poetry, which demanded that every prosodical exercise should begin with a description of a May morning in the fields, with a sufficiently lengthly list of birds singing in the boughs, & dewdrops hanging on every flower the poet could recall to mind. The rapture had been overdone by a swarm of rhyming clerks, & few of them could compress the beauty of such a landscape into lines such as these:

The bisy lerkë, messager of day,
Salueth in hir song the morwe grey;
And fyery Phebus ryseth up so brightë,
That all the orient laugheth of the lightë,
And with his stremës dryeth in the grevës
The silver dropës, hanging on the levës.

The country to Villon is a place where idle scholars may steal ducks out of ponds, where brambles grow that tear the clothes, where there are frozen rivers in winter & a hot sun in summer. He prefers to be a poet of the town. He performs his "observaunce to May" in the tavern; bubbles of wine delight his eyes more than dewdrops hanging

*on the thorn; & for him the minſter bells ringing the
Angelus take the place of feathered songſters. Yet
he had been haunted by the charm of echoes re-
turning across still lakes & rippling waters, & enshrined the experience in unforgettable lines. He
may not, like certain contemporary descendants of
the Lake School, exercise his ingenuity in making
poetry of seedsmen's catalogues & naturaliſts' note-
books, & prefers to concern himself with humanity;
but he never grows artificial or precious. When he
deals with the certainty of life's end & the uncertainty shrouding the further side of the gate through
which we all muſt pass, he rises far above the narrow
ſtreets & cramped dwellings wherein his life was
caſt. His verse swells up in a haunting dirge for
all the beauty, goodness & wisdom that have gone
the path of darkness before us. The beſt that life
holds, so runs his threnody, muſt have its exit
through this portal, leaving not a trace behind, no
more than do laſt year's snows.*

*Life is good, says his philosophy; & to be alive is
in itself a consolation. Better a living pauper than
a dead plutocrat; & for this reason he would not
change places with Jacques Coeur, who was the
Rothschild of his generation. This sentiment reminds us of those pathetic lines written by Heine on
his death-bed, wherein he bewails that the moſt miserable Philiſtine will soon be a better man than he,
the hero gone to a world of shadows.*

*Even on the very brink of the grave Villon muſt
have his jeſt, for he was no reſpecter of* **solemnities,**

*though he seems to have been orthodox enough as a
Christian. In one of his mordant bequests he leaves
to the hospital for the blind his large spectacles,
without their case, so that the bedesmen whose duty
was "in seemly sort their bodies to engrave" may
see how to bury the righteous apart from the sinners
in the cemetery. Then his very jest leads him back
to the old theme; all men are equal in death:*

.The clerk from master who can tell?

*Platitudes, doubtless, yet the type of reflection
that never fails to strike our self-conceit with all the
point of an epigram.*

*We are now led to consider two distinguishing
characteristics of our poet, wit, that volatile salt to
season the food of the gods, & the sense of humour,
a thing we all pride ourselves upon possessing, yet
find so hard to define. To pick out examples of
both will not be difficult; to choose the more decorous
is not so easy, for no demesne was too sacred for
Villon when in pursuit of a jest. He reached his
high-water mark, perhaps, in writing of the ladies
of Paris & Master Jehan Cotard; but it would be
captious to give the crown to one example of his
inimitable method of laying hard names under con-
tribution for rhymes to his ballades & illustrations
to his arguments. As a typical example of his irony
take the following stanza:*

These women too of tarnished fames
Grown old in poor and wretched state,

Beholding younger, pampered dames
Who still can charm and captivate,
Demand why God decreed their date
Of birth so soon, for they've grown old.
God holds His peace; for in debate
He could not match a female scold.

No one who reads the Grand Testament *will require proof of Villon's insight into the human heart;
enough would even be found in the two ballades
ostensibly addressed as sermons to those who were
following the wandering fires whereby he himself
had been misled. Truth to tell, these two poems
display more knowledge of iniquity than conviction
of remorse & rather abound in plain speaking than
in a tendency to edification. Yet there was nothing
of the Pharisee about Villon: while he did not hesitate to offer caustic comments on the mote in his
neighbour's eye, he makes no attempt to conceal the
beam in his own, otherwise we should not have made
the acquaintance of* la grosse Margot.
*A creature of impulse, while taking many wrong
paths he yet had longings & dissatisfactions, & he
summed up in one line his philosophic acceptance of
the riddle of life:*

I know everything, except myself.

*Thereto he was a keen observer of his fellow men,
& has painted for us the Falstaff of his days, the
pleasant lad changed into an old buffoon; the young*

*gallants strutting about to show off their fawn-col-
oured boots; Dalilah with her myriad wiles; Dr.
Slop with his lancets; mine host amid his barrels;
the magistrates among their papers; the police in
their habits as they lived; the underworld of old
Paris; the whole dance of life in a fifteenth-century
city.*

*We must add to the foregoing qualities his charity
in judging of others' faults & failings, a charity
never censorious & so wide that it might be interpreted as indifference, were it not that he condemns
the sin but not the sinner. It appears sometimes
with epigrammatic terseness, as when he asserts that
'tis need drives men to devilment & hunger wolves
to leave the wood; sometimes it accompanies a personal apology & excuse; sometimes it shrouds the
faults of a sinner, such as the fair Armouress, by
compelling us to throw the cloak of our pity over
all that has been done amiss.*

*All these traits are pleasing; & truly, while the
spirits of men continue to be moved by wit & pathos
blended together into melodious verse, so long will
the scapegrace singer find readers, lovers and apolo-
gists.*

*It is by a lover rather than an apologist that the
following translation of* The Testaments *has been
made. Even those with a fair knowledge of modern
French will be hard put to it at times to find out
Villon's meaning, & some little study is required to
master his language & tricks of style. This English version being intended as a guide for those who*

wish to know the poet better in the incomparable original is very literal, & while indulging in euphemistic circumlocutions at times on account of certain unsavoury puddles, yet endeavours to follow closely on the poet's footsteps. It is enough for the translator to indicate his object & let the judgment of others be the touchstone of his success.

THE LAY OF MASTER FRANCIS VILLON

COMMONLY KNOWN AS

THE LITTLE TESTAMENT.

Written in 1456.

THE LAY OF MASTER FRANCIS VILLON

COMMONLY KNOWN AS

THE LITTLE TESTAMENT.

Written in 1456.

I.

THIS year of fourteen fifty-six
    I *Francis Villon,* man of letters,
With might and main, full speed, prefix
Advice to all in Fortune's fetters,
To take the judgment of your betters
About your work, the truth to know;
Vegece has made us all his debtors,
The sage of Rome, by saying so.

II.

This winter, as was said before,
Near Christmas, season deathly old,
When wolves eat wind and nothing more,
And men are held indoors by cold
Where hearthstones glowing faggots hold,
The will I won to break a way
From Love's sweet gaol, whose walls enfold
My breaking heart this many a day.

III.

This way I take to end my anguish,
For She is there, before my eyes,
Quite satisfied to see me languish,
No happier in any wise:

3

My sorrows and complainings rise
Demanding vengeance from above
From amorous gods of every guise
And cure for all my pangs of love.

IV.

As I believe, she showed me favour
With soft regrets and fine deceit
To lend duplicity more savour
And make my overthrow complete;
But as a horse of four white feet
What seemed so fair but brought displeasure:
I must replant this pleasaunce sweet
And go to dig for other treasure.

V.

Full harsh and hard was her oppression;
For she who cast a spell on me,
Though I am guiltless of transgression,
Has doomed me die, and her decree
Is fixed that I shall cease to be.
I find no safety but in flight.
She means to break my life, I see,
Nor will take pity on my plight.

VI.

This danger to escape, I trow,
The best plan is to run away.
Adieu! I'm off to Angers now,
Since she ungraciously says nay,
Nor will a shred of ruth display.
Though free from bodily complaints,
I die Love's martyr, I might say,
Thus numbered with his band of saints.

VII.

Although departing brings despair,
Needs muſt, in truth, that I should fly,
As I conceive of the affair:
She loves another on the sly.
No kipper of Boulogne so dry
And taſteless as my wretched fate!
May God in mercy hear my cry:
For I am in a piteous ſtate.

VIII.

Well then, since go away I muſt,
And of return uncertain feel:
(Since I'm a being formed of duſt,
No more than others brass or ſteel;
Unſtable is all human weal
And death cannot be scared away:)
So, setting out, I now reveal
My will, these presents, in this lay.

IX.

Then firſt, in His our Father dear,
The Son, and Holy Spirit's name,
Our Lady's too, whom we revere,
Whose grace keeps all of us from shame,
I leave, God helping me, my fame
To *Guillaume Villon,* foſter sire,
My goods and chattels, and proclaim
The honour that those names inspire.

X.

To her who harried me so hard
And banished, as you'll call to mind,

From every joy in life debarred,
All pleasure being left behind,
To her I leave my heart enshrined,
Pale, piteous, shrivelled up and thin;
It perished by her deeds unkind,
May God forgive her this her sin!

XI.

And *Ythier Marchant* shall get,
Joint heir with *Master Cuckold John,*
To both of whom I'm much in debt,
My trenchant sword of steel; undrawn,
Because, by chance, it lies in pawn
For some small trifle, which when paid,
I order that mine host anon
Shall hand them back the trusty blade.

XII.

Item, the *White Horse* tavern sign
To *Saint Amant* and *Mule* as well.
Blaru, that diamond of mine
And baulking *Ass with Brindled Fell.*
The bull, whose opening letters spell
Omnis utriusque sexus,
That with the Carmelites played hell,
To parish priests for present use.

XIII.

To *Jehan Trouvé,* the butcher chap,
A sheep that's young and fat be brought,
Thereto a feather whisk to flap
The flies that taint his ox unbought

Or cow; and when the villain's caught
Who lifts her by the neck to thieve her,
Let him receive a collar taut
And perish of a gallows fever.

XIV.

To *Master Robert Vallée* now,
A clerk of Parliament, sans riches,
No hill or dale is his I trow.
He'll have a noble keepsake, which is
A special pair of under breeches,
That also lie in pawn, the stuff
To make a hood, with darns and stitches,
For *Jehanneton,* his bit of fluff.

XV.

Because he holds a decent post
He needs more pay, and might be led
Entirely by the Holy Ghost,
Because a trifle cracked, 'tis said;
The "Art of Memory" be read
To cure him, taken from Tom Fool;
For no more wisdom's in his head
Than lies within a wooden stool.

XVI.

And furthermore, I will bestow
Said *Robert's* livelihood, and tell,
(No need to let your envy grow!)
You friends of mine, that you must sell
My hauberk, spend the money well,
Some house near St. Jacques' steeple seek,
Wherein this popinjay may dwell
And copy deeds all Easter Week.

XVII.

To friend *Jacques Cardon* my bequeſt
Both absolute is and profuse:
To wit, my gloves and silken veſt;
With willow acorns for his use,
And, every day, a fatted goose,
A capon burſting through its skin,
Ten tots of milk-white vineyard juice,
And lawsuits two, to keep him thin.

XVIII.

René de Montigny, three hounds,
As nobly born, I dedicate;
And *Jehan Raguyer* shall have three pounds
As charge upon my whole eſtate;
Yet stay! I can't anticipate
How rich I may become ere long:
To friends be too considerate
And rob my heirs, were surely wrong.

XIX.

Item, I leave my lord of *Grigny*
Bicêtre in need of overhauling,
And six hounds more than to *Montigny,*
With *Nygon* tower that's near to falling;
And to that baſtard caterwauling,
Mouton, who summonses his betters,
I fain would give a proper mauling
And place for slumber, bound in fetters.

XX.

To *James Raguyer* the *Popin* Fountain,
With chickens and blancmange and brill,

In short, of food a very mountain;
A rabbit cooked with choicest skill,
The *Fir-Cone* cellar at his will
To ope and shut, with feet to fire
And hooded gown to guard from chill;
And tarlets too, should he desire.

XXI.

To *Master Jehan Mautaint* and *Peter
Bassenier,* for jointly sharing,
The Provost's favour, none is fleeter
To fine and punish without sparing;
To *Proctor Fournier* for his wearing
Light caps and shoes with toes embossed,
All of my cobbler's own preparing,
Meet fashion for this time of frost.

XXII.

Item, the Captain of the Guard
Shall with the *Helmet* be bedight;
His men who keep their watch and ward
And stumble over stalls at night,
I leave to them the *Lantern's* light
And rubies two; they are requested
With their best dungeon to requite
The donor, if he be arrested.

XXIII.

To *Perrenet Marchant* I give,
The *Bastard de la Barre* renowned,
(No better dealer e'er did live)
Of straw three trusses, sweet and sound,

To spread as mattress on the ground
His amorous calling to pursue,
Whereby his living muſt be found,
The only trade he ever knew.

XXIV.

Then to the *Wolf* and *Chollet* falls
As legacy the ducklings which
Are snatched at dusk, beneath the walls,
As is their cuſtom, from a ditch;
A mantle long and wide to hitch
About their prey, nor aught disclose,
Wood, charcoal, peas and gammon-flitch,
And my old waders lacking toes.

XXV.

I leave, in pity of their cases,
To three young boys by Fate derided,
All mentioned in their proper places,
Three orphans wholly unprovided,
All barefoot, all three hollow-sided,
And wormlike naked altogether,
My order is that they be tided
At leaſt o'er all this wintry weather.

XXVI.

Colin Laurens the firſt, the others
Girart Goussouyn and *Jehan Marceau,*
Devoid of goods and sires and mothers,
To each, who is not worth a row
Of pins, a slice of land shall go,
Or nimble fourpence paid in gold.
Good eating all these boys will know
In time to come, when I've grown old.

XXVII.

I here surrender and resign,
Two poor clerks from poverty to free,
Those high collegiate rights of mine,
The claim to be a nominee
Acquired on taking my degree;
Their names are here below included:
'Tis Charity that works in me
And Nature, seeing them denuded.

XXVIII.

They're *Guillaume Cotin,* I declare,
And *Thibault de Vitry,* for each
Is Latin scholar, poor and bare,
Not quarrelsome, of peaceful speech,
And fit in any church to preach.
For *Guillot Gueuldry's* house-rent yet
Incontinent their hands shall reach,
While waiting something more to get.

XXIX.

St. Antoine's Cross that all may view,
The tavern sign that hangs so plain,
I leave them too, with billiard cue
And daily draughts from out the *Seine:*
To those poor pigeons laws constrain
In cages barred to spend their life,
My mirror bright without a stain,
And favours from the gaoler's wife.

XXX.

Item, I leave the hospitals
My windows hung with cobweb-stuff;

To outcasts under butchers' stalls,
To each of them a hearty cuff,
To tremble at a visage gruff,
To go unshaven, starve and shiver,
Coat tattered, breeches scant enough,
Pinched, frozen, wet as any river.

XXXI.

My barber shall have this concession,
The shreds and clippings of my hair,
The whole in undisturbed possession;
My cobbler, shoes that need repair;
The ragman, clothes with many a tear;
And they shall have the residue
Of things that I have ceased to wear
For less than what they cost when new.

XXXII.

Item, I leave the begging friars
And nuns and tenders of the shrines,
All dainties that a man desires,
Flawns, capons and fat jellied chines;
Then let them preach the Fifteen Signs,
And keep on piling up the platter.
The *Carmelites* make concubines
Of our friends' wives, which doesn't matter.

XXXIII.

Jehan de la Garde, who's spiced too much,
The *Golden Mortar* sign shall claim,
From *St. Mor* church a votive crutch
To crush his mustard in the same.

But he who plays the lawyers' game
And threatens to begin a suit,
Saint Anthony set him aflame!
That's my bequest to him, the brute!

XXXIV.

To *Merebeuf* be handed down
And *Nicolas de Louviers* old,
An eggshell stuffed with many a **crown**
And franc, as full as it will hold.
While to the *Gouvieulx* porter bold,
Pierre Rousseville, without delay,
A larger sum of cash in gold,
Such crowns as princes give away.

XXXV.

At last, while sitting at my writing
To-night, alone, in humour prime,
This lay composing and enditing,
I heard the *Sorbonne* belfry chime
At nine o'clock, its proper time,
The Angelus rang through the air;
And so an end was made, for I'm
Accustomed then to say a prayer.

XXXVI.

Thereat, I fell into a doze,
But not from wine I swear to you,
My wits went wandering I suppose;
I saw Dame Memory review
Her shelves, collect in order due
Concurrent mental operations,
Opinions either false or true,
And other psychic ideations.

XXXVII.

Thereto our eſtimative motions,
Whereby prosperity we gain,
Cognition and conceptive notions,
Whence, when diſturbed, arises plain
A like disorder in the brain
And, monthly, men demented grow;
I read it, and the sense retain,
In *Ariſtotle* long ago.

XXXVIII.

My sensifacient syſtem drove
The loom Imagination plied
Which divers paradoxes wove,
My sovereign part was quite defied,
Suspended, even might have died,
Forgetful of all moods and tenses,
While I in Schoolmen's jargon tried
To prove th' alliance of the senses.

XXXIX.

Since now my senses were at reſt
And I had found the matter out,
I thought to finish my bequeſt;
My ink was frozen round about,
The wind had blown my candle out,
There was no fire to light it at,
So wrapped up in my mantle ſtout
I fell asleep, and that was that.

XL.

By *Francis Villon,* name renowned,
On date aforesaid made and writ,

No figs or dates with him abound.
Of all his chattels not one whit,
Though black as scrubbing-brush with grit,
But for some special friend is meant;
Some coppers make his only bit
Of cash, and they will soon be spent.

THE GREAT TESTAMENT

OF

MASTER FRANCIS VILLON.

Written in 1461.

Here beginneth the Great Testament of Master
Francis Villon.

I.

Not wholly fool nor wise man quite
I've come to this my thirtieth year
And drunk up all my shame outright,
In spite of many pains severe
Thibault D'Aussigny, as is clear,
Inflicted on me of design;
Although a spiritual peer
He certainly is none of mine.

II.

As lord or bishop he from me;
Shall neither faith nor homage find;
No land of his I hold in fee;
And I am not his hart or hind.
A summer's tide on crusts I pined
And water cold by his decree.
He starved me sorely, harsh or kind
God be to him as he to me.

16

III.

Though some may deem these things absurd
And say here sounds a sland'rous tone,
Indeed, I speak no lying word
And all abusive aims disown.
I wish him this mischance alone:
May Jesus from His heavenly seat
If mercy unto me was shown
To him an equal measure mete.

IV.

If he was harsh and hard to me
Yet more than I do here unfold,
God's own affair then let it be
To pay the debt incurred of old.
But since our Mother Church doth hold
Us bound to pray for all our foes:
That I am wrong then be it told;
Of all this coil let God dispose.

V.

Now, by the soul which late did part
From good *Cotard* for him I'll pray!
But stay, this muſt be learnt by heart,
For reading irks me every way.
I'll say it as the *Picards* say.
Who knows it not may liſt and learn,
And so it may some later day
At *Lille* or *Douai* serve his turn.

VI.

Thus, if that prelate claims this aid,
By my baptismal faith I swear

To heaven there shall be conveyed
A secret, unreluctant prayer.
My psalter, I shall find it there,
(Not leather-bound but none the worse) . . .
The *Deus Laudem* will declare
My feelings in the seventh verse.

VII.

So I the Son of God implore
That my poor prayers may make their ways
To Him who heard my plaints before;
Who mixed a spirit with my clays,
Who saved me, too, from great dismays
And sent to me deliverance;
His and Our Lady's be the praise
And *Louis'*; our good king of France.

VIII.

To whom may God give *Jacob's* dower,
The glory and the honour sure
Of *Solomon;* in point of power
He lacks not, nor for courage pure.
To keep his memory secure
While earth pursues her wonted ways
May our good monarch's reign endure
Methuselah's full span of days.

IX.

And grant his eyes may yet behold
A dozen royal children first,
Like *Charlemagne* both brave and bold
And good as was *Saint Martin* erst;

All males, at queenly bosom nursed.
Like joys the *Dauphin* too attend;
Of deſtined ills be these the worſt,
Then *Paradise* to make an end.

X.

But now since I am feeble grown,
With more of health than fortune **spent,**
And while I yet can call my own
The little sense that heaven lent,
To borrow more was not my bent,
My laſt will I have here expressed
In this my ſtablished teſtament,
And hereby do revoke the reſt.

XI.

I write in sixty-one, the year
Our noble king delivered me
From *Meung* and its harsh prison **cheer**
And life reſtored with liberty,
To whom in all humility,
While life blood warms my being's **core**
Or his, I'll bend a duteous knee,
Recalling benefits of yore.

XII.

The truth is many a sigh and moan
Were uttered, many a tear was shed,
And toils and griefs became my own,
And pains were on my pathway spread,
Before these very sorrows led
My dullish mind to wisdom's light
And brought more gain than all I read
In comment on the *Stagyrite.*

XIII.

But *God* who cheered the pilgrim's plight
At *Emmaus,* as the gospels say,
Just as my sorrow reached the height,
A waif without a plack to pay,
Did lead where this good city lay,
And gave me hope; my vile offence
So utterly was washed away
In *Heaven's* sight by penitence.

XIV.

A sinner I, as well is known;
Yet *God* doth not my death ordain
If heart and life be better grown;
And all whose sins did on them gain
Who be of better living fain
He sees with pity; mercy then,
When conscience brings remorseful pain,
Assoils the souls of sinful men.

XV.

Go read in famed romance's page
The faith of him who sang the *Rose:*
That ripened folk grown old and sage
Should find excuses pat for those
Mad hearts of youth where wisdom's snows
Yet never fell. Alack, 'tis truth!
But they who be my fiercest foes
Don't wish me to outlive my youth.

XVI.

Yet, if the world were bettered by
My death or story left untold,

I would condemn myself to die
For misdemeanours manifold:
I bring no harm to young or old
Alive or dead, in either case:
A man so needy never rolled
A mountain from its resting place.

XVII.

One day in *Alexander's* reign
A certain *Diomede,* 'tis said,
Was brought before the king, a chain
Enfettered him from heels to head
In felon guise; for he had led
A pirate's life upon the sea;
So came before the monarch dread
To hear the certain death decree.

XVIII.

"Why hast thou," came the query stern,
"Presumed to be a thief at sea?"
The other quickly made return:
"Why am I called a thief by thee?
Because I lived by piracy
With one small, feeble ship alone?
An emperor I now would be
Had I had armies like thine own.

XIX.

"But what's the odds? My fortune now
Has made me thus unfortunate.
Before its power I needs must bow
Accepting what was sent of fate.

Excuses are but idle prate,
But listen how the proverb goes:
When man's necessity is great
Small liking for the law he shows."

XX.

The king when he had made an end
Replied at once to *Diomede:*
"Thy fortunes shall be altered, friend,
From evil; I will help thy need."
'Twas done: the pirate, as we read,
Thenceforth paid everyone his due.
What goes before, in very deed,
The great *Valerius* tells as true.

XXI.

Had *Heaven* in my great diſtress
A pitying *Alexander* sent
To bring me into happiness
And had my life been ſtill misspent,
For such a sinner's punishment
To burn to ashes were too good!
'Tis need drives men to devilment
And hunger wolves to leave the wood.

XXII.

How I regret my time of *May,*
My days of riot, now no more,
That unperceived ſtole away
Till age was knocking at the door.
No sluggard foot nor charger bore
Them off. How then? As quick as **thought**
On eagle wings away did soar
My youth, and I am left with nought.

XXIII.

Yes, it is gone, and I remain
Right poor of learning and of sense,
But rotted fruit and blighted grain;
Devoid of power, or place, or pence;
And object of the most intense
Dislike from every relative.
The humblest even takes offence
Because I lack the means to live.

XXIV.

No spendthrift I of an estate
On banquets or in bawdy gear;
With loving at too fast a rate
They cannot blame me justly here,
Except that others paid too dear.
I tell the truth and nothing less,
And speak this boast with conscience clear;
Who did no wrong need not confess.

XXV.

In truth I've played the lover's part,
And fain would play it all my days;
But find a very heavy heart
And famished belly stop my craze
To wander in such amorous ways.
Well, let him thrive by my mischance
Whose ribs are lined with rich relays:
The bigger belt the better dance.

XXVI.

Had I but studied hard, in truth,
When I was young, nor played the fool,

But been a very virtuous youth,
I'd have a house and lie in wool.
But ah! I ran away from school,
A way that naughty children take.
The words are written; with the dule
Indeed my heart is like to break.

XXVII.

Alack, I took the *Preacher's* voice
To speak a most congenial truth
In that remembered text: "Rejoice,
My son, rejoice in this thy youth!"
But now another dish, forsooth,
He serves my riper years, ah me!
Declaring in his speech uncouth,
"Yea, youth and all are vanity!"

XXVIII.

My life has fled more swiftly than
A weaver's shuttle in the gloom,
As *Job* says, when the careful man
With burning straw lights up the room,
And, finding nothing on the loom,
Amiss, in mirk works on apace:
And I, I fear no future doom,
For death erases all disgrace.

XXIX.

Where is that graceful, gallant throng
Whose steps I followed in of yore,
So smooth of speech, so sweet in song,
With pleasant pranks and prate galore?

Ah, some of them are here no more,
But ſtiff and dead recline in clay;
For them be *Paradise* in ſtore,
And *God* preserve the reſt, I pray.

XXX.

And some, praise *God*, have poſts of truſt
As lords and maſters; some again
Go bare and never see a cruſt
But through the baker's window-pane;
Carthusian habits some maintain;
Or neath the Benedictine rule
In fishwives' footgear tramp the lane.
So wags the world with all the school.

XXXI.

To give all men of worth repose
And peace is surely *God's* own debt,
Which paid, he nothing further owes;
And mum's the word for what they get,
But to the poor with nought as yet
God grant the patience that endures;
Those others have no cause to fret,
Replete and rich in sinecures.

XXXII.

Good wine have they and noble roaſts,
Fish, sauces spiced that flavour lend,
Tarts, cuſtard, eggs served up on toaſts,
Poached, fried, all manners without end.
Not like the masons do they spend
Long weary years in heavy labours;
Nor flunkeys need the glass to tend,
Each fills his own and then his neighbour's.

XXXIII.

But this digression has to do
With present matters not a whit.
No judge am I to sift them through,
Or to condemn or to acquit.
Indeed, imperfect every bit
Am I; may *Jesu* healing send!
Let them be satisfied with it!
What I have penned, sirs, I have penned.

XXXIV.

But let the cloister sleep in peace
An speak of things in cheerier vein.
'Tis time for discontent to cease
Her song in this unpleasing strain.
Sad poverty will still complain
Aloud, and yet was never taught
From biting speeches to refrain;
If mute from fear, rebels in thought.

XXXV.

I met with poverty from birth,
Begotten poor, of humble race;
Among the great ones of the earth
Nor sire nor grandsire claimed a place.
Want followed after us apace.
Upon the tombstones of my line,
Whose souls may *God* receive in grace,
No kingly crowns or sceptres shine.

XXXVI.

Lamenting at this needy state
My heart betimes rejoins to me:

"O mortal, grumble not at fate
And sorrow not at what muſt be.
If *Jacques Cœur* held more in fee,
Yet better live in mean array
Than lie with those of high degree
That under coſtly tombs decay." . . .

XXXVII.

"Of high degree!" What have I said?
In vain this high degree they wore.
What says the *Psalmiſt?* They are fled
Their place shall know of them no more.
No will have I, a sinner sore,
With death to meddle in the leaſt:
Be that to clerics handed o'er,
For 'tis the office of the prieſt.

XXXVIII.

No son am I of angel bright
Who bears a ſtarry aureole
Or other diadem of light.
My sire is dead, God reſt his soul,
His bones are neath a tombſtone's scroll .
My mother, too, will die I know,
Poor thing, the bell muſt also toll
For her; and then the son will go.

XXXIX.

'Tis fated death shall be the rule
For poor and rich and low and high,
For prieſt or layman, sage or fool,
Fat, lean, tall, short, they all muſt die;

Yea, beauty no reprieve can buy;
And dames, both fair and foul, whose ruffs
In lofty braidings swept the sky
Must leave those costly padded stuffs.

XL.

To *Paris* and his *Helen* death
Brought anguish, as to every one.
He who suspires his latest breath
Must taste the gall his heart would shun;
God, how the sweats of terror run!
And nothing can the pain commute,
For brothers, sisters, children, none
Would answer as his substitute.

XLI.

The nostrils curl, the fingers clutch,
The hands are cold and moist as clay,
The flesh is clammy to the touch,
Death shakes the form, the face grows grey,
Must woman's tender shape decay,
So soft, so smooth, a precious prize,
And wait such evil ending? Yea,
Unless in life she scales the skies.

Ballade of the
Ladies of Byegone Times.

WHAT land afar, ah tell me where,
　　Doth *Flora, Rome's* delight, retain,
Archipiade, or *Thais,* ne'er
Were cousins a more lovesome twain;
Or Echo, answering again
Where mere lies still or river flows,
Whose beauty knew no human stain?
But where, ah where be last year's snows?

Where's *Eloise,* of wisdom rare,
Whose passion brought her lover pain?
For gelding *Abelard* must bear
And then in cloister monk remain.
And where the queen who did ordain
A sack should *Buridan* enclose
Before they dropped him in the *Seine?*
But where, ah where be last year's snows?

Queen Blanche, as lily pure and fair,
In voice so siren-sweet of strain,
With *Bietris, Bertha* debonair,
Alicia, Eremburge of *Maine,*
And *Joan,* the valour of *Lorraine,*
At *Rouen* burnt by English foes;
Where, Lady Blest, be all the train?
But where, ah where be last year's snows?

Prince, all enquiry will be vain
Of weeks or years where they repose;
No answer comes but this refrain:
But where, ah where be last year's snows?

Ballade of the
Lords of Byegone Times.

IN PURSUANCE OF THE FORMER THEME.

WHERE is the third *Calixtus,* late
    Deceased the bearer of the name,
Who held four years the papal State?
The king of Arragonian fame;
The *Duke of Bourbon,* void of blame;
Duke Arthur of the Breton hold;
The seventh *Charles* whom all acclaim?
But where is *Charlemagne* the bold?

Likewise the king of *Scots,* whose fate
Did half his face in spiteful game
As red as amethyst create,
From chin to forehead glowed the maim?
The great king that from *Cyprus* came;
Or that good Spanish king, unfold
His name I cannot, to my shame?
But where is *Charlemagne* the bold?

So further prattle I abate,
For all conclusions must be lame.
Death gains the day at any rate
And none can hope his rage to tame.
Yet but one question more I'll frame:
Bohemian *Ladislaus* enrolled
A king, where's he, or his grand-dame?
But where is *Charlemagne* the bold?

Where's *Breton Claquin's* patriot flame
The *Auvergne* dauphin, or the old
Alençon duke? The tale's the same:
But where is *Charlemagne* the bold?

Ballade on the Same Theme.

BUT where is every holy priest
    Whom alb and amice did array
And sacred stole, whose strength increased
To grip the devil's neck, they say,
Red-hot with evil plans, perfay?
For death both sons and servants find;
Their life is now blown out for aye:
And all that's left is merely wind!

Where be the rulers of the east,
The golden-handed emperors, pray;
Or *France's* monarchs, not the least
Of kings, o'er others bearing sway,
Who did for church and convent pay
To worship *God* with pious mind?
They once were honoured in their day:
And all that's left is merely wind.

Why hath the stout, wise *Dauphin* ceased
At *Vienne* or *Grenoble* to stay?
Where be the lords that used to feast
At *Dijon, Dolles* or *Sallins* way?
Their pursuivants, their trumpets gay
And heralds are they left behind?
With dainty fare they filled their clay:
And all that's left is merely wind.

Princes must meet with death's decay
And every man of human kind;
Some ruled while others did obey:
And all that's left is merely wind.

XLII.

So *Popes* and *Kings* and *Princes* brave
Conceived within a queenly womb
Muſt seek the narrow, silent grave,
While new successors fill their room.
I, shall I then escape the doom,
At *Rennes* a needy peddlar known?
God knows I shall not dread the tomb
When all my merry times are flown.

XLIII.

This world will not go on for ever,
Though wealthy grab-alls think it ought;
The fatal shears all lives dissever.
So thence some comfort may be taught
To one grown old and owning nought,
Whose tongue, when youthful, led the school
Of wits, whose railing now is thought
The prate of whoremonger and fool.

XLIV.

For now he needs muſt beg his bread;
The thought of death both day and night
Beside him ſtalks, a shape of dread;
Life offers him no more delight.
So, but for fear of *God,* he might
Be led to do a horrid deed.
Yea, some there be, in *God's* despite,
Despair to suicide did lead.

XLV.

For, though he were a pleasant lad,
An old buffoon appears a peſt,
The younger people scorn his sad
Grimaces and the threadbare jeſt.

When taciturn to please the rest
They deem the fool dumbfoundered found;
But when he speaks they swear with zest
That empty vessels make most sound.

XLVI.

These women too of tarnished fames,
Grown old, in poor and wretched state,
Beholding younger, pampered dames,
Who still can charm and captivate,
Demand why *God* decreed their date
Of birth so soon, for they've grown old.
God holds his peace: for in debate
He could not match a female scold.

*The Regrets of the Fair Armouress
at Having Grown Old.*

METHOUGHT I heard in great distress
That ancient woman thus complain
Who was the beauteous armouress
And wish herself a girl again:
"Ah age, so fell, whom all disdain,
Why hast thou conquered me so soon?
What hinders me to strike amain
And find the stroke of death a boon?

"The right to rule thou hast removed,
Rare beauty's dower to make men mad,
On merchants, clerks and clergy proved.
No man alive but then was glad
To give me freely all he had,
Whate'er repentance followed after,
So that I granted to the lad
What beggars now refuse with laughter.

"To many a man I did deny
The same (great folly you'll agree),
Through fancying a lover sly
Who had full many gifts from me.
Whoever else might cheated be
I loved him well, if truth be told,
But still his ways were rude to see,
He loved me only for my gold.

"Although he spurned and dragged me round,
I loved him, yea, would for his sake
Have gathered faggots from the ground;
When he but sought one kiss to take
I soon forgot all grief and ache;
The rake but needed to begin
To hug me. . . . So I gained my stake.
What's left me now?   But shame and sin.

"Well, he is dead gone thirty year
And I still live, old, white with care.
Ah when I think of byegone cheer,
My then estate with this compare,
When I behold myself all bare
And see myself transmuted quite,
All withered, wrinkled, lean and spare,
I almost do grow mad outright.

"Where be they now? the forehead fair,
The eyebrows arched, the hair so bright,
Large pupils and look debonair
That captured the most crafty wight;
The shapely nose of size aright;
The ears close clinging to the head;
The dimpled chin, skin clear and white,
And lovely lips of rosy red!

"Straight shoulders, arms both slim and long
With little hands and slender wrists,
Small nipples, haunches plump and strong,
High, smooth, where every charm assists
To make them meet for amorous lists;
Wide loins, fat thighs, and therein set,
Like love concealed amid the twists
Of silken curls, that amulet!

"The forehead wrinkled, ringlets gray,
The eyebrows hairless, dim the eyes
That smiled so saucily and gay
Entrancing men of merchandise,
The nose a hook whence beauty flies;
Ears limp, and mossy-like their skin;
The face pale, dead, in faded guise;
Lips coarse and swollen; shrunken chin;

"Thus human beauty ends its dream!
Stiff arms, and hands all claw-wise bent,
The shoulders fit for hunchback seem;
The breasts, they're withered now and spent;
The haunches shrunk a like extent.
The amulet, bah!   As for thighs,
They are but bags of discontent
And flecked like sausages by flies.

"Thus we the past good times regret
In company, each poor old trot!
Heaped close, as tennis balls are set,
Upon our hunkers, as we squat
Around a wretched fire, God wot,
Soon kindled and soon burnt away;
Yet we were once a dainty lot! . . .
So time makes men and women pay."

Ballade of the Fair Armouress
to all Gay Girls.

NOW think of it, gay glover's maid,
    Who used to be my pupil fair,
And you, *Blanche* of the slipper trade,
Of changing times and loves beware.
Take right and left, and do not spare,
I prithee, any man you see:
For age your value will impair,
Like coin cried down you then will be.

And you, sweet sausage-seller's aid,
Whose dancing is so debonair;
Costumier's *Guillemette*, you jade,
To flout your master do not dare;
To shut up shop you must prepare
When old and loathsome like to me:
All service priests grown old forswear;
Like coin cried down you then will be.

Hood-setting *Joan*, be much afraid,
Lest trouble catch you in a snare;
Purse-bearing *Katherine*, get paid,
Nor chase the lovers from your stair;
An ugly woman ne'er can share
Their boons, or from their jeers be free
And hideous age of love is bare,
Like coin cried down you then will be.

Girls, why I weep and rend my hair,
Just listen and you will agree:
No cure is known of anywhere,
Like coin cried down we all must be.

XLVII.

The good and fair who lived on earth
Aforetime teach this lesson terse,
So let it pass for what it's worth.
I've had it registered in verse
By *Fremin,* no one blunders worse,
Yet sober after my own mark . . .
If he denies it, how I'll curse!
For as the master so the clerk.

XLVIII.

The danger now is plain to see
How lovers purchase love too dear.
But some, be sure, will disagree
With this remark and say: "Give ear!
If love perverse and bad appear
These cheating women were to blame;
Thy sentence, sir, is too severe,
For they are known of evil fame.

XLIX.

"For if they only love for gold
A loving hour is all they reap.
To all the world their charms are sold
With laughter when the purses weep;
And none need sell her love wares cheap.
And every man who walks the sod
With dames of good repute should keep,
And shun the rest, so help me *God!*"

L.

But, faith, no pleading of the sort
Will pass for valid in my sight.
'Tis very easy to retort,
Provided I have heard aright
That we should love but virtue bright.
The question is, if those poor dears
I've sung at length were never white
And pure of soul in bygone years?

LI.

Aye, white and pure of soul were they,
And once without reproach or blame.
To every one there came a day,
Before she won her evil fame,
When love selected for the dame
A student, monk, or gentle squire
To quench of love the fiercer flame
Than is *Saint Anthony* his fire.

LII.

They only followed the decree
Of *Nature,* as is plainly shown:
And took their joys in secrecy
For those were shared by two alone.
But loves like these will droop full-blown;
They tire; they part; the song is done:
And she, who yet but one had known,
Loves better to love everyone.

LIII.

What moves them to it? 'Tis my creed,
(To speak no scandal of the fair)
That women when they love indeed
Wish all mankind to have a share.

(No other rhyme would suit me there!)
Besides all *Rheims* and *Troyes* agree
Backed up by *Lille* and *St. Omer,*
Six workmen do much more than three.

LIV.

Well, fools muſt ſtrike on the rebound,
While ladies volley in the air;
Collecting dues *Love* roams around;
All *Faith* is violated there,
Be hugs and kisses ne'er so rare.
Join hounds, arms, hawks and lovers' gains,
For all, at laſt, make mortals swear:
"For one short joy a thousand pains!"

Double Ballade
on the Same Theme.

NOW love on to your heart's desire,
    And go where feaſt and mob incite,
In the end nought better you'll acquire
Than heads well hammered in a fight:
Mad love makes fools of every wight:
Did *Solomon* to idols lead:
And *Samson's* peepers robbed of light . . .
Who misses such is bleſt indeed.

Sweet fiddling *Orpheus* who the lyre
And flute and bagpipe played aright
Through love ran danger from the dire
Dog *Cerberus'* three-headed bite;
Narcissus, too, of beauty bright
Was drowned in deep, dark well for greed
Of his own loveliness in sight . . .
Who misses such is bleſt indeed.

Sardana, too, it did inspire,
When *Crete* was won by that good knight,
To dress himself in girl's attire
And be a virgin spinner hight.
King David loſt *God's* favour quite
Although a prophet wise, we read,
Through seeing thighs washed plump and
        white . . .
Who misses such is bleſt indeed.

The same set *Ammon's* lust afire
His sister *Thamar* once by might
To ravish, feigning to require
Some tarts to eat, a foul despite;
And *Herod* (no vain tales I write)
John Baptist from his headpiece freed
Songs, leaps and dances to requite . . .
Who misses such is blest indeed.

So I, poor wretch, received my hire
Like clouts in stream no beating slight,
All naked, think me not a liar.
Who to such sour fruit did invite
But *Katherine de Vauselles* for spite?
And with a third was *Noë* fee'd.
Such gloves suit such a nuptial rite . . .
Who misses such is blest indeed.

Well, shall young fellows shun the choir
Of sweet young girls for very fright?
No, e'en if burnt upon a pyre
Like those who broomsticks ride by night.
Than civet they're more exquisite:
But fair or dark it is my creed
He's mad who trusts in them a mite . . .
Who misses such is blest indeed.

LV.

Had she, whom I have served of yore
So loyally with all my heart,
For whom much evil grief I bore
And suffered such tormenting smart,

Had she but told me at the ſtart
Her wishes, (Ah my vain regret!)
'Twould not have needed wizard's art
To draw back scatheless from her net.

LVI.

Whatever prattle poured from me
She always was prepared to hear,
Ne'er to concur or disagree;
Nay more, would let me linger near
Inclining unto me her ear;
And entertaining as before
Talk flowed like water through a weir:
She suffered it to fool me more.

LVII.

She fooled me well, and made me deem
That that was this and this was that;
Till flour did very cinders seem;
A worſted cap became a hat;
And ever when at dice we sat
Her aces changed to double threes . . .
So I and many another flat
Were made to think that chalk was cheese.

LVIII.

The sky appeared a brazen ball;
In calfskin clad the clouds would jump;
The mornings turn to evenings all;
A turnip be a cabbage ſtump;
Raw cider, wine unspilt by pump;
The hangman's rope, a silken scabbard;
A windmill seem a sow's fat rump;
An abbot's paunch, a herald's tabard.

LIX.

Thus love befooled me and o'erpowered
And blew by turns both hot and cold.
My faith is, any slyboots dowered
With cunning rare as finest gold
Would also have been bought and sold,
Nor had the luck to save his bacon,
But, just like me, this title hold:
"The lover flouted and forsaken!"

LX.

So, *Love,* in this rebellious mood
By blood and fire be defied!
Death nears me; she who sent him would
Not care a farthing if I died.
My hurdy-gurdy's laid aside;
I shall not follow as before
The loves whose badge was all my pride,
Their ranks shall know me nevermore.

LXI.

From such delights I now have flown,
Let those pursue who still are fain,
Henceforth I'll leave this theme alone.
And follow my own will again.
Should some ask how I dare complain
Of love, let this my answer be:
"A dying man need not refrain;
He has a charter to speak free."

LXII.

'Tis very plain the graveyard calls;
I spit, and from my mouth are thrown
Great gobs of white as big as balls;
What's more to tell? And I am grown

Quite useless as a squire to *Joan,*
Who scorns an old exhausted crock . . .
My voice sounds aged in its tone,
Though I should be a gay young cock!

LXIII.

'Twas that cold drink I had to swallow,
God willed it so and *Jacques Thibault,*
Deep underground in dungeon hollow,
And chew thereto the fruits of woe,
In chains. . . . When I recall it, lo,
I pray for him *et reliqua*
That *God* may send them . . . so and so,
Just what I think . . . *et cetera!*

LXIV.

I wish to him (oh dear me no!)
Or his lieutenant no mishap;
His henchman neither, who was so
Polite and always in the gap;
The rest concern me not a rap:
But little *Master Robert* . . . he?
I love them all, aye every chap,
As *God* does *Jews* from *Lombardy.*

LXV.

If memory is not playing tricks,
On leaving home I chanced to vent
Some rhymes in fourteen fifty-six
That some folk, maugre my dissent,
Are pleased to call my *Testament;*
Their pleasure 'tis, and theirs alone:
Yet why should I be discontent?
No man is master of his own.

LXVI.

Whoever has not had, I say,
The legacy I left him firſt
Muſt find my heirs some future day
And dun them after I'm enhearsed.
Who those may be?   Well, hear the worſt:
Turgis, Provins, Robin, Moreau;
By whom my goods will be disbursed
To this my very bed of woe.

LXVII.

No revocation I decree
Although my lands were all at ſtake,
My pity has not chilled towards thee,
Poor baſtard *De la Barre,* so take
Three wisps of ſtraw and mats to make,
Though old, a covering for thy shins;
Thus warmly gaitered cease to shake,
And ſtand up boldly on thy pins.

LXVIII.

In brief, I'll say but one more word
Before enditing this my will
To *Fremin,* who, as clerk, has heard
Me here proteſt, (if he is ſtill
Awake) that I desire no ill
To anyone in this bequeſt;
Nor shall its terms be published till
In *France* they are made manifeſt.

LXIX.

My heart grows weak and weaker ſtill;
The power to draw my breath has fled.
Come, *Fremin,* paper, ink and quill,
And take thy seat beside my bed

To keep away the spies I dread;
And write down quickly my intent,
Then copy all therein is said:

And here begins my Testament.
Here Villon beginneth his devises.

LXX.

Of *God* the *Father* in the name,
And *Son* conceived of *Virgin* sweet,
The *Godhead's* co-eternal flame
Together with the *Paraclete,*
Who keep in heaven a retreat
For souls by *Adam's* trespass flawed;
Who holds this faith will gain his seat
Where death makes many a demigod.

LXXI.

Their souls and bodies both were dead
And damned moreover in addition;
The bodies rotten, spirits sped
To flames, whatever their contrition;
But not a prophet found admission
Or patriarch, my faith declares,
Because I have a shrewd suspicion
Heat never tortured loins like theirs.

LXXII.

Should some one say: "How canst thou be
Cocksure of matters in debate
With no divinity degree?
Unwise presumption fills thy pate!"

Christ's parable doth demonstrate
How *Dives* had no bed of down
When dead, but met a fiery fate,
And *Lazarus* a heavenly crown.

LXXIII.

His finger was not seen aglow,
Or *Dives* had not sought the grace
That finger-tip should there bestow
A single drop to cool his face.
There sots will be in sorry case
Who swill both coat and shirt as well.
Since drink is dear in such a place
God keep us from the clutch of hell.

LXXIV.

In name of *God,* as was designed,
And in our *Blessed Lady's* name,
May I, though lean yet sound in mind,
Complete this writing void of blame;
That not a touch of fever came
I thank *God's* clemency of heart;
Of other grief and bitter shame
I'll say no more, but make a start:

LXXV.

First, to the holy *Three-in-One*
I do bequeath my wretched soul,
And to *Our Lady's* benison
Commend, in hope she may condole:
The charity, too, of the whole
Nine worthy *Orders* I entreat,
That they may bear it to its goal
Before the precious Mercy-seat.

LXXVI.

Item, my body's carrion
I leave to our great mother *Earth;*
The worms will not wax fat thereon,
For famine has reduced my girth.
Make haste: from dust it drew its birth
And unto dust it shall return.
Each thing its proper place with mirth
Regaineth, as the wise discern.

LXXVII.

Item, to *Guillaume Villon* . . . be
He more than foster-father styled . . .
Who ever kinder proved to me
Than mother to her swaddling child.
My bygone sorrows he beguiled,
And grieves about my present state;
I beg him to grow reconciled
And cease to be disconsolate.

LXXVIII.

I leave him all the books I boast
And that romance *"The Devil's Puff,"*
Which *Guy de Tabarie* engrossed,
A fellow of the proper stuff!
Though written in a style that's rough,
And tossed in sheets beneath the table,
The theme is notable enough
To lend some value to the fable.

LXXIX.

Item, I leave my mother dear,
Who suffered from my evil ways
God knows, the song ensuing here
Wherewith to give *Our Lady* praise;

Whose help is sent without delays
To soul and body; well I wot
To find none better all my days,
Nor will my mother, poor old trot.

Ballade that Villon Made
at the Request of
His Mother to
Invoke Our Lady.

L ADY of heaven, Queen of earth below,
      And Empress of the dread infernal shore,
Receive me your moſt humble Christian, so
That I with the eleƈt may you adore,
Although I ne'er was worthy heretofore.
Your bounties, oh my Lady and my Queen,
Are greater far than all my sins have been;
No souls without this bounty merit buy
Or heaven have, no quibbling here I mean.
And in this faith I wish to live and die.

Say to your Son I'm His for weal or woe;
Through him be cancelled my offences sore:
As pardoned was *Saint Mary* long ago,
Or clerk *Theophilus,* absolved of yore
And freed from debt, you did to grace reſtore,
Though paƈt was made him and the fiend be-
      tween.
'Twixt me and all such doings intervene,
Oh Virgin, in whose spotless breast did lie
The sacrament that at the mass is seen.
And in this faith I wish to live and die.

A woman old and poor I nothing know,
Unlearned, and ne'er on printed page did pore,
But at my parish church I see the show
Of heaven, with lutes and harps all painted o'er,

And hell where damned souls flame for ever-
      more :
This frights me, that gives joy and pleasure
      keen.
Grant, *Goddess* high, such joys I too may glean,
Oh you to whom all sinful folk must fly
With faith endowed, of sloth and feigning clean.
And in this faith I wish to live and die.

V irgin and Princess rare, you bore I ween
I *esus* who rules for aye each earthly scene.
L ord of all power He took our human screen,
L ike man to help us came from heaven high;
O ffered to death in beauteous youthful mien;
N o lord but Him, on no one else I lean.
And in this faith I wish to live and die.

LXXX.

Item, to my beloved *Rose*
Nor spleen nor heart of mine shall go:
She craves for something else than those,
Though heaps of money she can show:
For what?   A silken purse or so
Both wide and deep and filled with crowns.
But I'll be hanged if I beſtow
On her by will my bobs or browns.

LXXXI.

Indeed she does not need my stuff.
In no such way my thoughts aspire;
Of joys with her I've had enough;
No longer is my tail afire.

Of *Michault's* heirs she may enquire
In life as *Jolly Roger* known.
A prayer and leap would please this sire
At *Saint Satur* beneath his stone.

LXXXII.

Yet none the less to pay my debt
To Love, not to the merry maid,
(For that same damsel never yet
A spark of love to me conveyed:
If all the rest alike were paid
I know not, nor do greatly care;
Saint Mary knows when all is said
There's only stuff for laughter there;)

LXXXIII.

This next ballade to her I'll send
Whose rhymes all terminate in *R*.
Who'll bear it her, and serve my end?
It shall be *Pernet De La Barre*.
And he, when he espies afar
My lady's nose, so snub and scarlet,
Shall shout in the vernacular:
"Whence come you, oh you wanton harlot?"

Ballade of Villon to His Love.

F alse beauty, costing me so very dear,
R ight harsh in deeds and yet dissembling **fair**;
A h love, more sharp of wound than sword **or**
    spear.
N o deadlier these, whose name I could declare;
C harm stained with crime, my heart in twain
    to tear;
I ndocile pride, whence many wounded are;
S pare, eyes so pitiless, your rigour spare;
A poor man's fortune mend, and never mar.

M y better hap had been to seek, I fear,
A nother's grace, and so escaped this care:
R eflection warned me from her danger sphere;
T hus I must fly and be of honour bare.
H elp, one and all, help, help in my despair!
A h what? To die without one blow in war,
Since pity will not (hard the lot to bear)
A poor man's fortune mend, and never mar.

A time will come that shall turn dry and sere
Vainglorious beauty's blossoms now so rare:
I f still alive, 'twill give me cause to jeer.
Laugh? Ah but no; 'twould have too mad an
    air!
L o! I grown old, while ugliness you wear!
O n! Drink apace while streams do flow **afar**,
N or let us all alike this hardship share;
A poor man's fortune mend, and never mar.

Prince lover, of all loves beyond compare,
May nought from your good will me e'er debar;
But every true heart should, by *God* I swear,
A poor man's fortune mend, and never mar.

LXXXIV.

Item, ten lines of verse I've made
To merchant *Ythier* shall belong,
To whom before I left my blade,
(But he muſt set them in a song);
Thereto a *De profundis* ſtrong
For those he taught to play the whore,
Whose names to mention would be wrong,
Because he'd hate me evermore.

Lay or Rather Rondeau.

DEATH, from thy harshness I appeal
⎯ That did away my miſtress steal,
Nor yet doth any mercy deal,
But keeps me bound in languor's chain.
No force or ſtrength I may attain;
What harm then did her life conceal,
Death?
One heart we had, though we were twain
If it be dead, nought may me heal,
Or, if I live, muſt learn to feel
Like images who know no pain,
Death.

LXXXV.

Item, for *Maſter Jehan Cornu*
I wish to make another lay;
Because in needs and business too
He helped me on in every way:
So he shall have the garden gay
Pierre Bourgignon conveyed of yore,
With covenant that I should pay
To patch the wall and mend the door.

LXXXVI.

Because it lacked a door I loſt
A hone and handle of a hoe.
Eight hawks, not ten, might then have crossed
The ground with ne'er a lark to show.

The house is safe, but bar it so.
A hook as hatchment hung in sight;
Who stole the sign, a lodging low
I wish him and a bloody night.

LXXXVII.

Item, because the wanton wife
Of *Master Pierre Saint Amant* made
Me come to lead a beggar's life,
(If sin or blame for it be laid
To his account, *God's* pardon's prayed)
For her *White Horse's* sluggish mass
As mate I leave a fitting jade,
The *She-mule* too a red-hot ass.

LXXXVIII.

Item, to *Denys Hesselin,*
Elect of *Paris,* hogsheads large
Of *Aulnis* wine a full fourteen,
Supplied by *Turgis* at my charge.
Should drink enough to float a barge
His senses drown, then swiftly souse
In water to each barrel's marge;
Wine plays the deuce with many a house.

LXXXIX.

Item to *Guillaume Charruau,*
My advocate, be handed down,
However now his fortunes go,
My sheathless blade of rusty brown.
Thereto small change for half-a-crown
To swell whatever purse he bear,
All gathered up from streets in town
And from the cloistered *Temple square.*

XC.

Item, in wish to reimburse
My *Fournier*, his legal paws
Five times may plunge inside my purse
(Nor spare to clutch with all their claws!)
Because he won me many a cause,
By *Jesus Chriſt*, all juſt and right,
So found when teſted by the laws:
But right needs skill to make it might.

XCI.

Item, I unto *Maſter Jacques
Raguyer,* the *Grève's* great cup devise:
Provided he will pay four placks,
Though forced to sell to gain the prize
What covers up his legs and thighs;
And hurry bare-breeched in his shoes
Each morning early, as he hies
Unto the *Fir-cone Inn* for booze.

XCII.

Item, but as to *Merebeuf* now
And *Nicolas de Louviers* too,
I leave them neither bull nor cow,
As neatherds they would never do.
Indeed I make no jeſt of you,
They are as mighty falcon lovers
As ever from *Dame Maschecroue*
Took packs of partridges and plovers.

XCIII.

Item, let *Robert Turgis* come
To me at once, I'll pay my bill
For liquor, but to find my home
He'll need much more than wizard's skill.

I'll leave to him my right to fill,
As *Paris* bred, a civic chair . . .
The idiom's provincial, still
'Twas taught me by two ladies fair.

XCIV.

Two ladies very fair and dear!
By *Saint Genou* their dwellings be,
St. Julien des Voventes is near,
Where *Poitou* joins with *Brittany;*
No further hint shall come from me,
So guess all day and night as well;
I am not such a fool you see . . .
But mean to kiss and never tell.

XCV.

Item, to *Sergeant Jehan Raguyer,*
One of the Twelve, as donative
A cheesecake crisp his chops to cheer
Each day that he remains alive,
And *Bailly's* table shall contrive
To grant this cake; in *Maubue Street*
From pump his throttle will derive
Cool liquor to wash down his meat.

XCVI.

Item, the *Prince of Fools* shall take
Michault de Four as pantaloon,
Well practised many jests to make
And sentimental songs to croon:
With that I'll bid good-afternoon.
In short, in all, save girth, he's pleasant,
A very natural buffoon
Who pleases best where he's not present.

XCVII.

Item, of the Eleven Score
Two worthy sergeants, *Jehan Vallette*
And *Denis Richier*, to the core
Both good and honest men, shall get,
Yes each, a mighty aigulet
To hang down from the felten cap:
Foot-sloggers' fees, *videlicet;*
The horse-guards shall not have a rap.

XCVIII.

I leave to *Pernet*, in addition,
Three loaded dice that cannot err,
Or pack of cards to take position
Now filled by baton sinister,
And free his scutcheon from the slur . . .
Yet stay; he must be mute behind,
Or may a quartan ague stir
Him up and shake with every wind.

XCIX.

Item, of *Chollet* here I beg
To choose a trade that's more genteel,
And cease repairing stoup and keg
With staves and bits of board piecemeal,
But buy a sword of *Lyons* steel
To carve up brawlers unaware:
Though noise and riot don't appeal
To him, yet he can do his share.

C.

Item, to wolfish *John*, a man
Of merchandise and in good case,
Because he's thin and spare of span
And *Chollet's* rotten at the chase.

I leave a dog of setter race
Who'll pass no poultry on the way,
Thereto a mantle to embrace
Them all and hide the feathered prey.

CI.

Du Boys, the goldsmith, juſt five score
Of nail-shaped cloves, with point and head,
Of ginger from the Turkish shore;
That couples cunningly, instead
Of boxes, lovers in a bed,
And ham to sausages conjoins,
And makes the bosom swell and spread,
And vigour flow into the loins.

CII.

To *Captain Jehan Riou,* in wish
His archers and himself may dine,
Six heads of wolves to fill their dish,
No food for folk that herd the swine,
All choicely cooked in household wine
When caught by butcher's maſtiff-dog.
To gain such cheer one would decline
No sin in all the decalogue.

CIII.

As meat its weight is something more
Than feathers, cork, or thiſtledown.
'Tis fitted for a soldier's ſtore,
Or use in a beleaguered town.
If traps ensnare the vermin brown,
The maſtiffs should be flayed for curs,
I swear it, by my doctor's gown,
To make the soldiers winter furs.

CIV.

Item, to *Robin Troussecaille,*
Grown fat by services discreet,
To run afoot he is no quail,
A thick-set cob's his favourite seat;
I give him from my dresser neat
A bowl he dared not take on loan;
His household ware will be complete
With it, and everything his own.

CV.

Item, to *Perrot Girard* sworn
As barber unto *Bourg-la-Reine,*
Two basins and a lance be borne
Since he is sharp to gather gain.
Six years ago or so the swain
On porkers of a fatted growth
Did me a sennight entertain;
As *Pourras'* abbess can take oath

CVI.

Item, the many begging friars
And nuns with all their retinue
'Neath *Orleans* or *Paris* spires,
A farcical and scurvy crew,
With custards now I do bedew
And *Jacobins'* own greasy broth:
Then contemplation may ensue
Behind four-poster curtain cloth.

CVII.

They surely mother every child,
Although this boon my gift is not.
Because for *God's* sake oft reviled
From Him this rich reward they got.

These handsome priests must pay their shot
In *Paris* even, as we know.
They please our women quite a lot,
And prove their love to husbands so.

CVIII.

Jehan de Pontileu had much to say
Against the friars, but all he spoke
Was forced in public one fine day
In shame and sorrow to revoke.
Their ways to *Mathew* seemed a joke,
And *Jehan de Mehun* to mirth enticed,
But one must honour all the folk
That honoured have the *Church of Christ.*

CIX.

So I will play a humble part.
And never offer contradiction,
Their words and deeds with all my heart
Approve with uttermost conviction.
Their slanderers deserve affliction,
For whether in church or place apart
Or somewhere else there may be friction
With those inclined to take their part.

CX.

Item, to *Baulde,* monk resident
Within the cloister *Carmelite,*
Whose ways be tough and bold, be sent
A casque and halberts apposite.
De Tusca's ruffian soldiers might
Snap up his playmate any minute.
He's old: but if he will not fight,
The fiend of *Vauvert* must be in it.

CXI.

Item, because the chancellor's clerk
Has licked fly-droppings not a little,
I give, since he's a man of mark,
His seal anointment with my spittle,
And may his thumb be sealed with brittle
Official wax, to cut it short;
The rest concern me not a tittle,
I mean him of the Bishop's court.

CXII.

With wainscoating I will enrich
The room wherein the Council meets,
And all whose hinder portions itch
Shall sit on chairs with privy seats,
Provided heavy fining greets
Macée of Orleans who wore
My girdle in the public ſtreets
Againſt the law, the little whore.

CXIII.

Item, to *Francis Vacquerie,*
Promoter of the cowshed hight,
A high Scots gorget I decree,
But with no goldsmith's art bedight;
Because when he was made a knight
Saint George and *God* were roundly cursed.
Who hears of it in mad delight
Muſt laugh till he is fit to burſt.

CXIV.

Item, to *Maſter Jehan Laurens*
Whose eyes are ever red and sore
Because his parents gave offence
By swilling casks and flasks galore,

I hand my pocket-linings o'er
To wipe them with at break of day . . .
If made a prelate, he'd have store
Of silk for which there's more to pay.

CXV.

Item, to *Jehan Cotard* I owe,
My proctor of the church court kind,
The matter of a coin or so
That's due, as I recall to mind,
Since knavery *Denise* designed
And said I'd given her abuse:
His soul (be it with *God* enshrined)
Shall have this prayer writ in excuse.

Ballade & Prayer.

OLD *Noah,* you who first did plant the vine,
  You also, *Lot,* who drank so heartily
Within the cave till Cupid did incline
Your daughters both to come too close, perdie;
(Fear no reproaches on that score from me;)
Architriclin, renowned for drinking far;
I pray you harbour kindly, all you three,
The soul of worthy *Master Jehan Cotard.*
For he a scion was of your own line,
With best and dearest wine did well agree;
Without a sixpence wherewithal to dine
Would drink what came, no epicure was he:
Nor from his pots would separated be,
No laggard he to empty jug or jar.
Oh sirs, do not condemn by your decree
The soul of worthy *Master Jehan Cotard.*

With dotard's feet, that slip and intertwine,
When bound for bed full oft we might him see;
And once his pate acquired a scar as sign
That with a butcher's stall it made too free.
No better drinker could be found than he,
Search all the earth wherever topers are!
So, when it calls, admit without a fee
The soul of worthy *Master Jehan Cotard.*

Prince, though he oft was drunk as drunk could
    be,
He'd shout: "My throat's afire!" across the
    bar;

For thirſt could never find the knack to flee
The soul of worthy *Maſter Jehan Cotard.*

CXVI.

Item, I wish that *Merle* the youth
Shall at my money-changing ply;
I want to try exchange, in truth,
To gain some profit on the sly
At home, abroad, or where care I!
Six targets held to match three crowns;
Two angelets an angel buy;
For friends should not be ſtingy clowns.

CXVII.

Item, I heard while travelling here
My three poor orphan boys have grown,
Becoming riper every year,
No sheepshead on their shoulders shown.
From here to *Sallins* none is known
As better taught in all the schools.
Now, by all friars that wisdom own,
Such boys as these cannot be fools.

CXVIII.

My will is they should ſtudy thus:
Where? *Pierre Richier's* the very spot.
Donatus is too arduous:
Such tether shall not be their lot.
They'll know, and quite enough I wot,
Ave, Salus, tibi decus,
All other learning be forgot:
Great clerks are seldom prosperous.

CXIX.

These be their toils, then off they hie!
All surplus lore they muſt eschew.
The lengthy *Credo* be passed by,
For such young things 'tis much ado.
My tabard big I've cut in two,
And wish one half of it to sell
To purchase cuſtard for the crew,
For youth likes dainty morsels well.

CXX.

That they be drilled in manners good,
What e'er the coſt be, is my plan:
To go about with close-drawn hood
And thumbs ſtuck in the girdle's span;
With humble mien to every man;
Replying: "Eh? What? No indeed!"
Folk's thoughts will be none other than:
"These boys be of the proper breed!"

CXXI.

Item, those clerks so full of want
Fine fellows ſtraight as any reed,
Myself disseising with this grant,
To them my legal claims I cede,
(So be assigned each title-deed,
Sans charge, all safe as hand can get
With signature and date at need),
Againſt *Guillaume Gueuldry* his debt.

CXXII.

Although they're full of impudence
And youth, my anger does not rise.
Years twenty, thirty, forty hence,
Please *God*, they'll be quite otherwise.

Men are wrong-headed to despise
The charm and beauty of such youth,
And mad to buffet or chastise;
For boys like these turn men forsooth.

CXXIII.

A College bursary shall reap
Each one: its grant I undertake.
No dormice they to lie asleep
Three months on end and never wake.
At best but wretched sleepers make
Young hearts in youth, and later those
Perforce must age, for slumber's sake,
When old in vears they need repose.

CXXIV.

My letters to the bursars read
Exact in every turn and phrase:
Their prayers must for their patron plead
Or ears well pulled requite delays.
Some folk, indeed, are in amaze
My heart should love these two young men:
But, faith, church-wakes or holidays
Ne'er brought their mothers in my ken.

CXXV.

Item, *Charlot Taranne* shall share
Michault Culdou's bequest alone,
One hundred halfpence: gathered where?
No odds: like manna they'll be strown;
And cowhide boots they both shall own
With soles and uppers strongly girt,
Provided they will kiss my *Joan*
And such another piece of skirt.

CXXVI.

I leave my *Lord of Grigny* now,
To whom I left *Bicêtre* before,
The *Billy* tower, but he muſt vow
Each broken pane and fallen door
At his own charges to reſtore
And every part to overhaul:
On every side let money pour:
I need it, and have none at all.

CXXVII.

Item, to *Thibault de la Garde* . . . .
Thibault? I lie, his name is *John* . . . .
What can I give, he won't discard?
I've loſt enough the year that's gone.
God will provide, so carry on!
The Keg? But ſtay and let me think!
To *Genevois* it muſt be drawn
Who has a better head for drink.

CXXVIII.

Item, *Basanyer,* notary,
The Criminal Court Clerk as well,
A creel of cloves shall have from me
Supplied by *Maſter Jehan Ruel.*
The same to *Mautainêt* and *Rosnel;*
To serve like gift of cloves is due
That lord, whose graces all excel,
Saint Chriſtopher's own servant true,

CXXIX.

To whom I give this ballade now
To praise his dame, none better be.
If all alike Love can't endow
There's nothing ſtrange in that; for he,

When *René* king of *Sicily*
Dressed lists, did win his lady there
With deeds and silent modesty
No Trojan's ever could compare.

Ballade
that Villon gave to
a Gentleman Newly Married
that He might send it to His Wife won
by His Sword.

A T that same point of dawn, when falcons
      bate
M ade merry, as is then their noble ure
B espeaking joy, and on the wing elate
R eceive their food down-stooping to the lure,
O f all desires inflamed that fill a wooer
I offer what suits mates of every feather,
S ince Love prescribes it in no terms obscure
E 'en for this end we are alone together.

D ear, you shall rule my heart without debate,
E nthroned till death be my discomfiture,
L ike laurel crowning my victorious state,
O r olive of all bitterness the cure.
R est certain, faith, I never will abjure,
E namoured wholly of this pleasing tether,
(S o she and I the bondage sweet endure)
E'en for this end we are alone together.

And what is more, when met by grievous fate
Through Fortune that against me doth conjure,
Your gentle eye will banish all her hate
As wind doth chase away the smoky stour.

From such a field the harvest is secure,
God bids me plough and plant in every weather,
The fruit resembles me, no copy truer;
E'en for this end we are alone together.
My princess, these resolves of mine ensure
My heart will never part from your heart,
      whether
Come weal or woe: grant me a love as pure,
E'en for this end we are alone together.

CXXX.

Item: to *Jehan Perdryer* be paid
And to his brother *François* . . . nought!
For unto me just that much aid
And share of all their goods they brought;
Besides my comrade *François* thought
At *Bourges* with sharp and searing tongue,
Which half commanded half besought,
To gain me fame with old and young.

CXXXI.

'Twere vain in *Taillevent* to look;
The hashes chapter will not show
This dish, nor any other book
Before, behind, above, below.
But *Saint Macaire,* I'd have you know,
Who cooked the devil in his hide
Because the grill smelt better so,
He did this recipe provide.

Ballade.

IN arsenic, the white sort and the red,
Saltpetre, quicklime, causing countless aches,
To clean them better adding boiling lead;
In sulphur, pitch, and in those stinking lakes
You may discover in a ghetto jakes;
In lotions that have cooled a leper's heat;
In stuff scraped off from shabby shoes and feet:
In blood of asp and drugs with death allied;
In spleen of wolf and fox and pole-cat sweet
May all such envious tongues as these be fried!

In brain of coal-black cat, whose aged head
Has toothless gums, and fishing quite forsakes;
In foam and spittle, just as precious, shed
By an old mastiff that with madness quakes;
In phlegm a mule both worn and jaded makes
With a sharp pair of scissors chopped up neat;
In water where to dip the rats retreat,
With vermin, toads and all that harm betide,
With serpents, lizards and such noble meat
May all such envious tongues as these be fried.

In sublimate that all to handle dread;
With navels added cut from living snakes;
In blood at full-moon by the barbers shed
That on a little furnace dries and bakes,
Whereof some black some green as garlic cakes;
In cancers, sores and dirty tubs you meet

Where nurses wash their clouts in every street;
In basins such as harlots can provide,
(Who knows the stews will follow my conceit;)
May all such envious tongues as these be fried!

Prince, sift these morsels that entice to eat,
(If lacking sacking, gauze or bolting-sheet)
Through an old pair of breeches' foul backside;
But, firſt of all, in pig manure complete
May all such envious tongues as these be fried!

CXXXII.

Item, *Franc-Gontier Refuted*
To maſter *Jehan Courault* I send:
But on a Tyrant, so reputed,
I have no arguments to spend;
No poor, weak fellow should contend
Againſt the great, the wise declare,
Leſt nets be spread, and in the end
His feet should ſtumble in a snare.

CXXXIII.

I don't fear *Gontier;* neither men
Nor money has he more than I;
There's this dispute between us then:
He values poverty so high,
That to be poor neath any sky
As great good fortune he has rated;
Which claim of his I muſt deny.
Who's wrong?   Here be the point debated.

Ballade
Entitled:
Franc-Gontier Refuted.

A JOLLY canon on down cushions laid
  Beside a stove in room both neat and gay,
Dame Lovesome lying at his side displayed,
Fair, tender, smooth, and tricked in rare array :
A-drinking wine from dawn to eve were they,
Rejoicing, kissing, toying, full of glee,
And both all bared the easier to be,
I saw them through the keyhole on my knees :
Then knew, that if from care we would be free
No treasure is like living at our ease.

If *Franc-Gontier* and *Helen* his sweet maid
Had ever made of such delight assay,
Their hunger ne'er with brittle crusts were
    stayed,
Or onions that foul breath bestow alway.
Their buttermilk and other drinks, perfay,
Are in less worth than garlic held by me.
They boast of sleeping neath the woodland tree,
Doth not a chair-flanked bedstead better
    please?
What say you?   Does it need a longer plea?
No treasure is like living at our ease.

They feed on coarse brown bread and grain
    decayed,
And all the year drink water, yea or nay.

From here to *Babylon* no serenade
Of birds would hold me for a single day,
No not one morn, for fare like this to ſtay!
Franc-Gontier with *Helen* may agree
For joys beneath the eglantine to flee;
I need not frown, if such their hearts appease;
Whatever bliss in country life they see,
No treasure is like living at our ease.

Prince, judge between us all of each degree
For me, let none be wrath at what he sees,
Still young in years I learnt to touch this key,
No treasure is like living at our ease.

CXXXIV.

Item, ᴜecause her *Bible* knowledge
Gives *Dame Bruyeres* the right of speech,
I grant her and her female college
On all, save Gospel texts, to preach,
Those gossips better ways to teach
Whose tongues are sharp as anything,
But far outside the graveyard screech
Where people yarns to market bring.

Ballade of the Women of Paris.

THOUGH women skill in speech unfold
Neath Tuscan or Venetian sky,
Yea, even when they're waxen old
On confidential errands fly;
Let Roman dames or Lombards try,
Or Genoese, support to draw,
Bring Piedmontese, Savoyards nigh,
There's none to match a *Paris* jaw!

The *Naples* dames like doctors hold,
Discourses, and are never shy;
The Germans cackle, we are told,
The Prussian women shrilly cry;
But search all *Greece* or *Hungary*,
Or Gypsies of no land or law,
Castile, or *Spain*, and squeeze them dry,
There's none to match a *Paris* jaw!

All tongues of *Swiss* or *Breton* mould
Or from *Thoulouse* or *Gascony*,
Two wives of *Petit-Pont* would scold
Them dumb, and all *Lorraine* defy
With *England, Calais* hold thereby,
(Behold this list of names with awe!)
Valenciennes too and *Picardy*,
There's none to match a *Paris* jaw!

Prince, Paris ladies claim the high
Reward of speech without a flaw;
Italian lips in vain may vie,
There's none to match a *Paris* jaw!

CXXXV.

Just look at two or three at ease
Plumped down on kirtle's lowest pleat
In churches or in monasteries;
Draw near with cat-like silent feet;
You'll find *Macrobius* could compete
With none of these in powers of thought;
Mark, learn and bear off something meet;
For proper lessons there are taught.

CXXXVI.

Item, to *Montmartre* cloister-crowned
Which is a very ancient hill
I do convey and join the mound
That's known as *Mont Valerien* still;
A quarter-year too from the Bill
Of Pardon that I brought from *Rome;*
So, many Christians enter will
The walls where no man feels at home.

CXXXVII.

Item, to serving maids and men
In households rich, who make their diet
Of tarts and flawns and pastries when
At midnight lord and dame lie quiet,
And empty (wronging no one by it)
Much sooner eight than seven glasses,
My counsel is to make no riot
And not forget the sport of asses.

CXXXVIII.

Item, those heiresses with dozens
Of maids and men who crook the knee
And fathers, mothers, aunts and cousins,
Shall, by my soul, have nought from me:

'Tis suited well to their degree.
For scraps no *Jacobin* would measure
As worth the picking up may be
Great wealth to some poor girls of pleasure.

CXXXIX.

Monks *Benedictine* and *Chartreuse*,
Though strict their life in cloister cell,
At times a broader highway choose,
As these poor lasses know too well:
Perette and *Jacqueline* could tell,
Or *Isabeau* who swears: "I'facks!"
A man will scarcely merit hell
For wanting to supply their lacks.

CXL.

Item, to *Margot* fat and bloated,
In face and figure sweetly odd,
To all good works she's most devoted,
Faith, by our *Lady*, and by *God!*
She loves me well, the gentle bawd,
And I her every phase and feature.
Who meets her on his walks abroad
May read this ballade to the creature.

Ballade

Of Villon & Fat Margot.

IF I do serve my love, nor ask for hire,
    Mußt that be termed a vile or foolish trade?
For she possesses all that men desire.
I don for her the buckler and the blade.
When folks come in, with pot in hand displayed
I fetch the wine as silent as the dead,
Fruit, water, cheese, loaf, on the table spread,
And, if they pay well, show politeness great:
"Revisit us, when looking for a bed,
Within this brothel where we keep our ßtate!"

But other times the fat is in the fire,
Margot comes home without a penny made;
I hate her sight; my heart is filled with ire;
And swear her finery shall be conveyed
To pawn, since giving credit I forbade.
At that in scorn she tosses high her head
And, arms akimbo, swears in language dread,
By *Chrißt* I shan't! To finish the debate
A sudden slap upon her mouth is shed
Within this brothel where we keep our state.

Then fully charged my rearguard gun I fire
Of dunghill ßtench; when peace at laßt is made.
She pats my head all smiles, and coming nigher
We bill and coo like turtles in the shade.
As drunk as owls in bed together laid;
When we awake by longing she is led

To save love's fruit and cover me instead.
I groan below no burden light of weight;
Caressing her my strength and health are shed
Within this brothel where we keep our state.

Come wind, come hail, come froSt, I've baked
    my bread!
A brawling bully to a baggage wed.
Each worthy of the other be it said.
Like follows like; the beaSt muSt find its mate.
We sought the mire, and mire befouls our tread.
We fled from honour, honour now is fled,
Within this brothel where we keep our State.

CXLI.

Item, big *Joan* the *Breton* maid
Has leave to hold a public school
With *Marion* the *Idol's* aid
Where pupils over teachers rule.
Since, save in *Mehun's* prison cool,
Such markets are held everywhere,
No need for trade-signs fanciful,
I say, the work is no ways rare!

CXLII

Item, to *Noë,* called *The Beauty,*
No better gift in no event
Than willow rods prepared for duty,
And freshly cut, could I present.
Sweet are the alms of chaStisement;
Nor should his soul dread my command,
Eleven score of stripes be spent
On him by hangman *Henry's* hand.

CXLIII.

I know not what I can devise
For hospital's or hostel's care;
This is no time for sending lies;
The poor have ills enough to bear.
Each one may send his garlic there.
The begging friars have had my goose;
At best, the bones be pauper's share:
Small money for small people's use.

CXLIV.

Item, to pay my barber's labour,
(*Colin Galerne* who doth abide
The herbist *Angelot's* near neighbour)
A lump of ice . . . Whence? Marne supplied.
This clapped close to his belly's side
The winter he may spend at ease.
If wintry cures like this be tried
Next year no summer heats will tease.

CXLV.

Item, the *Foundlings* shall have nought:
But troops forlorn some comfort need;
At *Marion* the *Idol's* brought
Together nightly be the breed,
A lesson of my school I'll read
To all of them, both brief and fast.
Heads hard and foolish, pay good heed
Thereunto; for it is my last.

Villon's Good Counsel to the
Forlorn Hope.

FEAR lads, beware of letting fall
The faireſt rose you own today;
My clerks, like bird-lime gripping all,
When out upon the prigging lay
Or robbing, watch your skins I pray:
For following these paſtimes twain
Colin de Cayeulx had to pay,
Relying on appeals in vain.

Where lives and even souls are played
It truly is no paltry game:
If loſt, repentance will not aid,
But one muſt die in evil frame;
If won, no *Dido,* royal dame
Of *Carthage* comes within your clutch.
That man's a fool and loſt to shame
Who for so little ſtakes so much.

Give ear and learn my lesson right:
They truly say, as years expire
A lake of wine is drunk up quite
By summer glade or winter fire.
No coin that's fruitful you acquire;
But all you get is spent with speed.
Who profits by the devil's hire?
No man e'er throve by wicked deed.

Ballade
of Good Doctrine to Those of a
Naughty Life.

FOR if forged bulls about ye bear,
    Or let cogged dice your luck amend,
Or make false coins, of burns beware,
For traitors vile that so offend
In boiling water meet their end;
To theft or highway robbery fall:
Where, think ye, will the profits wend?
To taverns and to harlots all!

Make rhymes, brawls, music everywhere,
To wit of fools or clowns descend;
In farces, plays and concerts share;
In masques or shows of moral trend
The ears of town and city rend;
Or win at cards and games of ball:
Where goes the coin ye gain?   Perpend:
To taverns and to harlots all!

If for such filth ye do not care,
Dig, mow and o'er the sickle bend!
Or if ye be of learning bare,
Take service, mules and horses tend;
Be pleased if you have aught to spend;
Beat hemp or linen with a maul;
Where do your wages go, my friend?
To taverns and to harlots all!

Coat, jerkins, cloak belaced, you send
Each clout and garment great or small
Before they're worn or know a mend,
To taverns and to harlots all!

CXLVI.

My boon companions, this to you
Who make so free in every place;
Shun, shun the horrid sunburnt hue
That darkens the dead felon's face;
Avoid it, as a bad disgrace
As well as may be from it fly
Fore *God,* to heart this truth embrace,
An hour will come when you muſt die.

CXLVII.

Item, I give the Fifteen-Score,
Three-hundred were a name as good,
The *Paris,* not *Provincial,* Corps,
Because I owe them gratitude,
My spectacles; (but don't include
The case), because they lack the art
To set the decent and the lewd
At *Innocent's* in graves apart.

CXLVIII.

For here there are no smiles or play.
In vain they gained inheritances,
In richly valanced bedsteads lay,
Swilled wine, increased their girth-expanses,
Had revels, feſtivals and dances,
While death drew nearer every day.
Soon fade such pleasures and romances,
But all the sin of them will ſtay.

CXLIX.

These skulls whereon my vision reſts
Heaped up in charnel-houses dank
Perchance were Maſters of Requeſts,
Or once of Privy Council rank,
Or under market-baskets stank;
Since each and all speak juſt as little,
Of bishop or of mountebank,
I truly cannot tell a tittle.

CL.

And those who very lowly bowed
To one another in their day,
Whereof a few were rulers proud
While more did tremble and obey,
They've had their fill and now decay
Together in a heap pell-mell.
Their lordships all have flown away;
The clerk from maſter who can tell?

CLI.

They all are dead; their souls *God* cheer.
As for their flesh, 'tis rotted quite.
Those who were lords and ladies here
Whose nice and tender appetite
Rice, cream and paſtry nourished right,
Their bones have mouldered into duſt,
Unthrilled by laughter or delight . . .
Chriſt's pardon will be theirs I truſt!

CLII.

This song for those who vanished are
I've made, and do communicate
To regents, courts, both bench and bar,
The crime of avarice who hate,

And in their service to the ſtate
Both bones and bodies wither quick:
To them, when dead, commiserate
Be *God* and be *Saint Dominic.*

Lay.

IN turn from that vile cell to go
   Where life was almoŝt left by me,
Judge what an error there would be
If Fortune ŝtill remains my foe!
I should, by rights, it seemeth so,
Some of her smiles of favour see
In turn.

That I should reap death's fulleŝt woe
No man of reason will agree;
Please *God,* my spirit if set free
His mansion's joys above may know
In turn.

CLIII.

Item, since I am fairy-bred
I give to *Lomer* love's beŝt hap,
The art to turn each female head
Neath girlish snood or matron's cap,
And 'twill not coŝt a single rap
To him, nor warm his head at night
One hundred times to fill the gap
In *Danish Holgar's* great despite.

CLIV.

Item, *Jacques Cardon* not a mite,
(I've nought to suit him, more's the pity,
Nor mean to offer any slight)
Except this shepherd's song so pretty:

If it were *Marionette*, the ditty
Composed for *Marion Tawny-hide*,
Or that one, *Ope thy portal, Kitty*,
It would go well with mustard tried.

CLV.

Item, I leave Love's pining guild
Besides the lay of *Chartier* dead
A stoup for holy water filled
With tears and sobs above their bed,
With sprig of eglantine o'erspread,
Still evergreen, the drops to dole,
Provided fitting prayers be said
Or chanted for poor *Villon's* soul.

CLVI.

I grant this licence to *Jacques James*,
Who kills himself in gathering so,
To be betrothed to all the dames
He covets, but to marry, no!
Why hoards he? For his own I trow.
He'd grasp at scraps unfit for hogs;
What's gained by bitchery should go
By rights, I fancy, to the dogs.

CLVII.

Item, the *Seneschal Camus*
Who once from debt did me release
In recompense the blacksmith's dues
For shoeing little ducks and geese . . .
These silly tales all of a piece
I send to pass his time; at need
They may his stock of spills increase.
Good singing wearies one indeed.

CLVIII.

I leave the *Captain of the Guard*
Two little pages fair of face,
Philippe and *Marquet* fat as lard,
Who served, and thus grew wise apace,
The best part of their lives his Grace
The *Provost-Marshal Tristan* grim.
Alas, if they should lose this place
They must go bare both foot and limb.

CLIX.

Friend *Chappelain* shall have indeed
My chapel tonsured like his pate;
'Twill be no heavy task to read
A mass with nought to consecrate.
My cure, too, I would delegate,
But at no cure of souls he aims
And all confessions holds in hate.
Save those of dainty maids or dames.

CLX.

Because he knows my meaning clear
Jehan de Calays of honest fame,
(We have not met this thirty year,
He even does not know my name),
As arbiter I do proclaim;
If any puzzles people find
In this my will to make the same
As smooth as any apple-rind.

CLXI.

With glosses, comments, definitions,
Prescriptions also at command,
With diminutions or additions;
To cancel with his own right hand,

Transcribe what's hard to understand,
Or well or ill, pursue his bent,
Interpret and the sense expand;
To all these powers I give consent.

CLXII.

If anyone has passed away
To life through death unknown to me,
I do empower the said *Calays,*
So that my orders followed be
And my behests fulfilled, that he
Those legacies elsewhere apply
In modes from all self-seeking free;
For on his soul I do rely.

CLXIII.

In *Saint Avoye's* and not elsewhere
My sepulchre shall then be made;
And so that all may view me there,
If not in flesh by picture's aid,
My form and stature be portrayed
In ink, if cheap enough, no more.
A tomb? No; no such vain parade;
'Twould be too weighty for the floor.

CLXIV.

Item, I wish around my crypt
What follows, and no further tale,
Be written in no puny script;
And if supplies of ink should fail,
Let coal or charcoal draw the trail,
But so as not to hurt the plaster:
So shall my memory prevail
As one in wit and folly Master.

CLXV.

Heere lies & sleeps within this tomb
A scholar poor & never tall,
Slain by Love's fatal arrow, whom
Men's tongues did Francis Villon call.
No lands he owned however small.
He gave his all, the fact is plain:
Board, trestles, basket, bread & all.
For God's sake, sing him this refrain.

Rondeau.

ETERNAL rest be his for aye
  In clear and everlasting light;
No dish or platter worth a mite
He ever had, or sprig of bay.
His hair, beard, brows were shaved away,
Like turnip scraped and peeled aright.
Eternal rest be his for aye.

Harsh justice his behind did flay
And make him seek in exile flight;
In vain 'twas: "I appeal" to say,
A law term not too recondite.
Eternal rest be his for aye.

CLXVI.

The belfry great, of glass not fashioned,
Shall let a jangling peal be tolled;
All hearts will thrill at those impassioned,
Sweet songs from chimes full swing outrolled.
As stories tell, in days of old
They saved the homeland many times:
Nor thunder dire nor foemen bold
But fled the clangour of those chimes.

CLXVII.

The ringers shall receive four loaves;
If this seem mean, then double three
As much as a rich man behoves;
But of *Saint Stephen* shall they be.

For *Vollant* as his trouble's fee
One loaf.   Beholding him I claim
A week 'twill laſt him easily.
Who else?   *Jehan de la Garde* the same.

CLXVIII.

All to perfeét and to complete
Executors whose names ensue
I make; such tasks to them be sweet
And much content their debtors too.
Though boaſting never was their cue,
Yet each, thank *God,* has means to spend!
So they shall see this business through . . .
Six names I'll write: and then an end.

CLXIX.

Lieutenant *Martin Bellefaye*
Who in Crown cases doth excel.
And who as second? I should say
That 'tis a job for *Colombel.*
If he accepts and likes it well,
He'll all discharge in manner juſt.
Another? *Michel Jouvenel.*
These three alone shall take the truſt.

CLXX.

But if they seek to be excused
As dreading the first coſts to pay,
Or if the office be refused,
I do appoint this next relay,
All right good men in every way:
Philippe Brumeau, shall have the labour,
Brave knight, with him bear equal sway
Good Maſter *Jacques Raguyer,* his neighbour.

CLXXI.

As third, *Jacques James* with these have station,
Three men of means and honour known,
Desirous of their souls' salvation
And fearing *God* upon his throne.
They rather would expend their own
Than leave the trusts unsatisfied.
The whole they shall control alone
And, as seems best to them, divide.

CLXXII.

The *Master of the Wills,* so called,
Shall meddle not with *quid* or *quo;*
For in that office be installed
A youthful priest *Colas Tacot.*
To drink with him I fain would go,
Although my hat be sold to pay.
If he were able balls to throw,
I'd give him best at every play.

CLXXIV.

Guillaume du Ru shall manage all
The lights displayed around the bier.
To bear the corners of the pall
Let my executors appear.
Down, hair, beard, eyebrows more severe
Distresses feel and torture me.
My sickness grows; the time is here
To cry you mercy, all of ye.

Ballade

Wherein Villon Cries all Folk Mercy

TO *Benedictine* and *Chartreuse;*
    To begging friars and devotees;
To maids and wives and all who use
To wear the corset and chemise;
To lazy drones and worker bees;
To love-sick dandiprats who run
All buckskin-booted to the knees;
I cry you mercy, every one!

To little flirts who offer views
Of bosoms, in desire to tease;
To rioters and rowdy crews
And men with monkeys full of fleas;
To idiots, grouped in two and threes,
Who keep on whistling for fun;
To widows; flappers ripe for hes;
I cry you mercy, every one!

Who all but crusts did me refuse
With water cold enough to freeze,
No, those vile dogs I'll not excuse
Who robbed my belly of its ease!
I'd shame them with a downward **sneeze,**
But, sitting, I can summon none:
Well, well, then, to avoid a breeze,
I cry you mercy, every one!

Their fifteen ribs I fain would **grease**
With cudgel-oil, and senses stun
With bullets or such balls as these:
I cry you mercy, every one!

Ballade

To serve as Conclusion

SO here the teſtament doth end;
    Poor *Villon* his laſt word hath **said**.
Come to his burial, each friend,
By sound of belfry clamour led,
In clothes the hue of blood new shed,
Because he died Love's martyr dear:
He swore, by cock, Love ſtruck him **dead**
Preparing to depart from here.

On this as truth we may depend,
For he, perforce, in tatters fled
From her would not his plight amend.
No thorn or bramble lifts its head
From here to *Roussillon* outspread
That had not, let the truth appear,
Snatched from his clothes a scrap **or thread,**
Preparing to depart from here.

So when he died, we comprehend,
He scarce was worth a single shred.
What's more: Love keeneſt shafts did **send**
Againſt him on his dying bed;
To ſtrike their mark the arrows sped
More sharp than point of buckle's gear,
(Which truly is a marvel dread)
Preparing to depart from here.

Prince, as a falcon gently bred,
Know what he did when death was near:
He drank a draught of vintage red
Preparing to depart from here.

Here endeth The Great Testament.

Notes To

THE LITTLE TESTAMENT.

THE LITTLE TESTAMENT.—*M. Louis Thouasne, the latest & not the least erudite editor of Villon, is very insistent that this poem should be known as "The Lay of Master Francis Villon," pointing out that the more usual title was given contrary to the poet's wishes. I have given the alternative titles, & the reader can choose which he prefers.*

IV.   a horse with four white feet. *Proverbially untrustworthy.*

XI.   my trenchant sword. *Evidently pawned at a tavern.*

XII.   White Horse tavern sign. *In this verse & many others Villon drags in allusions to the tavern signs of old Paris, not forgetting the most notable of all, the Pomme de Pin, or Fir-Cone.*

the bull, etc. *This was a bull of Pope Calixtus III, ordering Christians to confess to their parish priests, & revoking a former bull of Pope Nicholas V, which had given the mendicant friars as wide powers of hearing confessions.*

XIV.   *The verse is satirical. Vallée, in reality, was a rich Clerk of the Parliament.*

XV.   "The Art of Memory." *A mediæval book, of a purport explained by the title, Villon's opinion of it may be gauged by the remark that it will be found in the hands of Tom Fool.*

XVIII. three hounds. *Nobles were the sole class privileged to keep hounds for the chase.*

XXI. The Provoſt. *Robert d'Eſtouteville, Provoſt of Paris, whose wife, Ambroise de Loré, was a patroness of the poet.*

XXV. *This & the following verse are satiric. The three orphan boys in reality were very rich men, the firſt-named a captain of finance, the second a money-lender, the third a profiteer.*

Every epoch has produced such hungry souls, whose ſtore of worldly possessions is ever in need of being increased.

XXVIII. *Similarly, the two poor clerks mentioned in this verse were in reality two wealthy prelates, lacking all the qualities wherewith the poet mockingly has inveſted them.*

XXX. *A fine piĉture of the fifteenth-century unemployed.*

XXXVI. *In this & the following verses Villon parodies the terminology of philosophers, whereof every age possesses its own particular jargon.*

XXXIX. *This gives us a glimpse into the garret of a man of letters in 1456.* "*Dans un grenier qu'on eſt bien à vingt ans!*"

Notes To
THE GREAT TESTAMENT.

V. Cotard. *For more information about the peculiar sanctity of this individual see the ballade later in The Great Testament.*

Picards. *The inhabitants of Picardy were supposed to be tainted with heresy, hence a prayer said in their manner might not be very efficacious.*

VI. Deus Laudem. *Psalm* 108, *verse* 7.

XV. *Villon is alluding to the* Roman de la Rose *by Jehan de Meung and Guillaume de Loris.*

XX. *The story is taken from Nonius Marcellus, not from Valerius Maximus.*

XXVIII. *This stanza paraphrases Job ch.* 7, *verse* 6.

XXXVI. Jacques Cœur. *The richest Frenchman of his day. He lent Charles VII money to carry on the wars against the English, was not repaid & died poor. A better patriot than financier.*

BALLADE OF THE LADIES OF BYEGONE TIMES.

Buridan. *This scholar's adventure with the naughty French queen in the Tour de Nesle was a popular fable of the times.*

Bertha debonair. *The mother of Charlemagne in the romances, which apply this epithet to her. Also known as Bertha "big-foot," the name used by Villon.*

Joan, the valour of Lorraine. *I take it that the*

original la bonne Lorraine conveys the idea of bravery still attached to the adjectives in the phrase "the good knight."

BALLADE OF THE LORDS OF BYEGONE TIMES.

King of Scots. *James II ob.* 1456. *His face was disfigured by a birthmark.*

Breton Claquin. *Duguesclin, the patriot leader against the English.*

BALLADE OF THE SAME THEME.

The golden-handed emperors. *The Byzantine emperors were often represented wearing gilded gauntlets.*

The stout, wise Dauphin. *The title of Dauphin was purchased by Philip of Valois who began his reign in* 1328. *Imbert or Hubert the last Count of Dauphiné and Viennois, who was called the Dauphin of Viennois, sold his title to the French king because he had no heir to succeed him. The first of the royal house to hold the title was Charles V during the lifetime of his father King John, whom he succeeded* 1364.

XLII.   At Rennes a needy peddlar known. *Mercerot de Rennes in original. See introductory essay for note on the fraternity of peddlars. Rennes may have been Villon's place of initiation into this doubtful society.*

THE REGRETS OF THE FAIR ARMOURESS.

It appears to have been the custom for the "bona robas" of Paris in Villon's day to have been known by the name of some trade, either as having sprung from that particular class, or from some idiosyncrasy in their costume. Cf. the epithets applied to the damsels in the ensuing ballade.

The beauteous Armouress. *She was a very real
personage. Born about* 1375 *she would have
been* 86 *in* 1461 *when Villon immortalized her
unhappy history. She was the mistress of
Nicolas d'Orgemont, Master of the Chamber
of Accounts & Canon of Notre-Dame, son to a
Chancellor & brother of a Bishop of Paris, who
actually installed her in a house in the cloister
of Notre-Dame, from which, however, she was
expelled by the indignant Chapter in* 1394. *In*
1416 *d'Orgemont having become implicated in
a plot against the State was thrown into prison,
despoiled of all his property, & died in a few
months. The Armouress, then a woman of*
40, *placed herself under the protection of a
despicable creature who exploited her till his
death in* 1426. *The remainder of her life was
a mere process of sinking from one degradation
to the next. It seems certain that Villon must
have known & conversed with her; hence this
unforgettable poem.*

What's come now to the forehead fair, etc.
*Readers of mediæval French should compare
this detailed description of feminine charms
with a very similar passage in "Aucassin &
Nicolette." The armouress in bewailing her
vanished charms falls naturally into the language of the romances she had heard sung by
minstrels in her youth.*

DOUBLE BALLADE.

Sardana. *Neither the name of this hero, nor yet
any account of a prototype is met with outside
of Villon's verse. The poet seems to have had*

vague recollections of Sardanapalus in describing a mythical worthy.

LVIII.   the fruits of woe.   *The choke-pear, a form of gag.*

LXVI.   *Turgis was the proprietor of the famous Pomme-dePin, the Fir-Cone Tavern, situated in the Rue de la Juiverie in the city.   Probably Villon's other heirs followed equally cheery trades.*

LXVII.   *In the Petit Testament Villon had left Perrenet Marchant, called the Bastard de la Barre, three trusses of straw for an indescribable purpose.   He now supplements that gift. This worthy appears to have been a crony of Villon, as there are several allusions to him in the poem; he receives two legacies & appears as a man fit to be sent on unpleasant errands.*

LXXVII.   *For Guillaume de Villon see introductory essay.*

LXXVIII.   that romance, etc.   *"Le pet au Diable" was a pillar stone which caused a famous town & gown riot in Paris.   Nothing is known of this romance, if indeed it ever was written.*

LXXXVI.   a lodging low, etc.   *Promptsault suggests that Villon's wish is that the thief may be broken on the wheel.*

LXXXVIII.   *Hesselin was a rich Parisian merchant of the day.   One can imagine the willingness wherewith mine host Turgis would have supplied wine to anyone on Master Francis' score!*

XCI.   *Jacques Raguyer, an ecclesiastic who became Bishop of Troyes in 1483.   Villon insinuates that he drank more than was good for him.*

The great cup was probably some tavern sign
hanging in the Place de Grève. For his brother
Jean Raguyer see stanza XCV.

XCV. Jean Raguyer was one of the twelve sergeants attached as guards to the Provost of
Paris. Brother to Jacques Raguyer. Bailly
was a clerk in the Chancery of the Ecclesiastical
Court of Notre Dame de Paris. The insinua-
tion may be that Jean was as great an eater as
his brother was a drinker.

XCVI. In 1457 Michault du Four held the office
of "sergent à verge" in the Châtelet prison.
He figures as such in the trial for the robbery
in the Collège de Navarre, & probably fell foul
of the poet, who now recommends him for employment to any leader of a troop of comedians
needing a clown.

XCVII. There were eleven score sergeants attached to the Provost of Paris. Vitu thinks
that the gift is chosen because the sergeants
were not allowed to wear such ornaments. The
eleven score appear to have been mounted police; perhaps that is the reason why Villon says
that the legacy is only intended for those who
go afoot.

XCIX. There was a Cholet associated with Guy
de Tabarie in a brawl in 1456, who later became a "sergent à verge" in the Châtelet &
was whipped publicly for riotous behaviour in
1465. The stanza might apply to him. In the
Petit Testament Villon left a joint legacy to a
Cholet & Jean le Loup, & the mention of Wolfish John in stanza C of the Great Testament
seems to indicate that the same pair are still in

his mind. The amusement of this pair of friends when the Petit Testament was written seems to have been stealing ducks & poultry outside the walls of Paris & hiding them under their clothes; but in the Grand Testament we seem to see a hint that Cholet has abandoned these courses for more warlike pursuits as the appropriate materials for the chase are left to Jean le Loup alone.

CI. *Du Boys was a famous goldsmith in Paris. His guild used to give a dinner to prisoners on Easter Day. Villon may have benefited by this good cheer during one of his incarcerations & for this reason have left a legacy of spices to a man who knew how to use them in preparing savoury food: but this is going deep into the hinterland of conjecture.*

CV. Pourras' abbess. *The abbess of Port Royal, the former being the popular pronunciation of the name. Villon hints a scandal, there having been some talk about the behaviour of the abbess in* 1455.

CVIII. Jean de Pontlieu, *Jean de Pouilli ("de Poliaco"), adversary of the friars in thirteenth century.*

Mathew; *there are several of this name in the field, Mathew Paris, Mathew of Westminster, etc.* Que scais-je?

Jean de Mehun, *the famous author of the "Roman de la Rose."*

CX. Baulde, *Baude de la Mare, a contemporary poet.*

the fiend of Vauvert, *an apparition of the times as famous as the later Cock-lane ghost.*

CXII.   the room wherein the council meets. *One of
the divisions of the Court which sat in the
Châtelet was known as the Cambre du Conseil.*
Macée of Orleans, etc. *There was a law againſt
silver girdles being worn by filles de joie.*
CXIII.   *François de la Vacquerie was "promoteur
de l'officialité," & later became vicar of Argen-
teuil. Villon is punning on "Vacquerie, vacherie
& vicairie." The scots gorget, according to M.
Vitu means a halter. Could the allusion to St.
George mean that Vacquerie had had treason-
able relations with the English?*
CXIV.   *Jean Laurens was one of the ecclesiastical
tribunal before whom Guy de Tabarie appeared
in 1458. No doubt Villon bore a grudge
againſt all his friend's judges, hence the uncom-
plimentary allusion to the personal appearance
of one of them.*
BALLADE & PRAYER.
Architriclin.   *Villon miſtook for a proper name the
Greek word in the New Teſtament meaning
ruler of the feaſt, & has enshrined it here as
the cognomen of yet another luſty drinker.*
CXXI.   Two young clerks, *Guillaume Cotin &
Thibault de Vitry, had received legacies in the
Petit Teſtament. These are now confirmed.
What Villon leaves them is all his legal claims
againſt the house of Guillaume Gueuldry,
which the commentators think means the pillory
or gallows.*
CXXIII.   *The Collège des Dix-huit received ſtu-
dents too poor to pay for themselves.*
CXXVI.   *In the Petit Teſtament Villon had lefт
Bicêtre caſtle to the Sieur de Grigny.   He now*

beſtows on him the Tower of Billy which was in a ruinous condition.

CXXVIII.   *Basanyer was notary at the Châtelet in* 1458. *Mautainſt and Rosnel were two of the examining magiſtrates who inveſtigated the criminal charges againſt Villon & his companions at the same time.*

that lord whose graces all excel, etc. *Robert d'Eſtouteville, Provoſt of Paris. He won the hand of his wife Ambroise de Loré at the celebrated tournament held at Saumur by King René in* 1446. *Clement Marot is reſponsible for the title of the ensuing ballade which contains a good deal of poetic licence, as the Provoſt had been married for years when it was written.*

CXXX.   *We are ignorant of the particular scurvy trick played by François Perdryer on Villon, happily so perhaps, if his mischief-making tongue deserved a tithe of the treatment prescribed for it in Villon's unsavoury recipe.*

CXXXI.   *Taillevent, the Mrs. Beeton of the day, wrote a "livre de cuisine."*

CXXXII.   *Clement Marot notes that in Villon's day appeared a little book called* The sayings of Franc-Gontier, *extolling the paſtoral life, & to refute it another book entitled* Franc-Gontier contradiſted, *which took a tyrant as its subject & wherein the life of a great lord of that time was satirised. Villon sets out to refute Franc-Gontier, but wisely determines not to meddle with tyrants.*

CXXXVI.   the walls where, etc. *Villon alludes to*

*the Abbaye des dames de Montmartre. The
stanza may contain a sneer at the nuns.*

CXL. by our Lady, etc. *Written "brelare bigod"
in the original. Villon's attempt at English has
proved a puzzle to commentators, but the first
of these Clement Marot explains properly,
par dieu et par notre Dame!*

CXLI. public school, *obviously a euphemism for an
establishment of quite another kind.*

CXLII. *It is probable that the Noë mentioned in
this stanza is the same person who took a third
of the whipping that Katherine de Vauselles
obtained for Villon. Henry Cousin was the
Paris hangman & executioner.*

VILLON'S GOOD COUNSEL.

Colin de Cayeulx, *one of the gang who robbed the
Collège de Navarre. He was finally hanged
after many crimes committed.*

CXLVII. *The blind man belonging to the hospital
of the Quinze-Vingts had to furnish a certain
number of helpers or mourners to escort dead
bodies that were buried in the cemetery of the
Saints Innocents.*

CLIII. Danish Holgar, *the hero of the romance
of Ogier the Dane, the great protector of female innocence.*

CLX. Jean de Calays, *patriot & anthologist. A
wealthy bourgeois of Paris who during the
English occupation formed a plot to rescue the
capital from them. It was discovered & he
saved his life by paying large sums. He com-
piled the "Jardin de Plaisance," a collection of
contemporary poems.*

CLXIII. A tomb? etc. *The chapel of St. Avoye*

*was the only one in Paris not situated on the
ground floor, hence no one could be buried in
the church.*

CLXVII.   loaves of St. Stephen, *i.e.,* ſtones.

CLXIX.   *As regards the executors named by Villon, Bellefaye was criminal lieutenant to the
Provoſt of Paris, Colombel & Jouvenel were
proſperous merchants, Jacques Raguyer we
have met before, & nothing much is known of
Bruneau or Jacques James, except that the latter was the owner of a bagnio, & is described as
a miser in a previous passage of the Grand
Teſtament. No doubt Villon had some satiric
purpose in coupling these names together, but
the secret of the jeſt seems loſt to us.*

CLXXIV.   Guillaume de Ru, *one of the prieſts associated with Guillaume de Villon at Saint
Benoît la Bientourné.*

**BALLADE WHEREIN VILLON CRIES ALL FOLK
MERCY.**

fifteen ribs, *one rib was supposed to be missing
from the male skeleton since the day when Eve
was created.*

SUPPLEMENT

PUBLISHER'S NOTE

In order to show the very real and individual merit of Mr. Lepper's translation of Villon's Testaments, and so that we may have in one volume a standard English translation of all of Villon's verse, the publishers include the following supplementary matter containing the unabridged translation by Mr. John Payne, including the Miscellaneous Poems; those verses which have been attributed to Villon, and Payne's masterly introduction to his edition of 1881.

We also include versions of Villon by Swinburne, Rossetti, Arthur Symons and Ezra Pound. The English and American reader because of this will now have a definitive edition of Villon's work.

The Poems of Master François Villon of Paris, now first done into English verse, with a biographical and critical Introduction

by

John Payne

(THE VILLON SOCIETY: 1892)

TO THE MEMORY
OF MY FRIEND
THÉODORE DE BANVILLE

INTRODUCTION *

By JOHN PAYNE

THERE are few names in the history of literature over which the shadow has so long and so persistently lain as over that of the father of French poetry. Up to no more distant period than the early part of the year 1877, it was not even known what was his real name, nor were the admirers of his genius in possession of any other facts relative to his personal history than could be gleaned, by a laborious process of inference and deduction, from such works of his as have been handed down to posterity. The materials that exist for the biography of Shakespeare or Dante are scanty enough, but they present a very harvest of fact and suggestion compared with the pitiable fragments which have so long represented our sole personal knowledge of Villon. That he had been twice condemned to death for unknown offences; that his father was dead and his mother still living at the time he reached his thirtieth year; that he attended the courses of the University of Paris in the capacity of scholar and presumably attained the quality of Licentiate in Arts, entitling him to the style of Dominus or Maître; above all, that his companions and acquaintances were of the lowest and most disreputable class and, indeed, that he himself wasted his youth in riot and debauchery and scrupled not to resort to the meanest and most revolting expedients to furnish forth that life of alternate lewd plenty and sheer

---

* The following essay was written in 1878 and was first published in 1881, by way of introduction to the expurgated edition of the Poems. I have thought it best to leave it substantially unaltered, incorporating such supplementary matter as is necessary to bring it up to date in the form of additional notes, distinguished by brackets.

starvation which, bohemian in grain as he was, he pre-
ferred to the decent dullness of a middle-class life; and
that he owed his immunity from punishment partly to ac-
cidents, such as the succession of Louis XI to his father's
throne, and partly to the intervention of influential pro-
tectors, probably attracted by his eminent literary merits,
amongst whom stood prominent his namesake and supposed
relative, Guillaume de Villon;—such were the main scraps
and parings of information upon which, until the publication of M. Longnon's "Étude Biographique," * we had alone
to rely for our conception of the man in his habit as he
lived.   Even now the facts and dates, which M. Longnon
has so valiantly and so ingeniously rescued for us from the
vast charnelhouse of mediæval history, are in themselves
scanty enough, and it is necessary to apply to their connection and elucidation no mean amount of study and labour
before anything like a definite framework of biography can
be constructed from them.   Such as they are, however, they
enable us for the first time to catch a glimpse of the
strange mad life and dissolute yet attractive personality
of the wild, reckless, unfortunate Parisian poet, whose
splendid if erratic verse flames out like a meteor from the
somewhat dim twilight of French fifteenth-century literature.

It is to be hoped that the example so ably set by M. Longnon will not be allowed to remain unfollowed and that
new seekers in the labyrinth of mediæval archives and
records will succeed in filling up for us those yawning gaps
in Villon's history which are yet too painfully apparent.†
M. Longnon, indeed, seems to imply a promise that he

---

* Étude Biographique sur François Villon, d'après les docu-
ments inédits conservés aux Archieves Nationales.   Par Auguste
Longnon.   Paris, 1877.
[† The hopes expressed in the above paragraph have now
to a certain extent been realised by the labours of MM. Bijvanck,
Schwob, Paris, Schöne and others, as well as by those of M.
Longnon himself; but much yet remains to be done.   *See* Prefa-
tory Note.]

himself has not yet said his last word upon the subject; and we may fairly look, within the next few years, for new help and guidance at the hands of M. Auguste Vitu, when he at last gives to the world his long and anxiously awaited edition of the poems, a work which, considering the special qualifications and opportunities of the editor and the devotion with which he has applied himself to the task, may be expected to prove the definitive edition of Villon.*

In putting together the following pages I should be sorry to allow it to be supposed that I contemplated any exhaustive study of the man or of his work. My sole object has been to present the facts and hypotheses, of which we are in possession on the subject, in such a plain and accessible form as may furnish to those readers of the translation of his strange and splendid verse who (and we know that they are as yet many) are unacquainted with the poems, and perhaps even with the name of Villon,† some unpre-

---

*I owe to the kindness of M. Vitu the following particulars of the scheme of his forthcoming edition of Villon, which will serve to show the great scope and importance of the work, now in an advanced stage of preparation. It will form four volumes, the first of which will consist wholly of notices upon Villon and his contemporaries, completing and correcting all that has been hitherto published on the subject. The second volume will comprise the complete text of Villon, augmented by several authentic poems hitherto unknown, an appendix containing pieces written in imitation of the old poet and a short treatise upon mediæval prosody and versification, in correction of the errors and laches of modern scholars. The text presented will be founded wholly upon the manuscripts, the gothic editions being all, according to M. Vitu, incorrect, garbled and incomplete. The third volume will comprise the "Jargon," with the addition of five unpublished ballads, besides a philological interpretation and a history of the work; and the fourth will contain an exhaustive glossary. [Since the above note was written (in 1881), M. Vitu has died, leaving his work uncompleted. *See* Prefatory Note.]

† The uncertainty that has so long obscured every detail of Villon's life has extended even to the pronunciation of the name by which he is known to posterity. It has been, and still

tentious introduction, as well as to his personality and habit
of thought as to the circumstance and local colouring of
his verse. The rest I leave to more competent hands than
my own, content if I have, in the following sketch and in
the translation to which it is intended to serve as preface,
set ajar one more door, long sadly moss-grown and ivy-
hidden, into that enchanted wonderland of French poetry,
which glows with such spring-tide glory of many-coloured
bloom, such autumn majesty of matured fruit.

I.

The year 1431 may, without impropriety, be styled the
grand climacteric of French national life. After a hundred
years' struggle for national existence against the great
soldiers produced in uninterrupted succession by England,
apparently with no other object than the conquest of the

---

is, the custom to pronounce the poet's adoptive name *Vilon,* as if
written with one *l,* and it is only of late years that this error
(no doubt due to the proverbial carelessness of the French, and
more especially of the Parisian public, with regard to the pronunciation of proper names) has been authoritatively corrected.
As M. Jannet remarks it is only in the Midi that folk know
how to sound the *ll mouillés* or liquid ll. It has now, however,
been conclusively demonstrated that the correct pronunciation of
the name is *Vilion,* the poet himself (as was first pointed out by
M. Jannet) always rhyming it with such words as *pavillon,*
tourbillon, bouillon, aiguillon, etc., in which the *ll* are liquid; and
a still more decisive argument is furnished by M. Longnon, who
has noted, in the course of his researches, that the Latin form
of the patronymic, as it appears in contemporary documents,
is *Villione,* and that the name is spelt in error *Vignon* in a record
of the Court of Parliament, dated 25th July, 1425, in which
Guillaume de Villon is shown by internal evidence to be the
person referred to, thus proving by inference that the *ll* of the
name, apparently imperfectly caught from dictation, must nec-
essarily have been liquid; otherwise they could hardly have been
mistaken for another liquid, *gn.* Moreover (and this information also we owe to M. Longnon) the name of the village which
gave birth to the Canon of St. Benoit is to this day pronounced
Vilion.

neighbouring continent, as well as against far more dangerous and insidious intestine enemies; after having seen three-
quarters of the kingdom, of which Charles VI was the
nominal king, bowed in apparently permanent subjection
to the foreign foe, the French people had at last succeeded
in placing on the head of Charles VII the crown of his
fathers, thanks to the superhuman efforts of two of the
noblest women that ever lived, Jeanne d'Arc and Agnes
Sorel, and to the unselfish devotion of the great-hearted
patriot Jacques Cœur. On the 31st of May, 1431, the
heroine of Domrèmy consummated the most glorious life of
which the history of womankind affords example by an
equally noble death upon the pyre of Rouen; not, however,
before she had fulfilled her sublime purpose. Before her
death she had seen the achievement of the great object, the
coronation of Charles VII at Rheims, which she had origi-
nally proposed to herself as the term of her unparalleled
political career: and the English, driven out of stronghold
after stronghold, province after province, were now obliged
to concentrate their efforts on the retention of the provinces
of Normandy and Guienne. Nor was it long ere even this
limited purpose was perforce abandoned. Paris, after six-
teen years of foreign occupation, opened her gates to her
legitimate king and four or five more years sufficed to complete the permanent expulsion of the English from France.
The heroic peasant girl of Lorraine had not only recovered
for the Dauphin his lawful inheritance; she had created the
French people. Until her time France had been inhabited
by Bretons, Angevins, Bourbonnais, Burgundians, Poitevins,
Armagnacs; at last the baptism of fire through which the
land had passed and the breath of heroism that emanated
from the Maid of Orléans had welded together the con-
flicting sections and had informed them with that breath of
patriotism which is the beginning of all national life. France
had at length become a nation. The change was not yet
complete: there remained yet much to be done and suffered
before the precious gift so hardly won could be definitively

assured: Louis XI, with his cold wisdom and his unshrinking determination, was yet to consolidate by the calculated severity of his administration and the supple firmness of his domestic and foreign policy (long so grossly misunderstood and calumniated) the unity and harmony of the young realm. Still the new national life had been effectually conquered and it only remained for time and wisdom to confirm and substantiate it.

One of the most salient symptoms of a national impulse of regeneration is commonly afforded by the consolidation and individualisation of the national speech. I should say rather, perhaps, that such a phenomenon is one of those most necessary to such a popular movement and therefore most to be expected from it, though it may not always be possible to trace the correspondence of the one with the other. However, it is certain that the converse generally holds true, and it was undoubtedly so in the present instance. Up to the middle of the fifteenth century France can scarcely be said to have possessed a *national* language; the Langue d'Oïl, for want of writers of supreme genius, had hardly as yet become fashioned into an individual tongue. It is to poets rather than to prose writers that we must look for the influences that stimulate and direct the growth of a national speech, and there is, perhaps, no instance in which the power of a true poet is more decisively visible than in his control over the creation and definition of a language, especially during periods of national formation and transition. Up to the time of which I speak, this influence had been wanting in France. During the fourteenth century and the earlier part of the next, her poetic literature had consisted mainly of imitations of the elder poets, especially of Guillaume de Lorris and Jehan de Meung, of the Chansons de Geste and other heroic romances and probably also of the Troubadours or poets of the Langue d'Oc. Abundance of sweet singers had risen and passed away, most of them modelled upon the Roman de la Rose, whose influence had been as that of the plane, beneath which, it is

said, no corn will ripen. Under its shadow there had
sprung up abundance of flowers, but they were those rather
of the hothouse and the garden than the robuster and
healthier denizens of the woods and fields. There was
hardly any breath of national life in the singers of the
time: Guillaume de Machau, Eustache Deschamps, Jehan
Froissart, Christine de Pisan, Alain Chartier, Charles
d'Orléans, were indeed poets of the second order, of whom
any country might be proud; but they were poets who
(if one should except from their verse its accidental local
colouring) might, for all that they evince of national life
and national spirit, have been produced in any country where
a like and sufficient culture prevailed. The thirteenth century had indeed produced one poet, Rutubeuf, in whose
"Complaintes" ran some breath of popular feeling, sorely
limited, however, by deficient power and lacking inspira-
tion in the singer; and in some of the productions of the
poets I have named above, notably in Deschamps' fine ballad
on the death of the great Constable du Guesclin, Christine
de Pisan's pathetic lament over the madness of Charles
VI and the state of the kingdom and in the anonymous
poem know as "Le Combat des Trente," there breathes
some nobler and stronger spirit, some distant echo of popular passion; nor is the sweet verse of Charles d'Orléans
wanting in patriotic notes, touched, unfortunately, with too
slight a hand. But these are few and far between; the
subjects usually chosen are love and chivalry, questions of
honour, gallantry and religion, treated allegorically and
rhetorically after the extinct and artificial fashion of the
"Roman de la Rose." Beautiful as is often the colour and
cadence of the verse, we cannot but feel that it is a beauty
and a charm which belong to a past age and which have
no living relation to that in which they saw the light. In
perusing the poetry of the time, one seems to be gazing
upon interminable stretches of antique tapestry, embroid-
ered in splendid but somewhat faded hues, wherein armed
knights and ladies, clad in quaintly-cut raiment and adorned

with ornaments of archaic form, sit at the banquet, stray a-toying in gardens, ride a-hawking in fields or pass a-hunting through woods, where every flower is moulded after a conventional pattern and no leaf dares assert itself save for the purpose of decoration. Here everything is prescribed: the bow of the knight as he kneels before his lady, the sweep of the châtelaine's robe through the bannered galleries, the fall of the standard on the wind, the career of the war-horse through the lists, the flight of the birds through the air, the motions of the deer that stand at gaze in the woods,—all are ordered in obedience to a certain strictly prescribed formula, in which one feels that nature and passion have ceased to have any sufficient part. Whether one wanders with Charles d'Orléans through the forest of Ennuyeuse Tristesse, conversing with Dangier, Amour, Beaulté d'Amours, Faux Dangier, Dame Merencolie and a host of other allegorical personages, or listens to Guillaume de Machau, as, with a thousand quaint conceits and gallant devices, he compares his lady to David's harp with its twenty-five strings, one feels that one is gazing upon phantoms and moving in a dead world, from which the colour and the glory are hopelessly faded. It is not poets of the trouvère or troubadour order who can have any decisive effect upon the new growth of a nation, as it emerges from the fiery furnace of national regeneration; it is for no mere sweet singer that the task of giving to the national speech that new impulse which shall correspond with its political and social advance is reserved. The chosen one may be rude, lacking in culture, gross in thought or form, but he must and will come with lips touched with the fire of heaven and voice ringing with the accents of the new world. Such a poet was called for by the necessities of the time and such an one was provided, by the subtle influences which order the mechanism of national formation, in the very year that saw the consecration of French nationality by the death of the Martyr of Rouen.

II.

François de Montcorbier, better known as Villon, from the name of his lifelong patron and protector, was born in the year 1431, within a few weeks or days of the capital political event of which I have just spoken. It is uncertain what place may claim the honour of his birth, but the probabilities appear to be in favour of his having been born at some village near (or at least in the diocese of) Paris, entitling him to the style of *Parisiensis* or *de Paris,* which he commonly adopts, and also, combined with residence and graduation at the Paris University, to certain municipal and other privileges of citizenship, such as the right of voting at the election of Échevins or notables. It seems probable that he belonged to a decayed and impoverished branch of the noble family of Montcorbier, who took their name from a fief and village (since disappeared) in the Bourbonnais, and that to this connection with the duchy he was indebted for the moderate countenance and assistance which he seems to have received at the hands of the princes of the ducal family of Bourbon. The only fact certainly known about his relatives is that he had an uncle, a priest established at Angers in Anjou, to whom he paid at least one visit with a sufficiently questionable purpose, and that the rest of his family (with the exception of his mother, as to whom we possess no biographical details whatever) utterly and consistently refused to recognise him—according to his own story, because of his lack of means,—but, it may rather be assumed, on account of the very unsavoury nature of his connections and the incessant scandal of his life. Decent people (as we may presume these relatives of his to have been) might well be allowed to consider their connection with Master Fran· çois Villon of brawling, wenching, lock-picking and cheat:- ing notoriety as anything but a desirable one, and history will hardly reproach them with their unwillingness to culti-· vate it. However this may be, it is certain that the only relative who appears to have had any share in Villon's life was his mother; and it is little likely that she, whom he describes as a poor old woman, unlettered and feeble, and who (as he himself confesses) suffered on his account "bitter anguish and many sorrows," could have exercised any considerable influence over her brilliant, turbulent, ne'er-do-weel son. Yet he seems always, in the midst of the mire of his life, to have kept one place in his heart white with that filial love which outlasts all others and which has so often been to poets the perfume of their lives. In the words of Théophile Gautier, his love for his mother shines out of the turmoil and ferment of his life like a white and serene lily springing from the heart of a marsh. His father he only mentions to tell us that he is dead, when or how there is nothing to show, and to state that he was poor and of mean extraction, nor have we any information as to his condition or to the position in which he left his family. We do not even know whether Villon's mother inhabited Paris or not, but it would appear probable that she did, from his mention in the ballad that bears her name of the *monstier* or convent church (probably l'Église des Celestins *) in which she was wont to say her orisons and which was decorated with paintings little likely to have then existed in any of the villages about Paris. However, the want of living and available family connections was amply compensated to Villon by the protecting care of a

---

* I cannot agree with M. Longnon in considering the Abbé Valentin Dufour wrong in his suggestion that the church to which Villon makes his mother refer might have been l'Eglise des Celestins, which was decorated with pictures of heaven and hell precisely answering to the description in the ballad. The very word used by Villon (*monstier,* i. e. *monasterium,* the old form of the modern *moûtier*) points to the probability of the church having been a conventual one; and we need not read the words *"dont je suis paroissienne"* as meaning more than that the convent where she made her orisons was situated in her own parish or that she was a regular attendant at the services held there and so looked upon it as practically her parish church.

patron who seems to have taken him under his wing and perhaps even adopted him at an early age. Guillaume de Villon, the patron in question, was a respectable and apparently well-to-do ecclesiastic, belonging to a family established at a village of the same name (which I believe still exists), Villon, near Tonnerre, in the dominions of the ducal house of Burgundy, and the worthy priest appears to have turned his origin to good account in securing the patronage of that princely family, which in all probability he was able in some measure to divert to the benefit of his protégé. We first hear of Messire Guillaume as one of the chaplains of the parish church of the little village of Gentilly, near Paris, during his occupancy of which cure he probably formed an acquaintance with the poet's family, which afterwards led to his undertaking the charge of their son. About the year of François' birth, Messire Guillaume obtained a long-awaited promotion: through the influence, probably, of the Burgundian family he was appointed to a stall in the cathedral church of St. Benoît le Bétourné or Bientourné at Paris, a lucrative benefice, involving, besides a handsome residence called L'Hotel de la Porte Rouge, in the Close or Cloister of St. Benoît, a considerable piece of land and a stipend enabling him to live at his ease. In addition to his official income, he must have had some private fortune, as he possessed, to our knowledge, at least two houses in the neighbourhood, which he let out to tenants, and a considerable rent-charge upon a third, which latter, however, the good easy man appears hardly to have troubled himself to collect, as, at the time it is mentioned in the archives of the Chapter, we find it stated that no less than eight years' rent was then in arrear. In this position he remained till his death, which occurred in 1468; and there is every reason to believe that he survived his protégé, towards whom, during the whole of his life, he appears never to have relaxed from untiring and unobtrusive benevolence. The disreputable nature of the poet's life and the perpetually recurring troubles in which he became involved seem to have had no effect in inducing the good Canon to withdraw his protection from so apparently unworthy an object, and (according to Villon himself) he was the ordinary *Deus ex machinâ* to whom the poet looked for deliverance from the consequences of his own folly and misconduct. Of no other person does Villon speak in the same unqualified terms of grateful affection as of the Canon of St. Benoît, calling him "his more than father, who had been to him more tender than mothers to their sucking babes." Indeed, such honour and affection did he bear him that we find him on one occasion (with a consideration little to have been expected from such a scapegrace) actually begging the good Canon to leave him to his fate and not compromise his own reputation by taking any steps in the interest of so disreputable a connection.

Of the early life of Villon we know nothing whatever, except that he must have entered at the University of Paris about the year 1446, when he was fifteen years of age. In March, 1449, he was admitted to the Baccalaureate and became Licentiate in Theology or Ecclesiastical Law and Master of Arts in the summer of 1452. During the six years of his studies, it is probable that he resided with Guillaume de Villon at L'Hotel de la Porte Rouge, which adjoined the Collège de Sorbonne, and the the weekly payment of two sols Parisis, which as a scholar he was bound to make to the collegiate authorities, and the fees incurred on the occasion of his proceeding to his degrees were provided by his patron. It frequently happened in mediæval times, when colleges were far less richly endowed than is now the case, that the want of official means for providing such aids as exhibitions and bursaries for the education of poor scholars was supplied by private charity, and this was, indeed, a favourite mode of benefaction with rich and liberal-minded folk. The special college at which Villon followed the courses of the University was probably not the Collège de Sorbonne, notwithstanding its immediate neighbourhood to L'Hotel de la Porte Rouge, but (and this I

am inclined to suppose from the intimate knowledge he
displayed of its internal arrangements on a later occasion)
the Collège de Navarre, also in close vicinity to the Canon's
residence. It is possible that the latter intended Villon
for the church, in which direction lay the interest he could
command: if so, his intentions were completely frustrated,
for Villon never (as he himself tells us) achieved the
necessary theological degree; and subsequent events, hardly
to be called beyond his own control, completely diverted
him from the pursuit of the liberal professions and caused
him to become the wolf that watches for an opportunity
of spoiling the fold, rather than the shepherd whose duty
it is to guard it. The interval between the matriculation
of Villon and the year 1455 is an almost complete blank
for us, the only materials we have to enable us to follow
him being the allusions and references to be gleaned from
a study of his poems; but it was certainly during this
period of his life that he contracted the acquaintances, disreputable and otherwise, which exercised so decisive an influence over his future history. Amongst those belonging
to the former category may be specially cited René de
Montigny, Colin de Cayeulx, Jehan le Loup, Casin Chollet
and Philip Brunel, Seigneur de Grigny, all scoundrels of
the first water; and for women, Huguette du Hamel, Abbess of Port Royal or Pourras, as shining a light in debauchery as any of his male friends, and la petite Macée
of Orleans, his first mistress ("avoit ma ceincture," says
he), whom he characterises as "très mauvaise ordure," a
thoroughly bad lot, to say nothing of the obscure rogues,
sharpers and women of ill-fame who defile in so endless
a procession through the pages. The two first mentioned,
who were fellow-students of our poet, were indeed rogues
of no mean eminence and appear both to have attained
that distinction of "dying upright in the sun" which was
at once so fascinating and so terrible a contingency to
Villon. René or Regnier de Montigny was the son of
a man of noble family at Bourges, who, possessing certain

fiefs in the neighbourhood of Paris and a charge in the royal household, accompanied Charles VII to his capital, on its reduction in 1436, and there died shortly after, leaving his family in poor circumstances. Regnier, who was two years older than Villon, early distinguished himself by criminal exploits, pursuing an ever ascending scale of gravity. In August, 1452, he was banished by the Provost of Paris for a disreputable nocturnal brawl, in which he had beaten the sergeants of the watch before the hostelry of La Grosse Margot; whereupon he betook himself to the provinces, and after there exercising his peculiar talents to such effect as to be imprisoned for various offences at Rouen, Tours, Bordeaux and Poitiers, he once more ventured to Paris, where he speedily again came under the notice of the authorities. After a condemnation for the comparatively trifling offence of card-sharping, he was sentenced to death as an accessory to a murder committed in the Cemetery of the Innocents; but for this he succeeded in obtaining the royal pardon. This narrow escape, however, seems to have produced no salutary effect on him, for in 1457, after having escaped punishment for various offences by virtue of his quality of clerk, of which he availed himself to claim protection at the hands of the Bishop of Paris, he was again condemned to death for divers sacrilegious thefts from the Parisian churches, and under this condemnation, notwithstanding a pardon obtained by family influence, which appears to have been quashed for irregularity, it seems certain that the world was at last made rid of him by that "longitudinal death" he had so richly deserved; and it is even possible that he had the honour of being the first to make essay of a new gibbet in that year erected by the city of Paris and afterwards known as le Gibet de Montigny.

Colin de Cayeulx was no less eminent as a scoundrel. The son of a Parisian locksmith, he made use of his knowledge of his father's trade to become one of the most artistic thieves presented by the criminal annals of Paris; and it is in this his especial quality of picklock that we shall again come across him in connection with Villon. After a long career of crime, he was in 1460 condemned to death as (in the words of the Procureur du Roi) "an incorrigible thief, picklock, marauder and sacrilegious scoundrel," unworthy to enjoy the much-abused benefit of clergy, by which he and rascals of his kidney had so often profited to escape the consequences of their crimes. Nevertheless, the sentence was, for reasons unknown, not carried into effect, and he appears even to have been set at liberty. But his immunity was not of long duration; we know from Villon himself that, certainly not later than the next year, his infamous companion was broken on the wheel for "esbats" or gambols (as he euphemistically styles them), the least of which appears to have been rape or highway robbery, perpetrated at the villages of Rueil near Paris and Montpippeau near Orleans.

Of the Seigneur de Grigny we know little but through Villon himself, who places him in the same category as Montigny by bequeathing to him the right of shelter in various ruins around Paris, which were then the favourite resorts and strongholds of the choicest thieves and vagabonds of the time, and speaks of him in such terms as leave little doubt that his "lay" or criminal specialty was the coining and uttering of false money.

Jehan le Loup and Casin Chollet were scoundrels of a lower rank or "sneak-thieves," dealing chiefly in petty thefts of poultry and other eatables: the former appears to have been a bargee and fisherman in the service of the municipality of Paris, by whom he was employed to keep the moats and wet ditches of the city clean and free from weeds, an occupation which afforded him peculiar facilities for marauding among the numerous herds of ducks and geese kept by the corporation and the adjacent commoners of the city upon the waters which he traversed in his dredging boat; the later, by the operation of that curious law of reciprocal attraction between the police and the criminal

classes, of whose prevalence in countries of the Latin race
so many instances exist, after a turbulent early life, became tipstaff at the Châtelet prison and was in 1465 deprived of his office, flogged at the cart's tail and imprisoned for having spread false reports (probably with a pro-
fessional eye to plunder) of the entry into Paris of the
Burgundians, who then lay leaguer at the gates, under the
command of Charles the Rash.

The Abbess of Port Royal is another curious figure in
the history of criminality. Of a good family and holding
a rich abbacy, she early distinguished herself by leading a
life of unbridled licentiousness, associating with all the
lewd characters of her time, frequenting houses of ill-
fame and debauchery in male attire, brawling and fighting
in the streets, holding orgies in the convent itself, which
remind us of the legends of Gilles de Retz, and selling
the nuns under her control for the purpose of prostitution.
So notorious were her excesses and misconduct in Paris
that she became the subject of a satirical popular song,
whose author she caused to be beaten to death. For these
and many other shameless acts she was at last brought to
account, imprisoned and finally, after many shifts of liti-
gation, definitively deprived of her abbey, when she doubtless sank to the lowest depths of degradation. By reason
of her wanton way of life, the people appear to have corrupted her title and to have dubbed her Abbesse de Poilras
or Shaven-poll, a slang name then given to women of ill-
fame who had been pilloried and had their heads shaved.
We know from Villon himself that she was a companion
of his on at least one occasion, and it was probably during
one of her excursions in man's attire that she and the poet
in 1455 paid their famous visit to Perrot Girard, the unfortunate barber of Bourg la Reine, near Paris, and lived
for a week at his expense and that of his brood of sucking
pigs.

However, besides these disreputable acquaintances, Villon seems to have become intimate with many persons to

whom his merry, devil-may-care disposition, and perhaps also his wit and genius, made him acceptable whilst he and they were young: of these some were fellow-students of his own, others apparently people of better rank and position, those "gracious gallants," "so fair of fashion and of show, in song and speech so excellent," whom, as he himself tells us, he frequented in his youth. Some of these, says he, after became "masters and lords and great of grace"; and it was no doubt to the kindly remembrance which these latter cherished of the jolly, brilliant companion of their youth that he owed something of his comparative immunity from punishment for the numberless faults and follies which he committed at a subsequent and less favoured period. Of these (M. Longnon has discovered for us) were Martin Bellefaye, Lord of Ferrières en Brie, afterwards Advocate of the Châtelet and Lieutenant-Criminel of the Provost of Paris; Pierre Basanier, Notary and afterwards Clerc-Criminel at the Châtelet; Pierre Blaru, Guillaume Charriau, Robert Valée, Thomas Tricot, all men of some importance in law or trade at Paris; and (possibly through his son) Robert d'Estouteville, Provost of Paris, to whom Villon, in his student-days, dedicated the curious ballad on the subject of his marriage with Ambroise de Loré. It is by no means impossible that from this time of pleasant companionship and comparative respectability dates Villon's connection with the royal poet, Charles d'Orléans; and that he may also have became known to the then Dauphin (afterwards Louis XI) is almost equally likely, in view of the habits of familiar intercourse of the latter with the burghers and clerks of Paris and his well-known love of and taste for literature. It appears certain that Louis had some knowledge of and liking for Villon, founded probably on admiration of his wit and genius; and it was assuredly owing to this, and not to any general amnesty *de joyeux avènement,* that the poet owed his last remission of the capital penalty at the hands of so severe a monarch as the titular author of the "Cent Nouvelles Nouvelles," for which he shows (in the Greater Testament) so special and personal a gratitude as almost to preclude the idea of its having been granted otherwise than as a matter of peculiar and personal favour.

This early period of Villon's life, extending at least up to his twenty-fourth year, appears to have been free from crime or misconduct of any very gross character. Although he himself laments that he had neglected to study in his youth, whereby he might have slept warm in his old age, and expressly states that he fled from school as bird from cage, we have seen that, if he did not achieve the presumable object of his college career, namely the Maîtrise or Doctorate of Theology, he yet paid sufficient attention to his studies to enable him to acquire the title of Master of Arts, and it would appear that he had even been presented to what he calls a simple-tonsure chapelry, possibly one of the numerous quasi-sinecure offices connected with the churches or ecclesiastical machinery of the diocese of Paris, which were reserved as prizes for the more industrious and deserving scholars. M. Longnon is of opinion that he eked out the small revenue of this office by taking pupils, and amongst them the three poor orphans to whom he so frequently alludes; but I confess I see no ground for this supposition with regard to the latter, of whom he always speaks in such terms as to lead us to suppose them to have been actually foundlings dependent wholly upon his bounty. In 1456 he describes them as "three little children all bare, poor, unprovided orphans, shoeless and helpless, naked as a worm," and makes provision for their entertainment for at least one winter; and I am unable, therefore, to discover how M. Longnon justifies his hypothesis that they were young men of good or well-to-do families confided to Villon's tuition. On the other hand it is by no means impossible that some of the numerous unidentified persons mentioned in the Testaments may have been pupils of the poet at the period of which I speak. At all events, however he may have earned his living, it seems certain that up to the early part of the year 1455 he committed no act which brought him under the unfavourable notice of the police; and we find, indeed, in a subsequent document under the royal seal, his assertion, that "he had till then well and honourably governed himself, without having been attaint, reproved or convicted of any ill case, blame or reproach," accepted without question, as would certainly not have been the case had he been previously unfavourably known to the authorities. Yet it is evident, both on his own showing and on the authority of popular report, especially of the curious collecton of anecdotes in verse known as "Les Repues Franches" or "Free Feeds" (of which he was the hero, *not* the author, and in which one phase of his many-sided character and career is recorded), that his life during this interval, if not actually trenching upon the limits of strictly punishable offences, was yet one of sufficiently disreputable character and marked by such license and misconduct as would assuredly, in more settled and law-abiding times, have early brought his career to a disgraceful close. He himself tells us that he lived more merrily than most in his youth; and we need only refer to the remarkable list of wine-shops, rogues and women of ill-fame with which he shows so familiar an acquaintance, to satisfy ourselves that much of his time must have been spent in debauchery and wantonness of the most uncompromising character. It is not likely that the supplies of money he could have obtained from legitimate sources, such as the kindness of Guillaume de Villon, the practice of tuition and the offices he may have gained as prizes during his scholastic career, would have sufficed for the prodigal expenditure naturally consequent upon his depraved tastes. On his own showing, he possessed a happy combination of most of the vices which lead a man to fling away his life in the quagmires of dissipation;—amorous, gluttonous, a drunkard, a spendthrift and a gambler,—no thought of future consequences seems ever to have been allowed to intervene between him and the satisfaction of his debased desires; and it was only in the intervals of disaster and depression (naturally of frequent occurrence in such a life) that the better nature of the man breaks out in notes of bitter anguish and heartfelt sorrow, of which it is difficult to doubt the genuineness, although the mercurial humour of the poet quickly allows them to merge into mocking cadences of biting satire and scornful merriment.

It was therefore to provide for the satisfaction of his inclinations towards debauchery that he became gradually entangled in complications of bad company and questionable dealings which led him step by step to that maze of crime and disaster in which his whole after-life was wrecked. In "Les Repues Franches"—a work not published till long after his death, whose assertions, apparently founded upon popular tradition (for Villon, quickly as his memory faded after the middle of the next century, seems to have been a prominent and favourite personality among his contemporaries of Paris) are amply endorsed by the confessions of the poet himself—we find him represented as the head of a band of scholars, poor clerks and beggars, "learning at others' expense," all "gallants with sleeveless pourpoints," "having perpetual occasions for gratuitous feeds, both winter and summer," who are classed under the generic title of "Les Sujets François Villon," and into whose mouth the author puts this admirable dogma of despotic equality— worthy of that hero of our own times, the British working-man himself—"Whoso hath nothing it behooves that he fare better than anyone else." "Le bon Maître François Villon" comforts his "compaignons," who are described as not being worth two sound onions, with the assurance that they shall want for nothing, but shall presently have bread, wine and roast-meat *à grant foyson,* and proceeds to practise a series of tricks after the manner of Till Eulenspiegel, by which, chiefly through the persuasiveness of his honeyed tongue, he succeeds in procuring them wherewithal to make merry and enjoy great good cheer. Provided with stolen bread, fish, meat and other victual to their hearts' desire, the jolly scoundrels remember that they owe it as a duty to themselves to get drunk and that if they would fain arrive at that desirable consummation, they must needs furnish themselves with liquor at some one else's expense. Master François is equal to the occasion; taking two pitchers of precisely similar appearance, one filled with fair water and the other empty, he repairs to the celebrated tavern of the Fir Apple, situate in the Rue de la Juiverie, (of which and its landlord, Robin Turgis, mention is so often made in Villon's verse), and requests to have the empty pitcher filled with the best of their white wine. This being done, in a twinkling the accomplished sharper changes the pitchers and pretending to examine the contents, asks the tapster what kind of wine he has given him, to which he replies that it is white wine of Baigneux. "Do you take me for a fool?" cries Villon. "Take back your rubbish. I asked for good white wine of Beaune and will have none other." So saying, he empties the pitcher of water into the cask of Baigneux wine—the tapster of course supposing it to be the liquor with which he had just served him—and makes off, in triumph, with the pitcherful of white wine, which he has thus obtained at the unlucky vintner's expense. The landlord of the Fir Apple seems to have been a favourite subject for the roguish tricks of the poet, who confesses in his Greater Testament that he had stolen from him fourteen hogsheads of white wine of Aulnis and adds insult to injury by offering to pay him, if he will come to him, but (says he slily) "if he find out my lodging, he'll be wiser than any wizard." This colossal theft of wine was probably perpetrated on a cartload on its way to Turgis, and perhaps furnished forth the great Repue Franche alluded to in Villon's Seemly Lesson to the Wastrils or Good-for-Noughts, apropos of which he so pathetically laments that even a load of wine is drunk out at last, " by fire in winter or woods in summer."

From tricks of this kind, devoted to obtaining the materials for those orgies in which his soul delighted, there is no reason to suppose that he did not lightly pass to others more serious or that he shrank from the employment of more criminal means of obtaining the money which was equally necessary for the indulgence of the licentious humours of himself and his companions. In the words of the anonymous author of "Les Repues Franches," "He was the nursing mother of those who had no money; in swindling behind and before he was a most diligent man." So celebrated was he, indeed, as a man of expedients, that he attained the rare honour of becoming a popular type and the word "villonnerie" was long used among the lower classes of Paris to describe such sharping practices as were traditionally attributed to Villon as the great master of the art; even as from the later roguish type of Till Eulenspiegel, *Gallicé Ulespiègle* (many of the traditional stories of whose rogueries are founded upon Villon's exploits), is derived the still extant word "espièglerie."

Villon, indeed, appears to have at once attained the summit of his roguish profession: ready of wit, eloquent of tongue, he seems to have turned all the resources of his vivid poetical imagination to the service of his debauched desires and so generally was his superiority admitted that, when he afterwards more seriously adopted the profession of "hook and crook," he seems to have been at once recognised by the knights of the road and the prison as, if not their actual chief, at least the directing and devising head, upon whose ingenious and methodical ordering was dependent the success of their more important operations.

At this period, in all probability, came into action another personage, whose influence seems never to have ceased to affect Villon's life and who (if we may trust to his own oft-repeated asseverations) was mainly responsible for his ill-directed and untimely career. This was a young lady named Catherine de Vaucelles or Vaucel and (according to M. Longnon's plausible conjecture) either the niece or cousin of one of the Canons of St. Benoît, Pierre de Vaucel, who occupied a house in the cloister, within a door or two of L'Hotel de la Porte Rouge. Her family inhabited the Rue St. Jacques, in which stood the Church of St. Benoît; and it is very probable that she may have altogether resided with her uncle for the purpose of ordering his household, in accordance with a custom of general prevalence among ecclesiastics, on whom celibacy was enforced,—or that through her connection with the cloister was afforded to Villon the opportunity of forming an intimate acquaintance with her, which speedily developed into courtship. Catherine de Vaucelles would appear (if we may accept Villon's designation of her as a demoiselle) to have been a young lady of good or at least respectable family and it would seem also that she was a finished coquette. Throughout the whole of Villon's verse the remembrance of the one chaste and real love of his life is ever present and he is fertile in invective against the cruelty and infidelity of his mistress. According to his own account, however, the love seems to have been entirely on his side; for, although she amused him by feigned kindness and unimportant concessions, he himself allows that she never gave him any sufficient reason to hope, reproaching her bitterly for not having at first told him her true intent, in which case he would have enforced himself to break the ties that bound him to her. She appears, indeed, to have taken delight in making mock of him and playing with his affections; but, often as he bethought himself to renounce his unhappy attachment, to

"Resign and be at peace,"

he seems, with the true temper of a lover, to have always returned before long to his vainly-caressed hope. No assertion does he more frequently repeat than that this his early love was the cause of all his misfortunes and of his untimely death. "I die a martyr to love," he says, "enrolled among the saints thereof"; and the expression of his

anguish is often so poignant that we can hardly refuse to
believe in the reality of his passion. Nevertheless, he does
not accuse the girl of having favoured others at his expense. "Though I never got a spark of hope from her,"
he says, "I know not nor care if she be as harsh to others
as to me"; and indeed he seems to imply that she was too
fond of money to be accessible to any other passion. One
of the persons mentioned in the poems was perhaps a rival
of his, as he tells us, in his Ballad of Light Loves, that
a certain Noé or Noel was present when he (Villon) was
beaten as washerwomen beat clothes by the river, all naked,
and that on account of the aforesaid Catherine de Vaucelles; and as he says "Noel was the *third* who was there,"
assuming the other person present to have been the lady,
we may fairly suppose that Noel was a more favoured lover
of Catherine's, by whom was administered to Villon the
correction of which he speaks so bitterly, probably on the
occasion of a sham rendezvous, in the nature of a trap, devised by Catherine to get rid of an importunate lover.
This presumption is strengthened by the fact that in the
Lesser Testament, speaking of his unhappy love affair, he
says, "Other than I, who is younger and can rattle more
coin, is in favour with her"; * and that in the Greater
Testament he bequeaths to Noel le Jolys (who may fairly
be taken to be the Noé mentioned above) the unpleasant
legacy of two hundred and twenty strokes, to be hand-
somely laid on with a handful of green osier rods by
Maître Henriot, the executioner of Paris. It is possible
that Catherine may, for a while, have encouraged Villon
out of cupidity, and after getting all she could out of him,
have thrown him off for a better-furnished admirer; but
of this we find no assertion in his poems, although, if we
may believe in the authenticity of certain pieces attributed
to him in the "Jardin de Plaisance," he accuses her of
compelling him to be always putting his hand in his pocket

* I quote a variant of Oct. vii.

to purchase her good graces, now asking for a velvet gown
and now for "high headgear" (*haults atours*) or the like
costly articles of dress; and (in a ballad coming under the
same category) he speaks of her "corps tant vicieux" and
reproaches her with having sold him her favours for twenty
rose-crowns and having, after draining him dry, transferred
her interested affections to a hideous but rich old man, although (says he) "I was so devoted to her, that had she
asked me to give her the moon, I had essayed to scale the
heavens." However, these pieces seem to be wrongly assigned to Villon; and in despite of the epithet, "foul
wanton," applied to her, probably in a passing fit of ir-
ritability and jealousy,—such as at times overcomes the most
respectful and devoted of unrequited lovers,—all the authentic evidence we possess points to the conclusion that
the young lady was guilty of no serious misconduct towards
Villon beyond that ordinary coquetry and love of admiration, and perhaps of amusement, which may have led her
to give some passing encouragement to the merry, witty
poet of the early days; and this hypothesis he himself con-
firms by the pure and beautiful ballad which he dedicates
to her, prefacing it, however, with the delicately depreca-
tory qualification that he had composed it to acquit himself
towards Love rather than her,—a ballad which breathes the
chastest and most romantic spirit of wistful love and anticipates for us Ronsard, as he pictures his lady in her old
age, sitting with her maidens at the veillée and proudly
recalling to herself and her companions that she had been
celebrated by her poet-lover "du temps que j'etais belle."

True and permanent as was the love of Villon for
Catherine, it does not seem to have restrained him from
the frequentation of those light o' loves, whose names so
jostle each other in his pages. La Belle Heaulmière, Blanche
the Slippermaker, Guillemette the Upholsteress, Macée of
Orléans, Katherine the Spurmaker, Denise, Jacqueline, Perrette, Isabeau, Marion the Statue, tall Jehanne of Brittany, a cloud of lorettes and grisettes, trip and chatter

through his reminiscences; and with two of them, Jehanneton la Chaperonnière and La Grosse Margot, he appears to have formed permanent connections. No doubt the *femmes folles de leur corps,* with whom Paris has ever abounded, were not wanting at the fantastic revels carried on by our bohemian and his band of scape-graces in the ruins of Nygeon, Billy and Bicêtre, or the woods to be met with at a bowshot in every direction round the Paris of his time. "Ill cat to ill rat," as he himself says; the feminine element was hardly likely to be wanting for the completion of the perfect disreputable harmony of his surroundings.

III.

This early period of comparative innocence, or at least obscurity, was now drawing to a close and its conclusion was marked for Villon by a disaster which in all probability arose from his connection with Catherine de Vaucelles and which fell like a thunderbolt on the careless merriment of his life. On the evening of the 5th June, 1455, the day of the Fête-Dieu, Villon was seated on a stone bench under the clock-tower of the Church of St. Benoît, in the Rue St. Jacques, in company with a priest called Gilles and the girl Isabeau above mentioned (who is noted in the Greater Testament as making constant use of a particular phrase, "Enné" or "Is it not?"),* with whom he had supped and sallied out at about nine o'clock to enjoy the coolness of the night air. As they sat talking, there came up to them a priest called Phillippe Chermoye or Sermoise and a friend of his named Jehan le Merdi, a graduate of the University. Chermoye, who was probably a rival of Villon for the good graces of Catherine de Vaucelles, appeared in a furious state of exasperation against the poet and swaggered up to him, exclaiming, "So I have found you at last!" Villon rose and courteously

---

* *Lat.* Anné? Isabeau would probably have used the French equivalent of "Ain't it?"

offered him room to sit down; but the other pushed him
rudely back into his place, saying, "I warrant I'll anger
you!" To which the poet replied, "Why do you accost me
thus angrily, Master Philip? What harm have I done
you? What is your will of me?" and would have retired
into the cloister for safety; but Chermoye, pursuing him
to the gate of the close, drew a great rapier from under
his gown and smote him grievously on the lower part of
the face, slitting his underlip and causing great effusion
of blood. At this Gilles and Isabeau took the alarm and
apparently fearing to be involved in the affray, made off,
leaving Villon alone and unsupported. Maddened by the
pain of his wound and by the blood with which he felt
himself covered, the latter drew a short sword that he
carried under his walking cloak and in endeavouring to
defend himself, wounded his aggressor in the groin, without being at the time aware of what he had done. At
this juncture Jehan le Merdi came up and seeing his friend
wounded, crept treacherously behind Villon and caught
away his sword. Finding himself defenceless against Chermoye, who persisted in loading him with abuse and sought
to give him the finishing stroke with his long sword, the
wretched François looked about for some means of de-
fence and seeing a big stone at his feet, snatched it up
and flung it in the priest's face with such force and pre-
cision that the latter fell to the ground insensible. Villon
immediately went off to get his wounds dressed by a barber
named Fouquet, who, in accordance with the police regu-
lations affecting such cases, demanded of him his name and
that of his assailant. To him Villon accordingly related
the whole affair, giving his own name as Michel Mouton
and stating his intention on the morrow to procure Chermoye's arrest for the unprovoked assault. Meantime, some
passers-by found the priest lying unconscious on the pavement of the cloiser, with his drawn sword in his hand, and
carried him into one of the houses in the close, where his
wounds were dressed and whence he was next day transferred

to the Hospital of L'Hotel Dieu, where on the Saturday following he died; the words of the record ("pour faute de bon gouvernement ou autrement") leaving it doubtful whether his death was not rather due to unskilful treatment than to his actual wounds. Before his death, however, he had been visited and examined by one of the apparitors of the Châtelet, to whom he related the whole affair, expressing a wish that no proceedings should be taken against Villon, to whom, he said, he forgave his death, "by reason of certain causes moving him thereunto"; words which seem to tell strongly in favour of the hypothesis that the quarrel bore some relation to Catherine de Vaucelles. However, Villon was summoned before the Châtelet Court to answer for Chermoye's death, but (as the record says) "fearing rigour of justice," he had availed himself of the interval to take to flight and appears to have left Paris. No record of the proceedings against him appears to be extant, but the probabilities point to his having been convicted in his absence and condemned, in default, to banishment from the kingdom. However, his exile did not last long. In January, 1456, he presented a petition to the Crown, setting forth that up to the time of the brawl "he had been known as a man of good life and renown and honest conversation and had in all things well and honourably governed himself, without having been attaint, reproved or convicted of any other ill case, blame or reproach whatsoever," and praying the king, in view of this and of the fact that the dead man had deprecated any proceedings against his adversary, to impart to him his grace and mercy in the remission of the sentence. Thanks, no doubt, to the assistance of Villon's powerful friends, as well as to the circumstances of the case, which appears to have been an unusually clear one of justifiable homicide in self-defence, reflecting no blame whatever on the poet, letters of grace and remission were in the same month accorded to him by Charles VII and he presently returned to Paris, where he perhaps endeavoured to resume his former

life of comparative respectability; at all events, we may be
sure that he so far resumed his old habits, as to renew his
acquaintance with Catherine de Vaucelles.

The six months of his banishment, which had in all probability been passed in the company of the thieves and vagabonds who infested the neighbourhood of Paris, had, however, sufficed hopelessly to compromise his life. It is impossible to suppose that he can, in the interval, have supported himself by any honest means; and it is clearly to
this period that may be traced his definitive affiliation to the
band or bands of robbers of which Guy Tabarie, Petit
Jean, Colin de Cayeulx and Regnier de Montigny were
the most distinguished ornaments and of which he himself
was destined to become an important member.* It is to
this time of need that Villon himself assigns the raid upon
the barber of Bourg-la-Reine, in company with Huguette
du Hamel; and excursions of this kind were doubtless
amongst the least reprehensible of his expedients to keep
body and soul together. On his return to Paris, he appears

[* The researches of M. Marcel Schwob have brought to
light the fact that the language, hitherto unidentified, in which
the "Jargon," or "Jobelin" of Villon is written, was a thieves'
slang or lingo peculiar to a notable association of robbers and
outlaws known as the Coquillarts or Compagnons de la Coquille,
a title probably derived from the circumstance that the Company
was largely recruited from the swarms of false palmers or pro-
fessional visitants to various shrines and especially to that of
St. James of Compostella (whose emblem was the scallop or
cockleshell habitually worn in the hat as a token of accomplishment of the pilgrimage to his shrine—hence the term *coquillart*
or cockleshell wearer vulgarly applied to the palmer—), who
availed themselves of the quasi-sacred character of the pilgrim
to rob and murder with impunity on all the high roads of
mediæval France. Of this lawless association Villon's comrades
Montigny and Cayeulx are known to have formed part and the
poet himself doubtless became affiliated to the Company during his
six months of exile. The generic name (Coquillarts) of the Companions of the Cockleshell figures in the poems composing the
"Jargon," which were doubtless written expressly for the members
of the band.]

to have been badly received by his lady-love and in despair quickly reverted to the habits of criminality which had now obtained a firm hold on him. We have it, on undoubted authority, that during the eleven months which followed his return to Paris he was concerned in three robberies committed or attempted by his band,—namely, a burglary perpetrated on the house of a priest called Guillaume Coiffier, by which they netted five or six hundred gold crowns; an attempt (frustrated by the vigilance of a dog) to steal the sacred vessels from the Church of St. Maturin; and the breaking open of the treasury of the Collège de Navarre, whence they stole another five or six hundred gold crowns, thanks to the intimate knowledge of its interior acquired by Villon during his scholastic career and to the lock-picking talents of Colin de Cayeulx. These were doubtless but a few of the operations undertaken by the band of desperadoes with whom Villon was now inseparably associated; and as they rejoiced in such accomplices as a goldsmith, who made them false keys and melted down for them their purchase or booty, when it assumed the inconvenient form of holy or other vessels, and in the protection of the Cloister of Notre Dame, of which sanctuary they seem to have made their headquarters, besides other refuges, to which they could flee when hard pressed, in the houses of priests and clerks, of whom several seem to have been affiliated to the band, the poet and his companions appear for a while to have pursued their hazardous profession to highly lucrative account. The successful attempt upon the Collège de Navarre took place shortly before Christmas, 1456, and almost immediately afterwards the poet, who seems to have thrown himself heart and soul into his new vocation and to have gained such appreciation among his comrades as led them to entrust him with the more delicate and imaginative branches of the craft, left Paris for Angers, where an uncle of his was (as I have already said) a priest residing in a convent; according to Villon's own account (see the Lesser Testament) in consequence of the despair to which he was driven by Catherine's unkindness and which led him to exile himself from Paris, for the purpose of endeavouring, by change of scene and occupation, to break away from the "very amorous bondage" in which he felt his heart withering away; but in reality (as we learn from irrecusable evidence) with the view of examining into the possibility of a business operation upon the goods of a rich ecclesiastic of the Angevin town and of devising such a plan as should, from a careful artistic study of the localities and circumstance, commend itself to his ingenious wit, for the purpose of enabling the band to relieve the good priest of the five or six hundred crowns * which they believed him to possess. Whether this scheme was carried out or not we have no information; however this may be, it does not appear that Villon returned to Paris for more than two years afterwards and his long sojourn in the provinces is probably to be accounted for on the supposition that he received warning from some of his comrades of the discovery of the burglary committed at the Collège de Navarre and feeling himself inconveniently well known to the Parisian police, thought it best to remain awhile in hiding where he was less notorious.

The discovery and consequent (at least temporary) break-up of the band was due to the drunken folly of Guy Tabarie, who could not refrain from boasting, in his cups, of the nefarious exploits of himself and his comrades, who (he said) possessed such powerful and efficient instruments of effraction that no locks or bolts could resist them. By a curious hazard, a country priest, the Prior of Paray-le-Moniau, a connection of Guillaume Coiffier, to whose despoilment by Villon and his companions I have already referred, became the chance recipient of the drunken confidences of Tabarie, whilst staying in Paris and breakfasting at the Pulpit Tavern on the Petit Pont, and by feigning a desire to take part in his burglarious operations, succeeded in eliciting from

---

* "Five or six hundred gold crowns" was decidedly the sacramental sum with the Companions. who apparently disdained to fly at more trifling game.

him sufficient details of the affaire Coiffier and that of the Collège de Navarre to enable him to procure Tabarie's arrest and committal to the Châtelet prison in the summer of 1458. Claimed by the Bishop of Paris in his quality of clerk, he was transferred to the prison of the ecclesiastical jurisdiction and after suffering the question ordinary and extraordinary, made a full confession, denouncing the various members of the band and naming Villon and Colin de Cayeulx as the acting chiefs. This happened more than two and a half years after the poet's departure from Paris, nor is it known when he was arrested in consequence of the revelations of Guy Tabarie; but it is probable, looking at the comparatively full manner in which his time may be accounted for between that date and 1461, that his arrest took place shortly afterwards. It is certain, on his own showing, that he was again tried and condemned to death, after having undergone the question by water, and that he made an appeal (the text of which has not reached us) to the High Court of Parliament, which, being probably supported by some of his influential friends, resulted in the commutation of the capital penalty into that of perpetual exile from the kingdom. It was apparently in the interval between the pronunciation of his condemnation to death and the allowance of the appeal that he composed the magnificent ballad, in which he imagines himself and his companions in infamy hanging dead upon the gibbet of Montfaucon, with faces dented with bird-pecks, alternately dried up and blackened by the sun and blanched and soddened by the rain, and in whose lines one seems to hear the grisly rattle of the wind through the dry bones of the wretched criminals "done to death by justice," as they swing to and fro, making weird music in "the ghosts' moonshine." This poem establishes the fact that five of his band were condemned with him and it is probable that these unhappy wretches, less fortunate than himself in possessing influential friends, actually realised the ghastly picture conjured up by the poet's fantastic imagination.

On receiving notification of the judgment commuting his sentence, he addressed to the Parliament the curious ballad (called in error his Appeal)* requesting a delay of three days for the purpose of providing himself and bidding his friends adieu, before setting out for the place of his exile, and presently left Paris on his wanderings. Of his itinerary we possess no indications save those to be laboriously culled from his poems; but, by a process of inference, we may fairly assume that he took his way to Orléans and followed the course of the Loire nearly to its sources, whence he struck off for the town of Roussillon in Dauphiné, a possession of the Duke of Bourbon, who had lately made gift of it to his bastard brother, Louis de Bourbon, Mareschal and Seneschal of the Bourbonnais, supposed to be the Seneschal to whom Villon alludes as having once paid his debts. Under the wing of this friend, he probably established his headquarters, during the term of his exile, at Roussillon, making excursions now and then to other places—notably to Salins in Burgundy, where it seems he had managed to establish the three poor orphans of whom he speaks in the Lesser Testament. In the Greater Testament he represents himself as having visited them, referring to them in such terms as to leave no doubt that they were still children, and moreover makes a bequest for the purpose of completing their education and buying them cates. To this period of exile (or perhaps, rather, to the time of his preceding visit to Angers) must also be assigned his stay at St. Generoux in the marches of Poitou, where he made the acquaintance of the two pretty Poitevin ladies—"filles belles

---

[* M. Longnon is manifestly in error in attributing the composition of this Ballad and that last before mentioned to the interval between Villon's condemnation for the homicide of Chermoye and his pardon, as is sufficiently evident from the fact that he describes himself in the latter as one of six done to death by justice. M. Longnon's statement of the judicial consequences of the prosecution in question is also at variance with the terms of the letters of remission, as set out in his appendix.]

et gentes," as he calls them—who taught him to speak the Poitou dialect; and his visit to Blois, where Charles d'Orléans was then residing and where Villon took part in a sort of poetical contest established by the poet-prince, from which resulted the curious ballad, "Je meurs de soif auprès de la fontaine," composed (as were poems of a like character by a number of other poets *) upon the theme indicated by the refrain and offering a notable example of the inferiority to which a great and original poet could descend, when forced painfully to elaborate the unsympathetic ideas of others and to bend his free and natural style to the artificial conceits and rhetorical niceties of the other rhymers of the day. A well-known anecdote of Rabelais attributes to the poet, at this period of his life, a voyage to England, where he is said to have ingratiated himself with the then regnant king and to have made him a celebrated speech distinguished equally by wit and patriotism; but the story carries in itself its own refutation and M. Longnon has shown that it is a mere modernisation of a precisely similar trait attributed to another French scholar of earlier date, Hugues le Noir, who is said to have taken refuge at the court of King John of England in the thirteenth century. It may be remarked, by the by, as a curious instance of the vitality of these old popular jests, that the trait above alluded to has, in our own times, become the foundation of one of the wittiest of modern Yankee stories. There is nothing whatever either in the works of Villon or in any contemporary documents, in which his name is mentioned, to show that he at any time visited England. Had he done so, the effect of so radical a change in his habits and surroundings would certainly have left no inconsiderable trace in the verse of so shrewd and keen an observer of men and manners: and it is probable that the whole story arose from the fact of his banishment from the

---

* Cf. Les Poésies de Charles d'Orléans. Ed. Guichard, 1842, pp. 128-138.

kingdom of France, the concoctor forgetting at that later period that the France of Villon's time was a comparatively small country, from which banishment was possible into many independent or tributary states, which afterwards became an integral portion of the French realm.

During the term of his banishment, Villon does not appear to have been under any kind of police supervision. At that time there existed no court exercising supreme authority over the whole kingdom; each province, nay, each ecclesiastical diocese possessed its own independent civil and criminal jurisdiction, having little or no connection with the better organised tribunals of Paris, which city had not yet begun to be that nucleus of centralisation it afterwards became. So that he appears to have been comparatively free to move about at will: and from a passage in his Greater Testament, in which he speaks of himself as "pauvre mercerot de Rennes"—poor hawker or pedlar of Rennes—it seems possible that he eked out the scanty doles to be obtained from the kindness of friends (such as the Duke de Bourbon, who lent him six crowns and to whom we find him again applying for a loan, and Jean le Cornu, a Parisian ecclesiastic, of whom says Villon, "he has always furnished me in my great need and distress") by travelling as a pedlar from town to town,—and this would explain his wanderings hither and thither.* However if he ever really essayed

---

[* Since the above was written, M. Vitu has shown in his learned introduction to his great work on the "Jargon" that the *mercerots* or *mercelots* formed the lowest grade of the great trades-guild of the *Merciers* and were mostly rogues and vagabonds of the lowest order, whose misdeeds, committed under the convenient cover of the pedlar's pack, were winked at and to whom protection was extended by the powerful parent society in consideration of the large addition to its revenues derived from the *redevances* or annual dues paid by them. The name of *mercelot* or pedlar appears to have been, indeed, practically synonymous with "sturdy rogue and vagabond"; many of the class were secretly affiliated to such criminal associations as the Gueux and the Coquillarts and it seems probable, therefore, that Villon's

this honest and laborious existence, he quickly tired of it
and there is no doubt that before long he came again in
contact with some of his old comrades in crime—members
of the dispersed band, either exiled like himself or hiding
from justice in the provinces—and was easily led to resume
in their company that career of dishonesty and turbulence
which had so fatal an attraction for him. Among these
was notably Colin de Cayeulx, in whose company he no
doubt assisted at some of those "esbats" for which, in the
year 1461, his old master in roguery was (as he tells us
in the Second Ballad of the Jargon) at last subjected to the
extreme penalty of the law, being broken on the wheel
probably at Montpippeau near Orléans, where the crimes
for which he suffered and of which rape seems to have
been the most venial were committed. At this last-named
place, Villon again appears in the centre of France, trusting apparently to lapse of time for the avoidance of his
banishment; and here it was not long before he again came
in collision with the authorities. In the early part of the
year 1461 we find him, in company with others of unknown condition, committing a crime (said to have been
the theft of a silver lamp from the parish church of Baccon
near Orléans) for which he was arrested by the police of
the ecclesiastical jurisdiction and brought before the tribunal
of the Bishop of Orléans, that Jacques Thibault d'Aussigny
against whom he so bitterly inveighs in the Greater Testament. We have no record of his conviction, but it cannot
be doubted that he was again condemned to death, although
(with his usual luck) a more powerful protector than had
ever before intervened in his favour appeared in time to
prevent the execution of the sentence. It appears from
his own statements that he was, during the whole summer

---

adoption of a nominally honest calling was only a mask for the
continuation of the career of lawlessness to which he must have
been irretrievably committed. Rennes was doubtless the headquarters of the provincial branch of the Mercers' Guild to which
he was directly affiliated.]

of 1461, confined in what he calls a "fosse" in the castle
of Meung-sur-Loire—a name reserved for the horrible dens
without light or air, dripping with water and swarming
with rats, toads, and snakes, adjoining the castle moat. Here
he was (if we may credit his own statements) more than
once subjected to the question of torture by water and
(what seems to have been a more terrible hardship than
all the rest to a man of Villon's passionate devotion to rich
and delicate eating and drinking) he was "passing scurvily
fed" on dry bread and water. At Meung, it can hardly
be doubted, he composed the curious ballad in which he
presents his heart and body, or soul and sense, arguing one
against the other, and sets before us, in a pithy and well-
sustained dialogue, the sentiments of remorse and despair—
not unrelieved by the inevitable stroke of covert satire—
which seem to have formed the normal state of his mind
during any interval of enforced retirement from the light
of the sun and the pursuit of his nefarious profession. To
this period also belongs the beautiful and pathetic ballad, in
which he calls upon all to whom Fortune has made gift of
freedom from other service than that of God in Paradise,
all for whom life is light with glad laughter and pleasant
song, to have compassion on him as he lies on the cold
earth, fasting feast and fast-days alike, in the dreary dungeon,
whither neither light of levin nor noise of whirlwind can
penetrate for the thickness of the walls that enfold him like
the cerecloths of a corpse. From an expression in this ballad, it would seem that there were no steps to Villon's
cell, but that he was let down into it by ropes, as was the
prophet Jeremiah in the dungeon of Malchiah the son of
Hammelech, in the reign of Zedekiah king of Judah. Here,
too, he seems to have been chained up in fetters ("enferré")
and (if we may believe him when he accuses the bishop
of having made him chew many a "poire d'angoisse") gagged
to prevent his crying out. To all this were added the
tortures of hunger, for even the wretched food supplied
to him seems to have been so small in quantity ("une petite

miche," says he) as barely to stave off starvation,—a
wretched state of things for a man who had always, on his
own confession, too well nourished his body; and it is very
possible that, had his imprisonment been of long duration,
hardship and privation might have ended his life. However,
this was not destined to be the case. In July, 1461, the old
King Charles VII died and was succeeded by the Dauphin,
Louis XI; and on the 2nd October following, the latter
remitted Villon's penalty and ordered his release by letters
of grace dated at Meung-sur-Loire, where he had probably
learnt the fate of the poet, whilst passing in the course
of the royal progress customary on a new king's accession.
It seems probable that he remembered Villon's name as
that of an old acquaintance, if not as that of a brilliant
and ingenius poet; and the saying is indeed traditionally
attributed to Louis XI, whose taste in literature was of the
acutest, that he could not afford to hang Villon. As
the kingdom could boast of 100,000 rascals of equal
eminence, but not of one other poet so accomplished in
"gentliz dictz et ingénieux sçavoir." At all events, it is
certain that Charles d'Orléans, to whom most commentators
have ascribed the merit of procuring Villon's release by
intercession with the king, could not have successfully intervened, as he was at that time in disgrace with the new
monarch, between whom and himself a bitter personal hos-
tility had long existed: and "Le Dit de la naissance Marie
d'Orléans"—by which poem, addressed to the father of the
new-born princess, Villon is conjectured to have secured his
good offices—is most assuredly the production neither of
Villon nor of any one else in any way worthy of the name
of poet.

IV.

Immediately upon his release, Villon seems to have returned to Paris and there appears to be some little warrant
for the supposition that he endeavoured to earn his living
as an *avoué* or in some similar capacity about the ecclesiasti-

cal courts. However this may be, he was probably speedily obliged to renounce all efforts of this kind on account of the failing state of his health and the exhaustion consequent upon the privations he had undergone and the irregularity of his debauched and licentious life. It would appear, too, from an allusion in his later verse, that his goods, little as they were ("even to the bed under me," says he), had been seized by three creditors, named Moreau, Provins and Turgis, in satisfaction apparently of debts due by him to them, or to reimburse themselves for thefts practised at their expense, at the time of "Les Repues Franches," two of which, carried out at Turgis' cost, I have already noticed: and as the scanty proceeds of the execution are not likely to have satisfied any considerable portion of his liabilities, it would seem that his creditors took further proceedings against him, from the consequences of which he was compelled to seek safety in some place of concealment, whither he defies Turgis to follow him. That he did not take refuge with Guillaume de Villon is obvious (as is also the honourable motive that prompted him to hold aloof from his old friend and patron) from Octave 77 of the Greater Testament, in which he begs his "more than father," who was (says he) saddened enough by this last scrape of his protégé, to leave him to disentangle himself as best he could. It is possible that he may have retired to one of the hiding-places before mentioned, whither he and his comrades were wont to resort when hard pressed by the police; but (*pace* M. Longnon) it seems to me that the probabilities are in favour of his having sheltered himself with the woman whom he calls "La Grosse Margot" and who, he implies, had alone retained a real and faithful attachment to him. That attachments of such a nature have never been rare among women of her class ("poor liberal girls!" as Villon calls them), in whom the very nature of their terrible trade seems to engender an ardent longing for real and unselfish affection which has often led them to the utmost extremities of devotion and self-sacrifice, none can doubt who knows anything of their history and habits as a class; and one need go no further than Dufour's curious History of Prostitution or Dumas' sympathetic study, "Filles, Lorettes et Courtisanes," for touching instances of the pathetic abnegation of which these unhappy creatures are capable. M. Longnon has endeavoured, with a motive in which all admirers of the poet must sympathise with him, to contend that Villon's connection with La Grosse Margot had no real existence and that his most explicit references to it should be taken as nothing but a playful and figurative description of his presumed devotion to some tavern, for which a portrait of the woman in question served as sign. With all respect for M. Longnon's most honourable intention and all possible willingness to accept any reasonable conjecture that might tend to remove from the poet's name a stigma of which his lovers must be painfully sensible, I am yet utterly at a loss to discover any warrant for the above-mentioned theory. It is of course possible that the ballad in which Villon so circumstantially exposes the connection in question may have been intended as a mere piece of bravado or mystification; but, failing evidence of this, I defy any candid reader to place such a construction upon the text as will justify any other conclusion than the very unsavoury one usually adopted.

Rejected by the only woman of his own rank whom he seems to have loved with a real and tender passion and even cast off by his sometime mistress Jehanneton la Chaperonniére, one can hardly blame Villon for not refusing the shelter of the one attachment, low and debased as it was, which remained to him.

In this retirement, whatever it was, deserted by all his friends and accompanied only by his boy-clerk Frémin,* Villon appears to have at once addressed himself to the composition of the capital work of his life, the Greater

---

* Possibly (and even probably) an imaginary character.

Testament. He had now attained the age of thirty, and young as he still was, he felt that he had not much longer to live. The terrible life of debauchery, privation and hardship he had led had at last begun to produce its natural effect. To the maladies contracted in his youth and to the natural exhaustion caused by an incessant alternation of the wildest debauch and the most cruel privation, appears now to have been added some disease of the lungs, probably consumption, which caused him to burn with insatiable thirst and to vomit masses of snow-white phlegm as big as tennis-balls (the student of our own old poets will recall the expression "to spit white," so commonly applied to those attacked with a fatal affection of the lungs, consequent upon excess), a disorder probably contracted in the reeking dungeon of the castle of Meung and aggravated by the terrible effects of the question by water, which he had so often undergone and from which the patient rarely entirely recovered. Indeed, he expressly attributes these latter symptoms to his having been forced by the Bishop of Orléans to drink so much cold water. He tells us, at the commencement of his Greater Testament, that his youth had left him, how he knew not, and that, though yet in reality a cockerel, he had the voice and appearance of an old rook. Sad, dejected and despairing, with face blacker, as he says, than a mulberry for stress of weather and privation, without hair, beard or eyebrows, bare as a turnip from disease, with body emaciated with hunger ("The worms will have no great purchase thereof," says he; "hunger has waged too stern a war on it"); and every limb one anguish for disease, with empty purse and stomach, dependent on charity for subsistence, so sick at heart and feeble that he could hardly speak, his eyes seem at last to have been definitively opened to the terrible folly of his past life. He renounces at last those delusive pleasures for which he retains neither hope nor capacity: "No more desire in me is hot," he cries; "I've put my lute beneath the seat": travail and misery have sharpened his wit: he

confesses and repents of his sins, forgives his enemies and
turns for comfort to religion and maternal love, consoling
himself with the reflection that all must die, great and
small, and that after such a life as he had led, an honest
death had nothing that should displease him, seeing that
in life, as in love, "each pleasure's bought with fifty pains."
After a long and magnificent prelude, in which he laments
the excesses of his youth, justifying himself by his favourite
argument that necessity compels folk to do evil, as want
drives wolves out of the brake, and sues for the favourable
and compassionate consideration of those whose lot in life
has placed them above necessity,—interrupted by numerous
episodes, some humourous, some pathetic, the individual
beauty of which is so great that (like the so-called diffuse
digressions which abound in the music of Schubert) one
cannot quarrel with their want of proportion to the general theme,—he commends his soul to the various persons
of the Trinity in language of the most exalted piety and
proceeds, in view of his approaching death, to dictate to
his clerk what he calls his Testament, being a long series
of huitains or eight-line octosyllabic stanzas, in each of
which he makes some mention, humorous, pathetic or satirical, of some one or more of the numerous personages
who had trodden with him the short but vari-coloured
scene of his life. Many of the men, women, places and
things he sets before us in a few keen and incisive words,
from which often spring the swiftest lightnings of humour
and the most poignant flashes of pathos, blending together
in inextricable harmony, with a careless skill worthy of Heine
or Laforgue, the maddest laugher and the most bitter tears.
Lamartine or De Musset contains no tenderer or more
plaintive notes than those which break, like a primrose,
from the Spring-ferment of his verse, nor is there to be
found in Vaughan or Christina Rossetti a holier or sweeter
strain than the ballad which bears his mother's name.
Among the lighter pieces, by which his more serious efforts are relieved, I may mention the delightfully humorous

orison for the soul of his notary, Master Jehan Cotard; the brightly-coloured ballad called "Les Contredictz de Franc-Gontier," in which, with comic emphasis, he denounces the so-called pleasure of a country life; and the tripping lilt that he devotes to the praise of the women of Paris. In the Ballad of La Grosse Margot he gives us a terrible picture of the degrading expedients to which he was forced by the frightful necessities of his misguided existence and dedicates to François Perdryer above named "The Ballad of Slanderous Tongues," perhaps the most uncompromising example of pure invective that exists in any known literature. Towards the end of his poem, in verses pregnant with serious and well-illustrated meaning, he addresses himself to the companions of his crimes and follies—"ill souls and bodies well bestead," as he calls them—and bids them beware of "that ill sun which tans a man when he is dead," warning them that all their crimes and extravagances have brought them nothing but misery and privation, with the prospect of a shameful death at last, that ill-gotten goods are nobody's gain, but drift away to wanton uses, like chaff before the wind, and exhorting them to mend their lives and turn to honest labour. When he has to his satisfaction exhausted his budget of memories, tears and laughter, he strikes once more the fatalist keynote of the whole work in a noble "meditation" on the equality of all earthly things before the inexorable might of Death and adds a Roundel, in which he deprecates the further rigour of Fate and expresses a hope that his repentance may find acceptance at the hands of God. Finally, he names his executors, gives directions for his burial, orders an epitaph to be scratched over him, to preserve his memory as that of a good honest wag ("un bon folâtre"), and concludes by determining, in view of his approaching death, to beg forgiveness of all men, which he does in a magnificent ballad, bearing the refrain, "I cry folk mercy, one and all" (from which, however, he still excepts the Bishop of Orléans), winding up with a second ballad, in which he solemnly repeats his assertion that he dies a martyr to Love and invites all lovers to his funeral.

No work of Villon's posterior to the Greater Testament, is known to us, nor is there any trace of its existence; indeed, from the date, 1461, with which he himself heads his principal work, we entirely lose sight of him: and it may be supposed, in view of the condition of mental and bodily weakness in which we find him at that time, that he did not long survive its completion. Indeed (as M. Longnon justly observes), in the case of so eminent a poet, there could be no stronger proof of his death than his cessation to produce verses. The Codicil (so named by some compiler or editor after the poet's death) is a collection of poems which contain internal evidence of having been composed at an earlier period; and the other pieces— Les Repues Franches, the Dialogue of Mallepaye and Baillevent and the Monologue of the Franc Archier de Baignolet—which are generally joined to the Testaments and Codicil, bear no trace whatever of Villon's handiwork. They were not even added to his works until 1532 and were in the following year summarily rejected as spurious by Clément Marot from his definite edition, prepared by order of Francis I. Nevertheless, I do not entirely agree with M. Longnon in supposing that Villon died immediately after 1461. This would be to assume that the whole of the Greater Testament was written at one time: and for this assumption there seems to me to be no warrant. On the contrary, even as the interpolated ballads and rondeaux bear for the most part signs of an earlier origin, there seems to me to exist in the body of the Greater Testament internal evidence that the principal portion of the poem (*i. e.,* that written in huitains) was composed at four or five, perhaps more, different returns; and it is, therefore, probable that Villon survived for two or three years after his release from Meung gaol.* Rabelais, in-

[* The opinion expressed in the above lines (which were written in 1878) has recently been completely confirmed by the

deed, states in his "Pantagruel" that the poet, in his old age, retired to St. Maixent in Poitou, where, under the patronage of an honest abbot of that ilk, he amused himself and entertained the people with a representation of the Passion "en gestes et en langage Poitevins"; but this tradition (if tradition it be) which Rabelais puts into the mouth of the Seigneur de Basché, is as completely improbable, destitute of confirmation and unworthy of serious attention as that of Villon's journey to England and seems to me to prove nothing, save, perhaps, that Villon at that time (1550), when his works had already begun to fall into disuse, had become a mere traditional lay-figure, on which to hang vague stories of "villonneries," adaptable to all kinds of heroes and mostly suggested by the "Rupues Franches." There occurs also, in a Gazetteer published in 1726, an assertion that Villon was burnt for impiety; but, although to a reader of his works this would seem by no means unlikely—not by reason of any real impiety on the part of Villon (for it is evident that, as is so often the case with men of loose and even criminal life, his faith in religion was sincere and deep-seated), but because of the continual jests and sarcasms he permits himself at the expense of the monks and secular clergy, always far more ready to pardon actual heresy or infidelity than such personal attacks, having no relation to religion, as tend to discredit themselves among the people—yet, looking at the utter want of confirmation and of any previous mention of the alleged fact and considering the grotesque ignorance of the eighteenth century with regard to the old writers and

terms of a judicial document discovered in the Archives Nationales and first published by M. Longnon (1892), to wit, the letters of Remission granted by Louis XI in November, 1463, to Robin Dogis for the wounding of one François Ferrebouç, in an affray which took place near the church of St. Benoît and at which Villon is mentioned as having been present, though not implicated therein, thus proving that the poet was still alive in 1463, two years after the date of the Greater Testament.]

especially the old poets of France, we are fully justified in treating the assertion as an absurd invention.

No edition of Villon's work is extant which is known to have been published in his lifetime and to which we might therefore have turned for information. The first edition, though undated, was evidently published without his concurrence and almost certainly after his death; and the second, published in 1489, affords no clue to the date of that event, though printed after the year mentioned as an extreme limit by those of his commentators who have ascribed to him the longest life. It is much to be regretted that the will of Guillaume de Villon is not extant, as it would almost certainly have contained some reference to the good Canon's unhappy protégé, whether dead or alive,—in the latter case, for the purpose of making some provision for him, and in the former, with some mention of his death and some pious wish for the repose of his soul. It probably perished, with many other valuable records and archives,— from which we might have fairly expected to glean important supplementary information relative to Villon,—in the Saturnalia of criminal and purposeless destruction which disgraced the French Revolution.

V.

There can be no doubt that Villon was appreciated at something like his real literary value by the people of his time. Little as we know of his life, everything points to the conclusion that his writings were highly popular during his lifetime, not only among those princes and gallants whom he had made his friends, but among that Parisian public of the lower orders, with which he was so intimately identified. Allusions here and there lead us to suppose that his ballads and shorter pieces were known among the people long before their publication in a collective form and it is probable, indeed, that they were hawked about in manuscript and afterwards printed on broadsheets in black-letter, as were such early English

poems as the "Childe of Bristowe" and the "History of Tom
Thumb." For many years after his death the Ballads were
always distinguished from the rest by the descriptive head-
ings of the various editions, in which the printers announce
"The Testaments of Villon *and his Ballads*," as if the latter had previously been a separate and well-known specialty
of the poet's. We may even suppose them to have been
set to music and sung, as were the odes of Ronsard a
hundred years later, and indeed many of them seem im-
peratively to call for such treatment. Who cannot fancy
the ballad of the Women of Paris—"Il n'est bon bec que de
Paris"—being carolled about the streets by the students and
street-boys of the day, or the Orison for Master Cotard's
Soul being trolled out as a drinking-song by that jolly toper
at some jovial reunion of the notaries and "chicquanous"
of his acquaintance?

The thirty-four editions, known to have been published
before the end of the year 1542,* are sufficient evidence
of the demand (probably for the time unprecedented) which
existed for his poems during the seventy or eighty years
that followed his death; and it is a significant fact that
the greatest poet of the first half of the sixteenth century
should have applied himself, at the special request of Francis
I (who is said to have known Villon by rote), to rescue
the works of the Parisian poet from the labyrinth of cor-
ruption and misrepresentation into which they had fallen
through the carelessness of printers and the indifference of
the public, who seem to have had his verses too well by
heart to trouble themselves to protest against misprints
and misreadings. In the preface to this edition (of which
twelve reprints in nine years sufficiently attest the estima-
tion in which Villon was held by the cultivated intellects
of the early Renaissance period) Marot pays a high tribute
to "le premier poëte parisien," as he styles Villon, declaring the better part of his work to be of such artifice, so

---

[* See M. Longnon's Bibliographie des Imprimés.]

full of fair doctrine and so emblazoned in a thousand bright colours, that Time, which effaces all things, had not thitherto succeeded in effacing it nor should still less efface it thenceforward, so long as good French letters should be known and preserved. Marot's own writings bear evident traces of the care and love with which he had studied the first poet of his time, who indeed appears to have given the tone to all the rhymers—Gringoire, Henri Baude, Martial D'Auvergne, Cretin, Coquillart, Jean Marot, Roger de Collerye, Guillaume Alexis—who continued, though with no great brilliancy, to keep alive the sound and cadence of French song during the latter part of the fifteenth and the first years of the sixteenth centuries. The advent of the poets of the Pleiad and the deluge of Latin and Greek form and sentiment with which they flooded the poetic literature of France seem at once to have arrested the popularity of the older poets: imitations of Horace, Catullus, Anacreon, Pindar took the place of the more spontaneous and original style of poetry founded upon the innate capacities of the language and ᵼthat "esprit Gaulois" which represented the national sentiment and tendencies. The memory of Villon, *enfant de Paris,* child of the Parisian gutter, as he was, went down before the new movement, characterised at once by its extreme pursuit of refinement at all hazards and its neglect of those stronger and deeper currents of sympathy and passion, for which one must dive deep into the troubled waters of popular life and activity. For nearly three centuries the name and fame of the singer of the Ladies of Old Time remained practically forgotten, buried under wave upon wave of literary and political movement, all apparently equally hostile to the tendency and spirit of his work. We find, indeed, the three greatest spirits of the sixteenth and seventeenth centuries, Rabelais, Regnier, and La Fontaine, evincing by their works and style, if not by any more explicit declaration, their profound knowledge and sincere appreciation of Villon; but their admiration had no effect

upon the universal consent with which the tastes and tendencies of their respective times appear to have decreed
the complete oblivion of the early poet. The first half
of the eighteenth century, indeed, produced three several
editions of Villon; but the critics and readers of the age
were little likely to prefer the robust and high-flavoured
food, that Villon set before them, to the whipped creams,
the rose and musk-scented confections with which the literary pastry-cooks of the day so liberally supplied them;
and it was not until the full development, towards the
end of the first half of the present century, of the Romantic
movement (a movement whose causes and tendencies bore
so great an affinity to that of which Villon in his own
time was himself the chief agent), that he began to be
in some measure restored to his proper place in the hier-
archy of French literature. Yet we can still remember
the compassionate ridicule with which the efforts of Théophile Gautier to revindicate his memory were received and
how even that perfect and noble spirit, in whose catholic
and unerring appreciation no spark of true genius or of
worthy originality ever failed to light a corresponding flame
of enthusiasm, was fain to dissimulate the fervour of his
admiration under the transparent mask of partial deprecia-
tion and to provide for his too bold enterprise of rehabili-
tation a kind of apologetic shelter by classing the first great
poet of France with far less worthy writers, under the
title of "Les Grotesques." In the country of his birth,
Villon is still little read, although the illustrious poet
Théodore de Banville did much to expedite the revival
of his fame by regenerating the form in which his greatest triumphs were achieved; and it is perhaps, indeed, in
England that his largest public (scanty enough as yet) may
be expected to be found. However, better days have definitively dawned for Villon's memory: he is at last recognised
by all who occupy themselves with poetry as one of the
most original and genuine of European singers; and the

spread of his newly-regained reputation can now be only a matter of time.

The vigorous beauty and reckless independence of Villon's style and thought, although a great, have been by no means the only obstacle to his enduring popularity. A hardly less effectual one has always existed in the evanescent nature of the allusion upon which so large a part of his work is founded. In the preface to the edition above referred to, Clément Marot allows it to be inferred that, even at so comparatively early a period as 1533, the greater part of his references to persons and places of his own day had become obscure, if not altogether undecipherable, to all but those few persons of advanced age, who may be said to have been almost his contemporaries. In Marot's own words, "Sufficiently to understand and explain the industry or intention of the bequests he makes in his Testament, it is necessary to have been a Parisian of his time and to have known the places, things and people of which he speaks, the memory whereof, as it shall more and more pass away, so much the less shall be comprehended the poet's intention in the references aforesaid." It is indeed difficult and in many cases impossible to understand the intent, based upon current and purely local circumstance, with which the poet made so many and such grotesque bequests to his friends and enemies. One can, by a stretch of imagination, to some extent catch his meaning, when he bequeaths to this and that hard drinker some of the numerous taverns or wine-shops—the White Horse, the Mule, the Diamond, the Jibbing Ass, the Tankard, the Fir-cone, the Golden Mortar—with whose names his verse bristles, or the empty casks that once held the wine stolen from this or the other vintner; to his roguish companions, the right of shelter in the ruins around Paris, a cast of cogged dice or a pack of cheating cards; to poultry-sneaks and gutter-thieves, the long gray cloaks that should serve to conceal their purchase; to his natural enemies, the sergeants of the

watch, the cotton nightcaps,* that they might sleep in
comfortable ignorance of his nocturnal misdeeds; and to
others of his dearest foes, the Conciergerie and Châtelet
prisons, with a right of rent-charge on the pillory, "three
strokes of withy well laid on and prison lodging all their
life"; to his barber, the clippings of his hair and to his
cobbler and tailor, his old shoes and clothes "for less than
what they cost when new." And we can more or less
dimly appreciate his satirical intention, when he bequeaths
to monks, nuns and varlets the means of dissipation and
debauch, of which he had good reason to know they so
freely availed themselves without the need of his permis-
sion; to notaries of the Châtelet the good grace of their
superior the Provost; to his friend the senechal and Maréchal de Bourbon, the punning qualification of *maréchal*
or blacksmith and the right of shoeing ducks and geese
(probably a hit at the prince's amorous complexion†); to
a butcher a fat sheep belonging to some one else and a
whisk to keep the flies off his meat; to the women of
pleasure, the right to hold a public school by night, where
masters should be taught of scholars; to one of his comrades, nicknamed (as is sure to be the case in almost every
band of thieves) "the Chaplain," "his simple-tonsure
chaplaincy"; or to the three hundred blind mutes of the
Hospital des Quinze-Vingts and the Cemetery of the Innocents, his spectacles, that, in the churchyards where they
served, they might see to separate the bad from the good;
these all have yet for us some glimmer, more or less sufficient, of sense and meaning. But why he should bequeath
to three different persons his double-handed or battle-sword
—an article it is not likely he ever possessed, the tuck ‡

[* *Cornetes.* This word should perhaps be read in its older
sense of "tippet" or "bandelet."]
[† Or perhaps at his simplicity, *ferrer les oies* being an old
phrase meaning "to waste time in trifling, to spend both time
and labour very vainly."—*Cotgrave.*]
[‡ Tuck (old Irish *tuca*), a clerk's short sword or hanger,

or dirk being the scholar's weapon of the time; why he
should gratify a clerk to the Parliament with a shop and
trade, to be purchased out of the proceeds of the sale of
his hauberk (another article, by the by, which he certainly never owned); why he should give to a respectable
Parisian citizen the acorns of a willow plantation and a
daily dole of poultry and wine; to René de Montigny three
dogs, and to Jehan Raguyer, a sergeant of the provostry
of Paris, one hundred francs; to his protector Fournier,
leather ready cut out for shoes and caps; to a couple of
thieves, "bacon, peas, charcoal and wood"; to two échevins
of Paris each an eggshell full of francs and crowns; to
three notaries of the Châtelet a basketful each of stolen
cloves; why he should will to his barber, Colin Galerne,
an iceberg from the Marne, to be used as an abdominal
plaster, or direct the joinder of Mount Valerien to Montmartre;—all these and others of the same kind—though
no doubt full of pertinence and meaning at the time when
the persons, things and places referred to were still extant or fresh in the memory of their contemporaries—
are now for us enigmas of the most hopeless kind, hidden
in a darkness which may be felt and which it can hardly
be hoped that time and patience, those two great revealers
of hidden things, will ever avail to penetrate with any
sufficient light of interpretation.*

Nevertheless, when we have made the fullest possible
allowance for obscurity and faded interest, there still remain in Villon's surviving verse treasures of beauty, wit
and wisdom enough to ensure the preservation of his mem-

---

not the long narrow thrusting weapon (rapier) after known by
the same name.]

[* The antithetical interpretation proposed by M. Bijvanck, according to which Villon may be supposed to have intended to
annul each legacy by the succeeding words, taken in their second-
ary meaning, seems hardly satisfactory; but see my notes to the
Poems, passim.]

ory as a poet what while the French language and literature endure.*

That which perhaps most forcibly strikes a reader for
the first time studying Villon's work is the perfect absence of all conventional restrictions. He rejects nothing
as common or unclean and knows—none better—how to
draw the splendid wonder of poetic efflorescence from the
mangrove swamps of the truanderie and the stagnant marish
of the prison or the brothel. His wit and pathos are like
the sun, which shines with equal and impartial light upon
the evil and the good, alike capable of illustrating the
innocent sweetness of the spring and summer meadows and
of kindling into a glory of gold and colour the foul canopy
of smoke which overbroods the turmoil of a great city.
He is equally at home when celebrating the valour of the
heroes of old time or when telling the sorry tragedy of
some ne'er-do-weel of his own day. His spirit and tendency
are eminently romantic, in the sense that he employed
modern language and modern resources to express and
individualise the eternal elements of human interest and
human passion, as they appeared, moulded into new shapes
and invested with new colours and characteristics by the
shifting impulses and tendencies of his time. He had in-

---

* I take this opportunity to protest against the fashion which
prevails among editors and critics of Villon, of singling out
certain parts of his work, notably his Ballads, for laudation, to
the detriment of the rest of his poems. No one is less inclined
than myself to begrudge his splendid Ballads the full tribute of
admiration they deserve; but, magnificent as they are, it is not,
(it seems to me) in them, but in the body of the Greater Testament, that Villon's last word as a poet is to be sought. Here
he put forth his full force and it is here (and more especially
in the magnificent passage, octaves xii to lxii inclusive) that
his genius shines out with a vigour and plenitude thitherto unexampled in French verse. The long passage last referred to
is one uninterrupted flow of humour, satire and pathos, glowing
with the most exquisite metaphor and expressed in a singularly
terse and original style; and it seems to me beyond question
that this was, if not his last, at least his most mature effort.

deed, in no ordinary degree, the capital qualification of the
romantic poet: he understood the splendour of modern
things and knew the conjurations which should compel
the coy spirit of contemporary beauty to cast off the rags
and tatters of circumstance, the low and debased seeming in which it was enchanted, and flower forth, young,
glorious and majestic, as the bewitched princess in the fairy
tale puts off the aspect and vesture of hideous and re-
pulsive eld, at the magic touch of perfect love. The true
son of his time, he rejected at once and for ever, with the
unerring judgment of the literary reformer, the quaint
formalities of speech, the rhetorical exaggerations and limi-
tations of expression and the Chinese swathing of allegory
and conceit that dwarfed the thought and deformed the
limbs of the verse of his day and reduced the art of poetry
to a kind of Tibetan prayer-wheel, in which the advent
of the Spring, the conflict of Love and Honour, the cry
of the lover against the cruelty of his mistress and the
glorification of the latter by endless comparison to all things
fit and unfit, were ground up again and again into a series
of kaleidoscopic patterns, wearisome in the sameness of their
mannered beauty, from whose contemplation one rises with
dazzled eyes and exhausted sense, longing for some cry of
passion, some flower-birth of genuine sentiment, to burst
the strangling sheath of affectation and prescription. Before Villon the language of the poets of the time had become almost as pedantic, although not so restricted and
colourless, as that of the seventeenth and eighteenth centuries. By dint of continual employment in the same
grooves and in the same formal sense, the most forceful
and picturesque words of the language had almost ceased
to possess individuality or colour; for the phosphorescence
that springs from the continual contact of words with
thought, and their reconstruction at the stroke of passion, was wanting, not to be supplied or replaced by the
aptest ingenuity or the most untiring wit. Villon did for
French poetic speech that which Rabelais afterwards per-

formed for its prose (and it is a singular coincidence, which I believe has not before been remarked, that the father of French poetry and the father of French prose were, as it were, predestined to the task they accomplished by the name common to both—*François* or *French* par excellence). He restored the exhausted literary language of his time to youth and health by infusing into it the healing poisons, the revivifying acids and bitters of the popular speech, disdaining no materials that served his purpose, replacing the defunct forms with new phrases, new shapes were wrung from the heart of the spoken tongue, plunging with audacious hand into the slang of the tavern and the brothel, the cant of the highway and the prison, choosing from the wayside heap and the street gutter the neglected pebbles and nodules in which he alone divined the hidden diamonds and rubies of picturesque expression, to be polished and faceted into glory and beauty by the regenerating friction of poetic employment. None better than he has known how to call forth the electric flash which has long lurked dormant, hidden in its separate polarities, till the hand of genius should bring into strange and splendid contact the words which had till then lain apart, dull and lifeless.

Villon was the first great poet of the people: his love of the life of common things, the easy familiarity of the streets and highways, his intimate knowledge and love of the home and outdoor life of the merchant, the hawker, the artisan, the mountebank, nay, even the thief, the prostitute and the gipsy of his time, stand out in unequivocal characters from the lineaments of his work. The cry of the people rings out from his verse,—that cry of mingled misery and humour, sadness and cheerfulness, which, running through Rabelais and Régnier, was to pass unheeded till it swelled into the judgment-thunder of the Revolution. The sufferings, the oppression, the bonhomie, the gourmandise, the satirical good-humour of that French people which has so often been content to starve upon a jesting ballad or a mocking epigram, its gallantry, its perspicacity and its innate lack of reverence for all that symbolises an accepted order of things—all these stand out in their natural colours drawn to the life and harmonised into a national entity, to which the poet gives the shape and seeming of his own individuality, unconscious that in relating his own hardships, his own sufferings, regrets and aspirations, he was limning for us the typified and foreshortened image and presentment of a nation at a cardinal epoch of national regeneration. "He builded better than he knew." His poems are a very album of types and figures of the day. As we read, the narrow, gabled streets, with their graven niches for saint and Virgin and their monumental fountains stemming the stream of traffic, rise before us, gay with endless movement of fur and satin clad demoiselles, "ruffed and rebatoed," with their heart or diamond shaped headdresses of velvet and brocade, fringed and broidered with gold and silver; sad-coloured burghers and their wives distinguished by the bongrace or *chaperon à bourrelet,* with its rolled and stuffed hem; gold-laced archers and jaunty clerks, whistling for lustihead, with the long-peaked hood or liripipe falling over their shoulders and the short bright-coloured walking-cloak letting pass the glittering point of the dirk; shaven, down-looking monks, "breeched and booted like oyster-fishers," and barefooted friars, purple-gilled with secret and unhallowed debauchery; light o' loves, distinguished by the tall helm or *hennin* and the gaudily coloured tight-fitting surcoat, square-cut to show the breasts, over the sheath-like petticoat, crossed by the demi-cinct or châtelaine of silver, followed by their esquires or bullies armed with sword and buckler; artisans in their jerkins of green cloth or russet leather; barons and lords in the midst of their pages and halberdiers; ruffling gallants, brave in velvet and embroidery, with their boots of soft tan-coloured cordovan falling jauntily over the instep; as they press through a motley crowd of beggars and mountebanks, jugglers with their apes and carpet, *culs-de-jatte,* lepers with clapdish and wallet. mumpers and chan-

ters, truands and gipsies, jesters, fish-fags, cut-purses, and
swash-bucklers, that rings anon with the shout of "Noël!
Noël!" as Charles VII rides by, surrounded by his heralds
and pursuivants, or Louis passes with no attendants save
his two dark henchmen, Tristan the Hermit and Oliver the
Fiend, and nothing to distinguish him from the burghers
with whom he rubs elbows save the row of images in his
hat and the eternal menace of his unquiet eye. Anon we
see the interior of the convent church at vespers, with
its kneeling crowd of worshippers and its gold-grounded
frescoes of heaven and hell, martyrdom and apotheosis,
glittering vaguely from the swart shadow of the aisles.
The choir peals out and the air gathers into a mist with
incense, what while an awe-stricken old woman kneels
apart before the altar in the Virgin's chapel, praying for
that scapegrace son who has caused her such bitter tears
and such poignant terrors. Outside, on the church steps,
sit the gossips, crouched by twos and threes on the hem
of their robes, chattering in that fluent Parisian speech
to which the Parisian poet gives precedence over all others.
The night closes in; the dim cressets swing creaking in
the wind from the ropes that stretch across the half-de-
serted streets, whilst the belated students hurry past to their
colleges, with hoods drawn closely over their faces "and
thumbs in girdle-gear," and the sergeants of the watch
pace solemnly by, lantern-pole in one hand and in the
other the halberd wherewith they stir up the shivering
wretches crouched for shelter under the abandoned stalls
of the street hawkers or draw across the ways the chains
that shall break the escape of the nocturnal brawler or the
stealthy thief. Thence to the Puppet wine-shop, where
truand and light o' love, student and soldier, hold high
revel, amidst the clink of beakers and the ever-recurring
sound of clashing daggers and angry voices; or the more
reputable tavern of the Pomme de Pin, where sits Master
Jacques Raguyer, swathed in his warm mantle, with his
feet to the blaze and hack resting against the piles of fag-

gots that tower in the chimney-corner; or the street in
front of the Châtelet, where we find Villon gazing upon
the great flaring cressets that give light over the gateway
of the prison with whose interior he was so well acquainted.
Anon we come upon him, watching with yearning eyes and
watering mouth, through some half-open window or door-
chink, the roaring carouses of the debauched monks and
nuns, or listening to the talk of La Belle Héaulmière and
her companions in old age, as they crouch on the floor, under
their curtains spun by the spiders, telling tales of the
good times gone by, in the scanty short-lived flicker of
their fire of dried hempstalks. Presently, Master Jehan
Cotard staggers past, stumbling against the projecting stalls
and roaring out some ranting catch or jolly drinking-song,
and the bully of La Grosse Margot hies him, pitcher in
hand, to the Tankard Tavern, to fetch wine and victual
for his clients. Anon the moon rises, high and calm, over
the hill churchyard of the Innocents, where the quiet dead
lie sleeping soundly in the deserted charnels, ladies and
lords, masters and clerks, bishops and water-carriers, all
laid low in undistinguished abasement before the equality
of death. Once more, the scene changes and we stand by
the thieves' rendezvous in the ruined castle of Bicêtre or
by the lonely gibbet of Montfaucon, where the poet wanders in the "silences of the moon," watching with a terri-
fied fascination the shrivelled corpses or whitened skeletons
of his whilom comrades, as they creak sullenly to and
fro in the ghastly aureole of the midnight star. All Paris
of the fifteenth century relives in the vivid hurry of his
verse: one hears in his stanzas the very popular cries and
watchwords of the street and the favourite oaths of the
gallants and women of the day. We feel that all the world
is centered for him in Paris and that there is no landscape can compare for him with those "paysages de métal
et de pierre" which he (in common with another ingrain
Parisian, Baudelaire) so deeply loved. Much as he must
have wandered over France, we find in his verse no hint

of natural beauty, no syllables of description of landscape or natural objects. In these things he had indeed no interest: flowers and stars, sun and moon, spring and summer, unrolled in vain for him their phantasmagoria of splendour and enchantment over earth and sky: men and women were his flowers and the crowded streets of the great city the woods and meadows wherein, after his fashion, he worshipped beauty and did homage to art. Indeed, he was essentially "the man of the crowd": his heart throbbed ever in unison with the mass, in joy or sadness, crime or passion, lust or patriotism, aspiration or degradation.

It is astonishing, in the midst of the fantastic and artificial rhymers of the time, how quickly the chord of sensibility in our poet vibrates to the broad impulses of humanity; how, untainted by the selfish provincialism of his day, his heart warms towards the great patriot, Jacques Cœur, and sorrows over his disgrace; how he appreciates the heroism of Jeanne d'Arc and denounces penalty upon penalty, that remind us of the 70,000 pains of fire of the Arabian legend, upon the traitors and rebels "who would wish ill unto the realm of France"; with what largeness of sympathy he anticipates the modern tenderness over the fallen and demonstrates how they "were once honest, verily," till Love, that befools us all, beguiled them to the first step upon the downward road; with what observant compassion he notes the silent regrets of the old and the poignant remembrances of those for whom all things fair have faded out, glossing with an iron pathos upon the "nessun maggior dolore" of Dante, in the terrible stanzas that enshrine, in pearls and rubies of tears and blood, the passion and the anguish, the "agony and bloody sweat" of La Belle Héaulmière.

The keenness of his pathos and the delicacy of his grace are as supreme as what one of his commentators magnificently calls "the sovereign rudeness" of his satire. When he complains to his unyielding mistress of her "hypocrite douceur" and her "felon charms," "la mort d'un pauvre cœur," and warns her of the inevitable approach of the days when youth and beauty shall no more remain to her, we seem to hear a robuster Ronsard sighing out his "Cueillez, cueillez votre jeunesse"; when he laments for the death of Master Ythier's beloved, "Two were we, having but one heart," we must turn to Mariana's wail of wistful yet undespiteous passion for a sweeter lyric of regretful tenderness, a more pathetic dalliance with the simpleness of love; and when he appeals from the dungeon of Meung or pictures himself and his companions swinging from the gibbet of Montfaucon, the tears that murmur through the fantastic fretwork of the verse are instinct with the salt of blood and the bitterness of death. Where shall we look for a more poignant pathos than that of his lament for his lost youth or his picture of the whilom gallants of his early memories that now beg all naked, seeing no crumb of bread but in some window-place? Where a nobler height of contemplation than that to which he rises, as he formulates the unalterable laws that make king and servant, noble and villein, equal in abasement before the unbending majesty of death, or a holier purity of religious exaltation than breathes from the ballad wherein, with the truest instinct of genius, using that mother's voice which cannot but be the surest passport to the divine compassion, he soars to the very gates of heaven on the star-sown wings of faith and song? He is one more instance of the potentiality of grace and pathos that often lurks in natures distinguished chiefly for strength and passion. Like the great realistic poet * of nineteenth-century France, he knew how to force death and horror to give up for him their hidden beauties; and if his own "Fleurs du Mal" are often instinct with the poisons that suggest the marshy and miasmatic nature of the soil to which they owe their resplendent colourings, yet the torrent of satire, mockery and invective, that laves their tangled roots, is

---

* Baudelaire.

often over-arched with the subtlest and brightest irises of
pure pathos and delicate sentiment. "Out of the strong
cometh sweetness," and in few poets has the pregnant
fable of the honeycomb in the lion's mouth been more
forcibly exemplified than in Villon.

Humour is with Villon no less pronounced a character-
istic than pathos. Unstrained and genuine, it arises mainly
from the continual contrast between the abasement of his
life and the worthlessness of its possibilities and the passionate and ardent nature of the man. He seems to be
always in a state of humorous astonishment at his own
mad career and the perpetual perplexities into which his
folly and recklessness have betrayed him; and this feeling
constantly overpowers his underlying remorse and the anguish which he suffers under the pressure of the deplorable
circumstances wherein he continually finds himself involved. The *spiel-trieb* or sport-impulse, which has been
pronounced the highest attribute of genius, stands out with
a rare prominence from his character, never to be altogether
suppressed by the most overwhelming calamities. The most
terrible and ghastly surroundings of circumstance cannot
avail wholly to arrest the ever-springing fountain of wit
and bonhomie that wells up from the inmost nature of
the man. In the midst of all his miseries, with his tears
yet undried, he mocks at himself and others with an astound-
ing good-humour. In the dreary dungeon of the Meung
moat we find him bandying jests with his own personified
remorse; and even whilst awaiting a shameful death, he
seeks consolation in the contemplation of the comic aspects
of his situation, as he will presently appear, upright in
the air, swinging at the wind's will, with face like a thimble
for bird-pecks and skin blackened of "that ill sun which
tans a man when he is dead." It is a foul death to die,
he says, yet we must all die some day, and it matters little
whether we then find ourselves a lord rotting in a splendid
sepulchre or a cut-purse strung up on Montfaucon hill.
He laughs at his own rascality and poverty, lustfulness and

gluttony, with an unexampled naïveté of candour, singularly
free from cynicism, yet always manages to conciliate our
sympathies and induce our pity rather than our reproba-
tion. "It is not to poor wretches like us," says he, "that
are naked as a snake, sad at heart and empty of paunch,
that you should preach virtue and temperance. As for us,
God give us patience. You would do better to address
yourselves to incite great lords and masters to good deeds,
who eat and drink of the best every day and are more open
to exhortation than beggars like ourselves that cease never
from want."

His faith in the saving virtues of meat and drink is
both droll and touching. One feels, in all his verse, the
distant and yearning respect with which the starveling
poet regards all manner of victual, as he enumerates its
various incarnations in a kind of litany or psalm of adora-
tions, in which they resemble the denominations and attributes of saints and martyrs to whom he knelt in un-
ceasing and ineffectual prayer. Wines, hypocras, roast
meats, sauces, soups, custards, tarts, eggs, pheasants,
partridges, plovers, pigeons, capons, fat geese, pies, cakes,
furmenty, creams, pasties and other "savoureux et friands
morceaux" defile in long and picturesque procession through
his verse, like a dissolving view of Paradise, before whose
gates he knelt and longed in vain. His idea of perfect
happiness is to "break bread with both hands," a potentiality
of ecstatic bliss which he attributes to the friars of the four
mendicant orders: no delights of love or pastoral sweetness,
"not all the birds that singen all the way from here to
Babylon" (as he says) could induce him to spend one
day amid the hard lying and sober fare of a country life;
and the only enemy whom he refuses to forgive at his
last hour is the Bishop of Orléans, who fed him so scurvily
a whole summer long upon cold water and dry bread (not
even manchets, says he piteously). If he cannot come at
his desire in the possession of the dainties for which his
soul longs, there is still some sad pleasure for him in caressing

in imagination the sacrosanct denominations of that "bien-heureux harmoys de gueule," which hovers for him, afar off, in the rosy mists of an apotheosis. In this respect, as in no few others, he forciby reminds one of another strange and noteworthy figure converted by genius into an eternal type, that *Neveu de Rameau,* in whom the *reductio ad absurdum* of the whole sensualist philosophy of the eighteenth century was crystallised by Diderot into so poignant and curious a personality. Like Jean Rameau, the whole mystery of life seems for Villon to have resolved itself into the cabalistic science "de mettre sous la dent," that noble and abstract art of providing for the reparation of the region below the nose, of whose alcahest and her-metic essence he so deplorably fell short; and as we make this unavoidable comparison, it is impossible not to be sur-prised into regret for the absence of some Diderot who might, in like manner, have rescued for us the singular individuality of the bohemian poet of the fifteenth century.

With all his faults, a most sympathetic and attractive personality detaches itself from the unsparing candour of his confessions. One cannot help loving the frank, witty, devil-may-care-poet, with his ready tears and his as ready laughter, his large compassion for all pitiable and his un-affected sympathy with all noble things. Specially attractive is the sweetness of his good-humour: so devoid of gall is he that he seems to cherish no enduring bitterness against his most cruel enemies, content if he can make them the subject of some passing jest or some merry piece of satire. He has no serious reproach for the cold-hearted woman to whom he attributes his misspent life and early death, nor does he allow himself the solace of one bitter word against the cruel creditors who seized the moment of his deliverance from Meung gaol, exhausted, emaciated and dy-ing, to strip him of the little that he possessed. Thibault d'Aussigny, the author of his duresse in Meung gaol, and François Perdryer, at the nature of whose offence against him we can only guess, are the only ones he cannot for-

give, and his invectives against the former are of a half-
burlesque character, that permits us to suspect a humorous
exaggeration in their unyielding bitterness.

Looking at the whole course of Villon's life and at the
portrait which he himself paints for us in such crude and
unsparing colours, we can hardly doubt that, under different circumstances, had his life been consecrated by successful love and the hope of those higher things to whose
nobility he was so keenly though unpractically sensitive, he
might have filled a worthier place in the history of his time
and have furnished a more honourable career than that
of the careless bohemian, driven into crime, disgrace and
ruin by the double influence of his own unchecked desires
and the maddening wistfulness of an unrequited love. Still,
whatever effect change of circumstance might have had
in the possible ennobling of the sorry melodrama of his
life, *we* at least cannot complain of the influences that
presided over the accomplishment of his destiny; for they
resulted in ripening and developing the genius of a great
and unique poet. The world of posterity is always and
rightly ready to accept the fact of a great artistic personality, even at the expense of morality and decency; and
instances are not wanting in which moral and material
amelioration has destroyed the mustard-seed of genius, that
poverty and distress, those rude and sober nurses, might
have fostered into a mighty tree, giving shelter and comfort to all who took refuge under its branches. To quote
once more the words of the greatest critic * of the nine-
teenth century, "We might perhaps have lost the poet, whilst
gaining the honest man; and good poets are still rarer than
honest folk, though the latter can scarce be said to be
too common."

---

* Théophile Gautier.

HERE BEGINNETH THE LESSER TESTAMENT

OF

MASTER FRANÇOIS VILLON

(Translated by John Payne)

I

THIS fourteen six and fiftieth year,
  I, François Villon, clerk that be,
Considering, with senses clear,
  Bit betwixt teeth and collar-free,
  That one must needs look orderly
Unto his works (as counselleth
  Vegetius, wise Roman he),
Or else amiss one reckoneth,—

II

In this year, as before I said,
  Hard by the dead of Christmas-time,
When upon wind the wolves are fed
  And for the rigour of the rime
  One hugs the hearth from none to prime,
Wish came to me to break the stress
  Of that most dolorous prison-clime
Wherein Love held me in duresse.

III

Unto this fashion am I bent,
  Seeing my lady, 'neath my eyes,
To my undoing give consent,
  Sans gain to her in any wise:

Whereof I plain me to the skies,
Requiring vengeance (her desert)
  Of all the gods and whom it lies,
And of Love, healing for my hurt.

IV

If to my gree, alack, I read
  Those dulcet looks and semblants fair
Of such deceitful goodlihead,
  That pierced me to the heart whilere,
  Now in the lurch they've left me bare
And failed me at my utmost need:
  Fain must I plant it otherwhere
And in fresh furrows strike my seed.

V

She that hath bound me with her eyes
  (Alack, how fierce and fell to me!),
Without my fault in any wise,
  Wills and ordains that I should dree
  Death and leave life and liberty.
Help see I none, save flight alone:
  She breaks the bonds betwixt her and me
Nor hearkens to my piteous moan.

VI

To 'scape the ills that hem me round,
  It were the wiser to depart.
Adieu! To Angers I am bound,
  Since she I love will not impart
  Her grace nor any of her heart.
I die—with body whole enough—
  For her; a martyr to Love's smart,
Enrolled among the saints thereof.

VII

Sore though it be to part from her,
  Needs must I go without delay.
(How hard my poor sense is to stir!)
  Other than I with her's in play;
  Whence never Bullen herring aye
Was drouthier of case than I.
  A sorry business, wellaway,
It is for me, God hear my cry!

VIII

And since (need being on me laid)
  I go and haply never may
Again return, (not being made
  Of steel or bronze or other way
  Than other men: life but a day
Lasteth and death knows no relent)
  For me, I journey far away;
Wherefore I make this Testament.

IX

First, in the name of God the Lord,
  The Son and eke the Holy Spright,
And in her name by whose accord
  No creature perisheth outright,
  To Master Villon, Guillaume hight,
My fame I leave, that still doth swell
  In his name's honour day and night,
And eke my tents and pennoncel.

X

Item, to her, who, as I've said,
  So dourly banished me her sight
That all my gladness she forbade
  And ousted me of all delight,

I leave my heart in deposite,
Piteous and pale and numb and dead.
She brought me to this sorry plight:
May God not wreak it on her head!

XI

Item, my trenchant sword of steel
    I leave to Master Ythier
Marchant—to whom myself I feel
    No little bounden,—that he may,
    According to my will, defray
The scot for which in pawn it lies
    (Six sols), and then the sword convey
To Jehan le Cornu, free of price.

XII

Item, I leave to Saint Amand
    The Mule and eke the Charger White;
And to Blaru, my Diamond
    And Jibbing Ass with stripes bedight;
    And the decretal, too, that hight
Omnis utrius—that, to wit,
    Known as the counter-Carmelite—
Unto the priests I do commit.

XIII

To Jehan Tronne, butcher, I devise
    The Wether lusty and unpolled
And Gad to whisk away the flies,
    With the Crowned Ox, that's to be sold,
    And Cow, whereon the churl hath hold,
To hoist it on his back. If he
    To keep the beast himself make bold,
Trussed up and strangled let him be.

XIV

To master Robert Vallée (who,
   Poor clerking to the Parliament,
Owns valley neither hill) I do
   Will first, by this my Testament,
   My hose be giv'n incontinent,
Which on the clothes-pegs hang, that he
   May tire withal, 'tis my intent,
His mistress Jehanne more decently.

XV

But since he is of good extract,
   Needs must he better guerdoned be
(For God His Law doth so enact)
   Though featherbrained withal is he;
   They shall, I have bethoughten me,
Since in his pate he hath no sense,
   Give him the Art of Memory,
To be ta'en up from Misprepense.

XVI

And thirdly, for the livelihood
   Of Master Robert aforesaid
(My kin, for God's sake, hold it good!)
   Be money of my hauberk made
   And (or most part thereof) outlaid,
Ere Easter pass, in purchasing
   (Hard by St. Jacques) a shop and trade
For the poor witless lawyerling.

XVII

Item, my gloves and silken hood
   My friend Jacques Cardon, I declare,
Shall have in fair free gift for good;
   Also the acorns willows bear

And every day a capon fair
Or goose; likewise a tenfold vat
Of chalk-white wine, besides a pair
Or lawsuits, lest he wax too fat.

XVIII

Item, a leash of dogs I give
To young René de Montigny;
And let Jehan Raguyer receive
One hundred francs, shall levied be
On all my goods. But soft; to me
Scant gain therefrom I apprehend:
One should not strip one's own, perdie,
Nor over-ask it of one's friend.

XIX

Item, to Baron de Grigny
The ward and keeping of Nygeon,
With six dogs more than Montigny,
And Bicêtre, castle and donjon;
And to that scurvy knave Changon,
A spy that holds him still in strife,
Three strokes of withy well laid on
And prison-lodging all his life.

XX

Item, I leave Jacques Raguyer
The 'Puppet' Cistern, peach and pear,
Perch, chickens, custards, night and day,
At the Great Figtree choice of fare
And eke the Fir-cone Tavern, where
He may sit, cloaked in cloth of frieze,
Feet to the fire and back to chair,
And let the world wag at his ease.

XXI

Item, to John the foul of face
  And Peter Tanner I devise,
By way of gift, that baron's grace
  That punishes all felonies;
  To Fournier, my proctor wise,
Leather cut out for caps and shoes,
  That now at the cordwainer's lies,
For him these frosty days to use.

XXII

The Captain of the Watch, also,
  Shall have the Helmet, in full right;
And to the crimps, that cat-foot go,
  A-fumbling in the stalls by night,
  I leave two rubies, clear and bright,
The Lantern of La Pierre au Lait.
  'Deed, the Three Lilies have I might,
Haled they me to the Châtelet.

XXIII

To Pernet Marchand, eke, in fee,
  (Bastard of Bar by sobriquet)
For that a good-cheap man is he,
  I give three sheaves of straw or hay,
  Upon the naked floor to lay
And so the amorous trade to ply,
  For that he knows no other way
Or art to get his living by.

XXIV

Item, to Chollet I bequeath
  And Loup, a duck, once in a way
Caught as of old the walls beneath
  Upon the moat, towards end of day;

And each a friar's gown of gray—
Such as fall down beneath the knees—
My boots with uppers worn away,
And charcoal, wood, bacon and peas.

XXV

Item, this trust I do declare
For three poor children named below:
Three little orphans lone and bare,
That hungry and unshodden go
And naked to all winds that blow;
That they may be provided for
And sheltered from the rain and snow,
At least until this winter's o'er.

XXVI

To Colin Laurens, Jehan Moreau
And Girard Gossain, having ne'er
A farthing's worth of substance, no,
Nor kith nor kindred anywhere,
I leave, at option, each a share
Of goods or else four blanks once told.
Full merrily they thus shall fare,
Poor silly souls, when they are old.

XXVII

Item, my right of nomination
Holden of the University,
I leave, by way of resignation,
To rescue from adversity
Poor clerks that of this city be,—
Hereunder named, for very ruth
That thereunto incited me,
Seeing them naked all as Truth.

XXVIII

Their names are Thibault de Vitry
   And Guillaume Cotin—peaceable
Poor wights, that humble scholars be.
    Latin they featly speak and spell
    And at the lectern sing right well.
I do devise to them in fee
    (Till better fortune with them dwell)
A rent-charge on the pillory.

XXIX

Item, the Crozier of the street
   Of St. Antoine I do ordain,
Also a cue wherewith folk beat
    And every day full pot of Seine
    To those that in the trap are ta'en,
Bound hand and foot in close duresse;
    My mirror eke and grace to gain
The favours of the gaoleress.

XXX

Item, I leave the hospitals
   My curtains spun the spiders by;
And to the lodgers 'neath the stalls
    Each one a buffet on the eye
    And leave to tremble, as they lie,
Bruised, frozen, drenched, unshorn and lean,
    With hose shrunk half way up the thigh,
Gowns all too-clipt and woeful mien.

XXXI

Unto my barber I devise
   The ends and clippings of my hair;
Item, on charitable wise,
   I leave my old boots, every pair,

Unto the cobbler and declare
My clothes the broker's, so these two
　May when I'm dead my leavings share,
For less than what they cost when new.

XXXII

Unto the begging Orders four,
　The nuns and sisters (tibits they
Dainty and prime) I leave and store
　Of flawns, poults, capons, so they may
　Break bread with both hands night and day
And eke the fifteen Signs declare:
Monks court our neighbours' wives, folk say,
　But that is none of my affair.

XXXIII

To John o' Guard, that grocer hight,
　The Golden Mortar I make o'er,
To grind his mustard in aright;
　Also a pestle from St. Maur;
　And unto him that goes before,
To lay one by the legs in quod,
　St. Anthony roast him full sore!
I'll leave him nothing else, by God.

XXXIV

Item, to Mairebeuf, as well
　As Nicholas de Louvieux,
Each one I leave a whole eggshell
　Full of old crowns and francs, and to
　The seneschal of Gouvieux,
Peter de Ronseville, no less;
　Such crowns I mean, to tell you true,
As the prince giveth for largesse.

XXXV

Finally, being here alone
  To-night and in good trim to write,
I heard the clock of the Sorbonne,
  That aye at nine o'clock of night
  Is wont the Angelus to smite:
Then I my task did intermit,
  That to our Lady mild I might
Do suit and service, as is fit.

XXXVI

This done, I half forgot myself,
  What while I felt Dame Memory
Take in and lay upon her shelf
  (The wit, as 'twere, being bound in me,
  Though not for wine-bibbing, perdie,)
Her faculties collateral,
  Th' opinative in each degree
And others intellectual.

XXXVII

And on likewise th' estimative,
  —Whereby prosperity we gain,—
Similative and formative,
  By whose disorder folk remain
  Oft lunatic, to wit, insane,
From month to month; which aforesaid
  I mind me often and again
In Aristotle to have read.

XXXVIII

Then did the sensitive unleap
  And gave the cue to fantasy,
That roused the organs all from sleep,
  But held the sovereign faculty

Still in suspense for lethargy
And pressure of oblivion,
　　Which had dispread itself in me,
To show the senses' union.

XXXIX

Then, when my senses in due course
　　Grew calm and understanding clear,
I thought to finish my discourse,
　　But found my inkpot frozen sheer
　　And candle out, nor far nor near
Fire might I find, so must of need,
　　All muffled up for warmer cheer,
Get me to sleep and end my rede.

XL

Done at the season aforesaid
　　Of the right well-renowned Villon,
Who eats nor white nor oaten bread,
　　Black as a malkin, shrunk and wan.
　　Tents and pavilions every one
He's left to one or t'other friend;
　　All but a little pewter's gone,
That will, ere long, come to an end.

HERE ENDETH THE LESSER TESTAMENT OF
MASTER FRANÇOIS VILLON

HERE BEGINNETH THE GREATER TESTAMENT

OF

MASTER FRANÇOIS VILLON

I

In the year thirty of my age,
    Wherein I've drunk so deep of shame,
Neither all fool nor yet all sage,
    For all my misery and blame—
    Which latter all upon me came
Through Bishop Thibault d'Aussigny:
    (If bishop such an one folk name;
At all events, he's none for me:

II

He's nor my bishop nor my lord;
    I hold of him nor land nor fee,
Owe him nor homage nor accord,
    Am nor his churl nor beast, perdie).
    A summer long he nourished me
Upon cold water and dry bread;
    God do by him as he by me,
Whom passing scurvily he fed.

III

If any go about to say
    I do miscall him—I say no:
I wrong him not in any way,
    If one aread me rightly. Lo!
    Here's all I say, nor less nor mo;
If he had mercy on my dole,
    May Christ in heaven like mercy show
Unto his body and his soul!

IV

And if he wrought me pain and ill
   More than herein I do relate,
God of His grace to him fulfil
   Like measure and proportionate!
   But the Church bids us not to hate,
But to pray rather for our foes:
   I'll own I'm wrong and leave his fate
To God that all things can and knows.

V

And pray for him I will, to boot,
   By Master Cotard's soul I swear!
But soft: 'twill then be but by rote;
   I'm ill at reading; such a prayer
   I'll say for him as Picards' were.
(If what I mean he do not know—
   Ere 'tis too late to learn it there—
To Lille or Douai let him go.)

VI

Yet, if he needs must have't that I
   Should, willy nilly, for him pray,
(Though I proclaim it not on high)
   As I'm a chrisom man, his way
   He e'en shall get; but, sooth to say,
When I the Psalter ope for him,
   I take the seventh verse alway
Of the psalm called "Deus laudem."

VII

I do implore God's blessèd Son,
   To whom I turn in every need,
So haply my poor orison
   Find grace with Him—from whom indeed

Body and soul I hold—who's freed
Me oft from blame and evil chance.
Praised be our Lady and her Seed
And Louis the good King of France!

VIII

Whom God with Jacob's luck endow,
   And glory of great Solomon!
Of doughtiness he has enow,
   In sooth, and of dominion.
   In all the lands the sun shines on,
In this our world of night and day,
   God grant his fame and memory wonne
As long as lived Methusaleh!

IX

May twelve fair sons perpetuate
   His royal lineage, one and all
As valorous as Charles the Great,
   Conceived in matrix conjugal,
   As doughty as Saint Martial!
The late Lord Dauphin fare likewise;
   No worser fortune him befall
Than this and after, Paradise!

X

Feeling myself upon the wane,
   Even more in goods than body spent,
Whilst my full senses I retain,
   What little God to me hath sent
   (For on no other have I leant)
I have set down of my last will
   This very stable Testament,
Alone and irrevocable.

XI

Written in the same year, sixty-one,
  Wherein the good king set me free
From the dour prison of Mehun
  And so to life recovered me:
  Whence I to him shall bounden be
As long as life in me fail not:
  I'm his till death; assuredly,
Good deeds should never be forgot.

*Here Beginneth Villon to Enter Upon Matter Full
of Erudition and of Fair Knowledge*

XII

Now is it true that, after years
   Of anguish and of sorrowing,
Travail and toil and groans and tears
   And many a weary wondering,
   Trouble hath wrought in me to bring
To point each shifting sentiment,
   Teaching me many another thing
Than Averrhöes his Comment.

XIII

However, at my trials' worst,
   When wandering in the desert ways,
God, who the Emmäus pilgrims erst
   Did comfort, as the Gospel says,
   Showed me a certain resting-place
And gave me gift of hope no less;
   Though vile the sinner be and base,
Nothing HE hates save stubbornness.

XIV

Sinned have I oft, as well I know;
   But God my death doth not require,
But that I turn from sin and so
   Live righteously and shun hellfire.
   Whether one by sincere desire
Or counsel turn unto the Lord,
   HE sees and casting off HIS ire,
Grace to repentance doth accord.

XV

And as of its own motion shows,
  Ev'n in the very first of it,
The noble Romaunt of the Rose,
  Youth to the young one should remit,
  So manhood do mature the wit.
And there, alack! the song says sooth:
  They that such snares for me have knit
Would have me die in time of youth.

XVI

If for my death the common weal
  Might anywhere embettered be,
Death my own hand to me should deal
  As felon, so God 'stablish me!
  But unto none, that I can see,
Hindrance I do, alive or dead;
  The hills, for one poor wight, perdie,
Will not be stirred out of their stead.

XVII

Whilom, when Alexander reigned,
  A man that hight Diomedes
Before the Emperor was arraigned,
  Bound hand and foot, like as one sees
  A thief. A skimmer of the seas
Of those that course it far and nigh
  He was, and so, as one of these,
They brought him to be doomed to die.

XVIII

The emperor bespoke him thus:
  "Why art thou a sea-plunderer?"
The other, no wise timorous:
  "Why dost thou call me plunderer, sir?"

Is it, perchance, because I ear
Upon so mean a bark the sea?
Could I but arm me with thy gear,
I would be emperor like to thee.

XIX

"What wouldst thou have? From sorry Fate,
    That uses me with such despite
As I on no wise can abate,
    Arises this my evil plight.
    Let me find favour in thy sight
And have in mind the common saw:
    In penury is little right;
Necessity knows no man's law."

XX

Whenas the emperor to his suit
    Had hearkened, much he wonderèd;
And "I thy fortune will commute
    From bad to good, "to him he said;
    And did. Thenceforward Diomed
Wronged none, but was a true man aye.
    Thus have I in Valerius read,
Of Rome styled Greatest in his day.

XXI

If God had granted me to find
    A king of like greatheartedness,
That had fair Fate to me assigned,
    Stooped I thenceforward to excess
    Or ill, I would myself confess
Worthy to die by fire at stake.
    Necessity makes folk transgress
And want drives wolven from the brake.

XXII

My time of youth I do bewail,
  That more than most lived merrily,
Until old age 'gan me assail,
  For youth had passed unconsciously.
  It wended not afoot from me,
Nor yet on horseback. Ah, how then?
  It fled away all suddenly
And never will return again.

XXIII

It's gone, and I am left behind,
  Poor both in knowledge and in wit,
Black as a berry, drear and dwined,
  Coin, land and goods, gone every whit;
  Whilst those by kindred to me knit,
The due of Nature all forgot,
  To disavow me have seen fit,
For lack of pelf to pay the scot.

XXIV

Yet have I not my substance spent
  In wantoning or gluttony
Nor thorow love incontinent;
  None is there can reproach it me,
  Except he rue it bitterly;
I say it in all soothfastness—
  Nor can you bate me of this plea—
Who's done no wrong should none confess.

XXV

True is it I have loved whilere
  And willingly would love again:
But aching heart and paunch that ne'er
  Doth half its complement contain,

The ways of Love allure in vain;
'Deed, none but those may play its game
  Whose well-lined belly wags amain;
For the dance comes of the full wame.

XXVI

If in my time of youth, alack!
  I had but studied and been sage
Nor wandered from the beaten track,
  I had slept warm in my old age.
  But what did I? As bird from cage,
I fled the schools; and now with pain,
  In setting down this on the page,
My heart is like to cleave in twain.

XXVII

I have construed what Solomon
  Intended, with too much largesse,
When that he said, "Rejoice, my son,
  In thy fair youth and lustiness":
  But elsewhere speaks he otherguess;
"For youth and adolescence be"
  (These are his words, nor more nor less)
"But ignorance and vanity."

XXVIII

Like as the loose threads on the loom,
  Whenas the weaver to them lays
The flaming tow, burn and consume,
  So that from ragged ends (Job says)
  The web is freed,—even so my days
Are gone a-wand'ring past recall.
  No more Fate's buffs nor her affrays
I fear, for death assuageth all.

XXIX

Where are the gracious gallants now
   That of old time I did frequent,
So fair of fashion and of show,
   In song and speech so excellent?
   Stark dead are some, their lives are spent;
There rests of them nor mark nor trace:
   May they in Heaven have content;
God keep the others of His grace!

XXX

Some, Christ-a-mercy, are become
   Masters and lords of high degree;
Some beg all naked and no crumb
   Of bread save in some window see;
   Some, having put on monkery,
Carthews, Celestines and what not,
   Shod, breeched like oysterfishers be;
Look you, how divers is their lot!

XXXI

God grant great lords to do aright,
   That live in luxury and ease!
We cannot aught to them requite,
   So will do well to hold our peace.
   But to the poor (like me), that cease
Never from want, God patience give!
   For that they need it; and not these,
That have the wherewithal to live,—

XXXII

That drink of noble wines and eat
   Fish, soups and sauces every day,
Pasties and flawns and roasted meat
   And eggs served up in many a way.

Herein from masons differ they,
That with such toil their bread do earn:
These need no cupbearer, folk say,
For each one pours out in his turn.

XXXIII

To this digression I've been led,
  That serves in nothing my intent.
I am no Court, empanellèd
  For quittance or for punishment:
  I am of all least diligent.
Praised be Christ! May each man's need
  By me of Him have full content!
That which is writ is writ indeed.

XXXIV

So let that kite hang on the wall
  And of more pleasing subjects treat;
For this finds favour not with all,
  Being wearisome and all unsweet:
  For poverty doth groan and greet,
Full of despite and strife alway;
  Is apt to say sharp things in heat
Or think them, if it spare to say.

XXXV

Poor was I from my earliest youth,
  Born of a poor and humble race:
My sire was never rich, in sooth,
  Nor yet his grandfather Erace;
  Want follows hard upon our trace
Nor on my forbears' tombs, I ween,
  (Whose souls the love of God embrace!)
Are crowns or sceptres to be seen.

XXXVI

When I of poverty complain,
  Ofttimes my heart to me hath said,
"Man, wherefore murmur thus in vain?
  If thou hast no such plentihead
  As had Jacques Cœur, be comforted:
Better to live and rags to wear
  Than to have been a lord, and dead,
Rot in a splendid sepulchre."

XXXVII

(Than to have been a lord! I say.
  Alas, no longer is he one;
As the Psalm tells of it,—to-day
  His place of men is all unknown.)
  As for the rest, affair 'tis none
Of mine, that but a sinner be:
  To theologians alone
The case belongs, and not to me.

XXXVIII

For I am not, as well I know,
  An angel's son, that crowned with light
Among the starry heavens doth go:
  My sire is dead—God have his spright!
  His body's buried out of sight.
I know my mother too must die—
  She knows it too, poor soul, aright—
And soon her son by her must lie.

XXXIX

I know full well that rich and poor,
  Villein and noble, high and low,
Laymen and clerks, gracious and dour,
  Wise men and foolish, sweet of show

Or foul of favour, dames that go
Ruffed and rebatoed, great or small,
  High-tired or hooded, Death (I **know**)
Without exception seizes all.

XL

Paris or Helen though one be,
  Who dies, in pain and drearihead,
For lack of breath and blood dies he,
  His gall upon his heart is shed;
  Then doth he sweat, God knows how **dread**
A sweat, and none there is to allay
  His ills, child, kinsman, in his stead,
None will go bail for him that day.

XLI

Death makes him shiver and turn pale,
  Sharpens his nose and swells his veins,
Puffs up his throat, makes his flesh fail,
  His joints and nerves greatens and strains.
  Fair women's bodies, soft as skeins
Of silk, so tender, smooth and rare,
  Must you too suffer all these pains?
Ay, or alive to heaven fare.

BALLAD OF OLD-TIME LADIES

I

Tell me where, in what land of shade,
  Bides fair Flora of Rome, and where
Are Thaïs and Archipiade,
  Cousins-german of beauty rare,

And Echo, more than mortal fair,
That, when one calls by river-flow,
  Or marish, answers out of the air?
But what is become of last year's snow?

II

Where did the learn'd Heloïsa vade,
  For whose sake Abelard might not spare
(Such dole for love on him was laid)
  Manhood to lose and a cowl to wear?
  And where is the queen who willed whilere
That Buridan, tied in a sack, should go
  Floating down Seine from the turret-stair?
But what is become of last year's snow?

III

Blanche, too, the lily-white queen, that made
  Sweet music as if she a siren were;
Broad-foot Bertha; and Joan the maid,
  The good Lorrainer, the English bare
  Captive to Rouen and burned her there;
Beatrix, Eremburge, Alys,—lo!
  Where are they, Virgin debonair?
But what is become of last year's snow?

Envoi

Prince, you may question how they fare
  This week, or liefer this year, I trow:
Still shall the answer this burden bear,
  But what is become of last year's snow?

BALLAD OF OLD-TIME LORDS

(Following on the same subject)

No. 1

I

There is Calixtus, third of the name,
  That died in the purple whiles ago,
Four years since he to the tiar came?
  And the King of Aragon, Alfonso?
  The Duke of Bourbon, sweet of show,
And the Duke Arthur of Brittaine?
  And Charles the Seventh, the Good? **Heigho!**
But where is the doughty Charlemaigne?

II

Likewise the King of Scots, whose shame
  Was the half of his face (or folk say so),
Vermeil as amethyst held to the flame,
  From chin to forehead all of a glow?
  The King of Cyprus, of friend and foe
Renowned; and the gentle King of Spain,
  Whose name, God 'ield me, I do not know?
But where is the doughty Charlemaigne?

III

Of many more might I ask the same,
  Who are but dust that the breezes blow;
But I desist, for none may claim
  To stand against Death, that lays all low.
  Yet one more question before I go:
Where is Lancelot, King of Behaine?
  And where are his valiant ancestors, trow?
But where is the doughty Charlemaigne?

ENVOI

Where is Du Guesclin, the Breton prow?
  Where Auvergne's Dauphin and where again
The late good duke of Alençon?   Lo!
  But where is the doughty Charlemaigne?

BALLAD OF OLD-TIME LORDS

No. 2

I

Where are the holy apostles gone,
  Alb-clad and amice-tired and stoled
With the sacred tippet and that alone,
  Wherewith, when he waxeth overbold,
  The foul fiend's throttle they take and hold?
All must come to the self-same bay;
  Sons and servants, their days are told:
The wind carries their like away.

II

Where is he now that held the throne
  Of Constantine, with the bands of gold?
And the King of France, o'er all kings known
  For grace and worship that was extolled,
  Who convents and churches manifold
Built for God's service?   In their day
  What of the honour they had?   Behold,
The wind carries their like away.

III

Where are the champions every one,
  The Dauphins, the counsellors young and old?
The barons of Salins, Dôl, Dijon,
  Vienne, Grenoble?   They all are cold.

Or take the folk under their banners enrolled,
Pursuivants, trumpeters, heralds, (hey!
 How they fed of the fat and the flagon trolled!)
The wind carries their like away.

Envoi

Princes to death are all foretold,
 Even as the humblest of their array:
Whether they sorrow or whether they scold,
 The wind carries their like away.

XLII

Since, then, popes, princes great and small,
 That in queens' wombs conceivèd were,
Are dead and buried, one and all,
 And other heads their crownals wear,
 Shall Death to smite poor me forbear?
Shall I not die? Ay, if God will.
 So that of life I have my share,
An honest death I take not ill.

XLIII

This world is not perpetual,
 Deem the rich robber what he may:
Under death's whittle are we all.
 Old men to heart this comfort lay,
 That had repute in their young day
Of being quick at jest and flout,—
 Whom folk, if, now that they are gray,
They should crack jokes, as fools would scout.

XLIV

Now haply must they beg their bread,
 (For need thereto doth them constrain;)
Each day they wish that they were dead;
 Sorrow so straitens heart and brain

That, did not fear of God restrain,
Some dreadful deed they might essay;
    Nay, whiles they take HIS law in vain
And with themselves they make away.

XLV

For if in youth men spoke them fair,
    Now do they nothing that is right;
(Old apes, alas! ne'er pleasing were;
    No trick of theirs but brings despite.)
    If they are dumb, for fear of slight,
Folk them for worn-out dotards hold;
    Speak they, their silence folk invite,
Saying they pay with others' gold.

XLVI

So with poor women that are old
    And have no vivers in the chest,
When that young wenches they behold
    Fare at their ease and well addrest,
    They ask God why before the rest
Themselves were born. They cry and shout:
    God answers not; for second best
He'd come off at a scolding-bout.

THE COMPLAINT OF THE FAIR
HELM-MAKER GROWN OLD

I

Methought I heard the fair complain
    —The fair that erst was helm-maker—
And wish herself a girl again.
    After this fashion did I hear:

"*Alack! old age, felon and drear,*
Why hast so early laid me low?
   What hinders but I slay me here
And so at one stroke end my woe?

II

"*Thou hast undone the mighty thrall*
   In which my beauty held for me
Clerks, merchants, churchmen, one and all:
   For never man my face might see,
   But would have given his all for fee,—
Without a thought of his abuse,—
   So I should yield him at his gree
What churls for nothing now refuse.

III

"*I did to many me deny*
   (Therein I showed but little guile)
For love of one right false and sly,
   Whom without stint I loved erewhile.
   Whomever else I might bewile,
I loved him well, sorry or glad:
   But he to me was harsh and vile
And loved me but for what I had.

IV

"*Ill as he used me, and howe'er*
   Unkind, I loved him none the less:
Even had he made me faggots bear,
   One kiss from him or one caress,
   And I forgot my every stress.
The rogue! 'twas ever thus the same
   With him. It brought me scant liesse:
And what is left me? Sin and shame.

V

"Now is he dead this thirty year,
  And I'm grown old and worn and gray:
When I recall the days that were
  And think of what I am to-day
  And when me naked I survey
And see my body shrunk to nought,
  Withered and shrivelled,—wellaway!
For grief I am well-nigh distraught.

VI

"Where is that clear and crystal brow?
  Those eyebrows arched and golden hair?
And those bright eyes, where are they now,
  Wherewith the wisest ravished were?
  The little nose so straight and fair;
The tiny tender perfect ear;
  Where is the dimpled chin and where
The pouting lips so red and clear?

VII

"The shoulders gent and strait and small;
  Round arms and white hands delicate;
The little pointed breasts withal;
  The haunches plump and high and straight,
  Right fit for amorous debate;
Wide hips and dainty quelque chose
  Betwixt broad firm thighs situate,
Within its little garden close.

VIII

"Brows wrinkled sore and tresses gray;
  The brows all fall'n and dim the eyne
That wont to charm men's hearts away;
  The nose that was so straight and fine,

Now bent and swerved from beauty's line;
Chin peaked, ears furred and hanging down;
Faded the face and quenched its shine
And lips mere bags of loose skin grown.

IX

"Such is the end of human grace:
The arms grown short and hands all thrawn;
The shoulders bowed out of their place;
The breasts all shrivelled up and gone;
The haunches like the paps withdrawn;
The thighs no longer like to thighs,
Withered and mottled all like brawn,

X

"And so the litany goes round,
Lamenting the good time gone by,
Among us crouched upon the ground,
Poor silly hags, to-huddled by
A scanty fire of hempstalks dry,
Kindled in haste and soon gone out;
(We that once held our heads so high!)
So all take turn and turn about."

THE DOCTRINE OF THE FAIR HELM-MAKER TO THE LIGHT O' LOVES

I

Now think on't, Nell the glover fair,
That wont my scholar once to be,
And you, Blanche Slippermaker there,
Your case in mine I'd have you see:
Look all to right and left take ye;
Forbear no man; for trulls that bin
Old have nor course nor currency,
No more than money that's called in.

II

You, Sausage-huckstress debonair,
*   That dance and trip it brisk and free,*
And Guillemette Upholstress, there,
*   Look you transgress not Love's decree:*
*   Soon must you shut up shop, perdie;*
Soon old you'll grow, faded and thin,
*   Worth, like some old priest's visnomy,*
No more than money that's called in.

III

Jenny the hatter, have a care
*   Lest some false lover hamper thee;*
And Kitty Spurmaker, beware;
*   Deny no man that proffers fee;*
*   For girls that are not bright o' blee*
Men's scorn and not their service win:
*   Foul eld gets neither love nor gree,*
No more than money that's called in.

Envoi

Wenches, give ear and list (quo' she)
*   Wherefore I weep and make this din;*
'Tis that there is no help for me,
No more than money that's called in.

XLVII

This lesson unto them gives she,
    The bellibone of days gone by.
Ill said or well, worth what they be,
    These things unregistered have I
    By my clerk Fremin (giddy fry!),
Being as composed as well I may.
    I curse him if he make me lie:
Like clerk, like master, people say.

XLVIII

Nay, the great danger well I see
    Wherein a man in love doth fall . . .
Suppose that some lay blame on me
    For this speech, saying, "Listen, all:
    If this do make you love miscall,
The tricks of wantons named above,
    Your doubts are too chimerical,
For these are women light o' love.

XLIX

"For if they love not but for gain,
    Folk do but love them for a day;
In sooth, they roundly love all men,
    And when purse weeps, then are they gay:
    Not one but questeth after prey.
But honest men, so God me spare,
    With honest women will alway
Have dealing, and not otherwhere."

L

I put it that one thus devise:
    He doth in nothing me gainsay;
In sooth, I think no otherwise,
    And well I ween that one should aye
    In worthy place love's homage pay.
But were not these, of whom I rhyme
    (God wot) and reason all the day,
Once honest women aforetime?

LI

Aye, they *were* honest, in good sooth,
    Without reproach or any blame;
But, in her first and prime of youth,
    Ere she had loren her good name,

Each of these women thought no shame
To take some man for her desire,
Laic or clerk, to quench love's flame,
That burns worse than St. Anthony's fire.

LII

Of these, as Love ordains, they made
Their lovers, as appeareth well:
Each loved her gallant in the shade
And none else had with her to mell.
But this first love's not durable;
For she, that loved but one erewhen,
Soon tires of him to her that fell
And sets herself to love all men.

LIII

What moves them thus? I do opine,
Without their honour gainsaying,
That 'tis their nature feminine,
Which tends to cherish everything:
No other reason with the thing
Will rhyme, but if this saw it be,
That everywhere folk say and sing:
Six workmen do more work than three.

LIV

The shuttlecock light lovers be;
Their ladie-loves the battledore.
This is love's way in verity:
Spite clips and kisses, evermore
By constancy it sets small store.
For everyone this wise complains
Of dogs and horses, love and war:
Each pleasure's bought with fifty pains.

DOUBLE BALLAD TO THE LIKE PURPORT

I

Serve love and ladies day and night,
  Frequenting feasts and revelries;
You'll get nor profit nor delight,
  But only broken heads and sighs;
  Light loves make asses of the wise,
As witness Solomon, God wot;
  And Samson thereby lost his eyes.
Happy is he who knows them not.

II

Orpheus, the minstrel fair and wight,
  That fluted in such dulcet guise,
Did hardly 'scape the deadly bite
  Of Cerberus, in love's emprize;
  Narcissus did so idolize
His own fair favour that (poor sot)
  He drowned himself, as none denies.
Happy is he who knows them not.

III

Sardana also, the good knight,
  That conquered Creté, did disguise
Him as a wench and so bedight,
  Span among maids; and on like wise
  David the king, for palliardize,
The fear of God awhile forgot
  At sight of white well-shapen thighs.
Happy is he who knows them not.

IV

And David's son, that Ammon hight,
  Deflowered his sister, for with lies,
Feigning desire for manchets white,
  Incest most foul he did devise;

And Herod (history testifies)
Paid with John Baptist's head the scot
For a girl's dancing deviltries.
Happy is he who knows them not.

V

And even I, poor silly wight,
  Was beaten as linen is that lies
In washers' tubs for bats to smite;
  And who gat me this sour surprise
  But Vaucel's Kate, the cockatrice?
And Noël, too, his good share got
  Of cuffs at those festivities.
Happy is he who knows them not.

VI

And yet before a young man might
  Be brought to leave this merchandise,
Well might you burn him bolt upright,
  Witch-like that on a besom flies.
  Above all, wenches doth he prize:
But there's no trusting them a jot;
  Blonde or brunette, this rhyme applies,
Happy is he who knows them not.

LV

If she whom I did serve of old
  So whole of heart and loyally,
For whom I wasted years and gold
  And only won much misery,—
  If she at first had told to me
(But no, alas!) her true intent,
  I had essayed assuredly
To cast off my entanglement.

LVI

Whatever I to her would say
   She always ready was to hear
Nor ever said me ay or nay;
    Nay more, she suffered me draw **near,**
    Sit close and whisper in her ear,
And so with me played fast and **loose**
   And let me tell my all to her,
Intending only my abuse.

LVII

She fooled me, being in her power;
   For she did make me think, alas!
That one was other, ashes flour,
    That a felt hat a mortar was;
    Of rusty iron, that 'twas brass;
Of double ace, that it was trey.
   So would she make a man an **ass**
And lead him by the nose alway.

LVIII

On this wise did she me persuade,
   Till heaven a brazen canopy,
The clouds of calfskin to be made
    And morning evening seemed to **be:**
    Ill beer new wine, a hank of three
A halter, navews cabbage-plant,
   A sow a windmill was for me
And a fat priest a pursuivant.

LIX

Thus Love hath wrought me to deceive
   And bandied me from cold to hot:
There is no man, I do believe,
   Were he as cunning as I'm not,

But he would leave with Love for scot
Pourpoint and hose, and fare as I,
That everywhere am called, God wot,
The lover flouted and laid by.

LX

Love now and wenches I forswear;
War to the knife to them I mete;
For death (and not a rap they care)
Through them treads hard upon my feet.
I've put my lute beneath the seat;
Lovers no longer I'll ensue;
If ever I with them did treat,
I'm none henceforward of their crew.

LXI

'Gainst Love my standard I've unfurled;
Let those that love him follow still;
I'm his no longer in this world;
For I intend to do my will.
Wherefore if any take it ill
That I Love venture to impeach,
Let this content him, will or nill,
"A dying man is free of speech."

LXII

I feel the droughts of death draw nigh:
Gobbets of phlegm, as white as snow
And big as tennis-balls, spit I;
By token Jehanneton no mo'
Doth me for squire and servant owe,
But for a worn-out rook. Ah, well!
I have the voice and air, I know;
Yet am I but a cockerel.

LXIII

Thanks be to God and Jacques Thibault,
 Who made me drink of water cold
So much within a dungeon low
 And also chew gags manifold.
 When on these things I think of old,
I pray for him, . . . et reliqua;
 God give him . . . what at heart I hold
To be his due . . . et cætera.

LXIV

Yet do I mean no ill to him
 Or his lieutenant; nought but well
Of his official eke I deem,
 Who's merry and conformable.
 Nor with the rest have I to mell,
Save Master Robert . . . Great and small,
 As God loves Lombards, sooth to tell,
I love the whole lot, one and all.

LXV

I do remember (so God please)
 In the year '56 I made,
Departing, sundry legacies,
 That some without my leave or aid
 To call my Testament essayed.
(Their pleasure 'twas, and theirs alone.
 But what? Is't not in common said
That none is master of his own?)

LXVI

And should it happen that of these
 Some peradventure be unpaid,
I order, after my decease,
 That of my heirs demand be made.

Who are they? If it should be said;
To Moreau, Provins and Turgis
    By letters sealed I have conveyed
Even to the mattress under me.

LXVII

Towards the Bastard de la Barre
    Compassion still at heart I bear.
Beside his straw, (and these words are
    His old bequest, though more it were,
    Not to revoke) I do declare
I give him my old mats for seat:
    Well will they serve him to sit square
And keep him steady on his feet.

LXVIII

In fine, but one more word I'll say
    Or ever I begin to test:
Before my clerk, who hears alway
    (If he's awake), I do protest
    That knowingly I have opprest
No man in this my ordinance:
    Nor will I make it manifest
Except unto the realm of France.

LXIX

I feel my heart that's growing dead
    Nor breath for further prate have I.
Fremin, sit down close to my bed,
    And look that no one us espy.
    Take pen, ink, paper, by and by
And what I say write thou therein;
    Then have it copied far and nigh:
And this is how I do begin.

Here Beginneth Villon to Test

LXX

In the eternal Father's name
 And His that's present in the Host,
One with the Father and the same,
 Together with the Holy Ghost,—
 [By whom was saved what Adam lost,
And in the light of heaven arrayed,
 (Who best believes this merits most,)
Dead sinners little gods were made:

LXXI

Dead were they, body and soul as well,
 Doomed to eternal punishment:
Flesh rotted, soul in flames of hell,
 What way soe'er their lives were spent.
 But I except, in my intent,
Prophets and Patriarchs all and sheer:
 Meseems they never could have brent
With over-muckle heat arear.

LXXII

If any ask, "What maketh thee
 With questions such as this to mell,
That art not of theology
 Doctor, or therein capable?"
 'Tis Jesus His own parable,
Touching the rich man that did lie,
 Buried in burning flames of hell,
And saw the leper in the sky.

LXXIII

If he had seen the lazar burn,
 He had not asked him, well I wot,
To give him water or in turn
 To cool his dry and parchèd throat.

There folk will have a scurvy lot
That to buy drink their hosen sell;
    Since drink is there so hardly got,
God save us all from thirst in hell!]

LXXIV

Now, in God's name and with His aid
    And in our lady's name no less,
Let without sin this say be said
    By me grown haggard for duresse.
    If I nor light nor fire possess,
God hath ordained it for my sin;
    But as to this and other stress
I will leave talking and begin.

LXXV

First, my poor soul (which God befriend)
    Unto the blessed Trinity
And to our Lady I commend,
    The fountain of Divinity,
    Beseeching all the charity
Of the nine orders of the sky,
    That it of them transported be
Unto the throne of God most high.

LXXVI

Item, my body I ordain
    Unto the earth, our grandmother:
Thereof the worms will have small gain;
    Hunger hath worn it many a year.
    Let it be given straight to her;
From earth it came, to earth apace
    Returns; all things, except I err,
Do gladly turn to their own place.

LXXVII

Item, to Guillaume de Villon,—
  (My more than father, who indeed
To me more tenderness hath shown
  Than mothers to the babes they feed,
  Who me from many a scrape hath freed
And now of me hath scant liesse,—
  I do entreat him, bended-kneed,
He leave me to my present stress,—)

LXXVIII

I do bequeath my library,—
  The "Devil's Crake" Romaunt, whilere
By Messire Guy de Tabarie,—
  A right trustworthy man,—writ fair.
  Beneath a bench it lies somewhere,
In quires. Though crudely it be writ,
  The matter's so beyond compare
That it redeems the style of it.

LXXIX

I give the ballad following
  To my good mother,—who of me
(God knows!) hath had much sorrowing,
  That she may worship our Ladie:
  I have none other sanctuary
Whereto, when overcome with dole,
  I may for help and comfort flee;
Nor hath my mother, poor good soul!

BALLAD THAT VILLON MADE AT THE REQUEST OF HIS MOTHER, WHEREWITHAL TO DO HER HOMAGE TO OUR LADY

I

Lady of Heaven, Regent of the earth,
   Empress of all the infernal marshes fell,
Receive me, Thy poor Christian, 'spite my dearth,
   In the fair midst of Thine elect to dwell:
   Albeit my lack of grace I know full well;
For that Thy grace, my Lady and my Queen,
Aboundeth more than all my misdemean,
   Withouten which no soul of all that sigh
May merit Heaven. 'Tis sooth I say, for e'en
   In this belief I will to live and die.

II

Say to Thy Son I am His,—that by His birth
   And death my sins be all redeemable,—
As Mary of Egypt's dole He changed to mirth
   And eke Theophilus', to whom befell
   Quittance of Thee, albeit (So men tell)
To the foul fiend he had contracted been.
Assoilzie me, that I may have no teen,
   Maid, that without breach of virginity
Didst bear our Lord that in the Host is seen.
   In this belief I will to live and die.

III

A poor old wife I am, and little worth:
   Nothing I know, nor letter aye could spell:
Where in the church to worship I fare.forth,
   I see Heaven limned, with harps and lutes, and **Hell,**
   Where damned folk seethe in fire unquenchable.

One doth me fear, the other joy serene:
Grant I may have the joy, O Virgin clean,
  To whom all sinners lift their hands on high,
Made whole in faith through Thee their go-between.
  In this belief I will to live and die.

ENVOI

Thou didst conceive, Princess most bright of sheen,
Jesus the Lord, that hath nor end nor mean,
Almighty, that, departing Heaven's demesne
  To succour us, put on our frailty,
Offering to death His sweet of youth and green:
Such as He is, our Lord He is, I ween!
  In this belief I will to live and die.

LXXX

Item, upon my dearest Rose
  Nor heart nor liver I bestow:
Thereat she would turn up her nose,
  Albeit she hath coin enow,—
  A great silk purse, as well I know,
Stuffed full of crowns, both new and old.
  May he be hanged, or high or low,
That leaves her silver aught or gold!

LXXXI

For she without me has enow:
  To me it matters not a jot:
My salad days are past, I trow;
  No more desire in me is hot:
  All that I leave unto Michot,
That was surnamed the good gallant—
  Or rather to his heirs; God wot
At St. Satur his tomb's extant.

LXXXII

This notwithstanding, to acquit
    Me toward Love rather than her,
(For never had I any whit
    Of hope from her: I cannot hear,
    Nor do I care, if a deaf ear
To all she turns as well as me:
    But by Saint Maudlin I aver,
Therein but laughing-stuff I see.)

LXXXIII

This ballad shall she have of me,
    That all with rhymes in R doth end:
Who shall be bearer? Let me see:
    Pernet the Bastard I will send,
    Provided, if, as he doth wend,
He come across my pugnosed frow,
    This question he to her commend;
"Foul Wanton, wherefrom comest thou?"

BALLAD OF VILLON TO HIS MISTRESS

I

False beauty, that hath cost me many a sigh;
    Fair-seeming sweetness in effect how sour;
Love-liking, harder far than steel, that I
    May sister name of my defeasance dour;
    Traitorous charms, that did my heart devour;
Pride, that puts folk to death with secret scorn;
    Pitiless eyes, will rigour ne'er allow her,
Ere worse betide, to succour one forlorn?

II

Well were it for me elsewhere to apply
 For succour: well I know that in her bower
The load of love I never shall lay by;
 Sure 'twere no shame to fly from such a stoure.
 Haro! I cry—both great and small implore.
But what avails me? I shall die outworn,
 Without blow struck, excepting pity bow her,
Ere worse betide, to succour one forlorn.

III

A time will come to wither and make dry,
 Yellow and pale, thy beauty's full-blown flower:
Then should I laugh, if yet my heart were high.
 But no, alas! I then shall have no power
 To laugh, being old in that disastrous hour.
Wherefore drink deep, before the river's frorne;
 Neither refuse, whilst grace is still thy dower,
Ere worse betide, to succour one forlorn.

Envoi

Great God of Love, all lovers' governour,
 Ill falleth thy disfavour to be borne:
True hearts are bound, by Christ our Saviour,
 Ere worse betide, to succour one forlorn.

LXXXIV

Item, to Master Ythier,
 To whom I left my sword of yore,
I give (to set to song) this lay,
 Containing verses half a score;
 Being a De profundis for
His love of once upon a day:
 Her name I must not tell you, or
He'd hate me like the deuce alway.

LAY OR RATHER ROUNDEL

Death, of thy rigour I complain,
  That hast my lady torn from me
  And will not yet contented be,
Save from me too all strength be ta'en,
For languishment of heart and brain.
  What harm did she in life to thee,
      Death?
One heart we had betwixt us twain;
  Which being dead, I too must dree
Death, or, like carven saints we see
In choir, sans life to live be fain,
      Death!

LXXXV

Item, a new bequest I will
  To make to Master Jehan Cornu;
Who in my need hath helped me still
  And done me favours, not a few;
  Wherefore the garden him unto
I give that Peter Bobignon
  Leased me, so but he hang anew
The door and fix the gable on.

LXXXVI

I there did lose, for lack of door,
  A hone and handle of a hoe:
Thenceforward, falcons half a score
  Had not there caught a lark, I trow.
  The hostel's safe, but keep it so.
I put a hook there in sign-stead:
  God grant the robber nought but woe,
A bloody night and earthen bed!

LXXXVII

Item, considering that the wife
  Of Master Peter St. Amant
(Yet if therein be blame or strife,
  God grant her grace and benison)
  Me as a beggar looks upon,
For the White Horse that will not stir,
  A mare, and for the Mule, anon,
A Brick-red Ass I give to her.

LXXXVIII

Item, I give unto Denis
  (Elect of Paris) Hesselin,
Of wine of Aulnis, from Turgis
  Taken at my peril, casks fourteen.
  If he to drink too much begin,
That so his wit and sense decline,
  Let them put water therewithin:
Many a good house is lost by wine.

LXXXIX

Item, upon my advocate,
  Whose name is Guillaume Charriau,—
Though he's a chapman by estate,
  My sword, (without the scabbard, though,)
  And a gold royal I bestow,
In sous, to swell his purse's space,
  Levied on those that come and go
Within the Temple cloister-place.

XC

Item, my proctor Fournier
  Shall handfuls four—for all his pain
And travail for me night and day,—
  Have from my purse; for suits amain

He hath ywrought to gar me gain,—
Just ones, by Jesus be it said!
Even as the judgment did ordain:
The best of rights has need of aid.

XCI

Item, to Jamy Raguyer
  The Muckle Mug in Grève give I,
Provided always that he pay
  Four placks for livery of it; ay,
  Even though what covers calf and thigh
To make the money up sell he
  And fare each morn bare-legged thereby
Unto the Fir-cone Hostelry.

XCII

Item, for Mairebeuf (I vow)
  And Nicholas de Louviers,
I give them neither ox nor cow,
  For drovers neither herds are they,
  But folk that ride a-hawking may,
(Think not I'm making mock of you)
  Partridge and plover night and day
To fake from Mother Maschicoue.

XCIII

Item, if Turgis come to me,
  I'll pay him fairly for his wine:
But soft; if where I lodge find he,
  He'll have more wit than any nine.
  I leave to him that vote of mine,
As citizens of Paris see:
  If sometimes I speak Poitevine,
Two Poitou ladies taught it me.

XCIV

Damsels they were, both fair and free,
  Abiding at St. Generou,
Hard by St. Julian of Brittany
  Or in the Marches of Poitou.
  Natheless, I tell you not for true
Where all their days and nights they **dwell;**
  I am not fool enough, look you,
My loves to all the world to tell.

XCV

Item, Jehan Raguyer I give
  (That's Sergeant,—of the Twelve, **indeed)**
Each day, so long as he shall live,
  A ramakin, that he may feed
  Thereon and stay his stomach's need;
(From Bailly's table be it brought).
  Let him not ask for wine or mead,
But at the fountain quench his drought.

XCVI

Item, I give the Prince of Fools
  A master-fool, Michault du Four,
The jolliest jester in the Schools,
  That sings so well "Ma douce amour."
  With that of him I'll speak no more.
Brief, if he's but in vein some jot,
  He's a right royal fool, be sure,
And still is witty, where he's not.

XCVII

Item, I give unto a pair
  Of sergeants here whose names I've set—
For that they're honest folk and fair—
  Denis Richer and Jehan Vallette,

A tippet each or bandelet,
To hang their hats of felt unto;
  I mean *foot*-sergeants, for as yet
Nought with the horse have I to do.

XCVIII

Item, to Pernet I remit
  For that he is a cogging jack,
(The Bastard of La Barre, to wit,)
    Three loaded dice or else a pack
    Of cheating cards, marked on the back,
To arms, in lieu of bend. But what?
    If he be heard to fyst or crack,
The quartan ague catch the sot!

XCIX

Item, I order that Chollet
  No longer hoop or saw or plane
Or head up barrels all the day.
    Let him his tools change for a cane
    (Or Lyons sword), so he retain
The cooper's mall; for, sooth to tell,
    Though noise and strife to hate he feign,
At heart he loves them but too well.

C

Item, I give to Jehan le Loup—
  For that he's lean and lank and spent,
(Though good-cheap man and comrade true)
    And Chollet too, is slow of scent,
    A setter, young, but excellent,
(No chick he'll miss afield, I trow)
    And a long cloak, 'gainst 'spial meant
To cover them from top to toe.

CI

Item, to Duboys, goldworker,
  An hundred cloves, both head and tail,
Of Saracenic zinziber;
  Not cases therewithal to nail.
Or boxes join, but breach and tail
  To knit and couple yard and thigh,
So to the cods the blood derail
  And in the teats the milk mount high.

CII

To Captain Riou, as a treat
  For him and for his archers, too,
I give six wolvis-heads (a meat
  No swineherds' fare that is, look you)
  Coursed with great dogs and set to stew
In tavern wine. In sooth, to feed
  Upon these dainties rare and new,
One might do many an ill deed.

CIII

'Tis meat a trifle heavier
  Than either feathers, cork or down:
For folk afield 'tis famous fare,
  In camp or leaguer of a town.
  But (failing dogs to hunting boun)
An' if the beasts in trap be ta'en,
  The skins, to fur his winter gown,
As a right tanner, I ordain.

CIV

Item, to Robinet Trousseçaille
  (Who's thriven rarely in his trade;
He scorns to go afoot like quail,
  But sits a fat roan stoutly made)

My platter, that he is afraid
To borrow, I on him bestow;
So will he now be all arrayed:
He needed nothing else, I know.

CV

To Perrot Girard I will well
(That's barber sworn at Bourg la **Reine**)
Two basins and a fish-kettle,
Since he's so eager after gain.
Six years ago, the man was fain
For seven whole days (God have his soul!)
Me with fat porkers to sustain;
Witness the Abbess of Shaven-poll.

CVI

Item, unto the Begging Frères,
The Devotees and the Beguines,
At Paris, Orleans and elsewhere,
Both Turpelin and Turpelines,—
Of stout meat soups with flawns beseen
I make oblation. Let them eat
Their fill and then, the sheets between,
The rogues! of contemplation treat.

CVII

Nay, 'tis not I that give them this;
But from their loins all children spring
Through God that guerdons them ywis
For their much swink and travailing.
Each one of them must live, poor thing,—
E'en monks of Paris, if they go
Our cummers still a-pleasuring,
God wot, they love their husbands so.

CVIII

Whatever Master Jehan Poullieu
 Missaid of them, et reliqua,
Constrained in public place thereto,
 His words perforce he did unsay:
 Meung of their fashion in his day,
Made mock, and Matheolus too:
 But honour unto that alway
Which God's Church honoureth is **due.**

CIX

So I submit me, for my part,
 In all that I can do or say,
To honour them with all my heart
 And yield them service, as I may.
 Fools only will of them missay:
For or in pulpit or elsewhere
 None needeth to be told if they
Are wont their enemies to spare.

CX

Item, I give to Brother Baude,
 In the Mount Carmel Convent **who**
Good cheer doth make and his abode,
 A morion and gisarms two,
 Lest anything Decosta do
To steal from him his wench away.
 He's old; unless he quit the stew,
There'll be the deuce and all to **pay.**

CXI

Item, for that the Chancellor
 Hath chewed fly-droppings off and **on**
Full many a time, his seal yet more
 (I give and grant) he spat upon;

And let him sprain his thumb anon,
(Him of the diocese, I mean,)
　To put my wishes all in one:
God keep the others all from teen.

CXII

I give my Lords the Auditors
　Wainscot to make their chamber fair;
And each whose buttocks in the wars
　Have been, a hollow-bottomed chair,
　Provided that they do not spare
Macée of Orleans, who, God wot,
　Had my virginity whilere,
For she's a thoroughly bad lot.

CXIII

To Master Francis (if he live),
　Promoter de la Vacquerie,
A Scotchman's collaret I give,
　Of hemp without embroidery;
　For, when he put on chivalry,
God and St. George he did blaspheme
　And ne'er hears speak of them but he
Doth with mad laughter shout and scream.

CXIV

I give Jehan Laurens, whose poor eyes
　Are still so red and weak, (I ween,
The fault o't with his parents lies,
　Who drank withouten stint or mean),
　My hose-linings, to wipe them clean
O' mornings, lest they waxen blear;
　Had he of Bourges archbishop been,
He had had sendal; but that's dear.

CXV

Item, to Master Jehan Cotard,
  My Church-court proctor, since some **groat**
Or two for fees yet owing are,
    (That had till now escaped my thought)
    When action 'gainst me Denise brought,
Saying I had miscallèd her,—
    I have this Orison ywrought
So God to heaven his soul prefer.

BALLAD AND ORISON

I

Noah, that first the vine plantéd;
  Lot, too, that in the grot drank high,
By token that Love (the trickster!) led
  Your daughters lewdly to draw you nigh,
  (I say't not to flout you withal, not I)
Architriclinus, learn'd in the bowl,—
  I pray you all three to set in the sky
Good Master Cotard, honest soul.

II

He was of your lineage born and bred;
  He drank of the best and dearest; ay,
Though he'd never a stiver to stand him in
        stead,
  The best of all topers he was: for why,
  Never good liquor found him shy,
None could the pot from his grasp cajole.
  Fair Lords, do not suffer in hell to sigh
Good Master Cotard, honest soul.

III

I've seen him oft, when he went to bed,
Totter for tipple as like to die;
And once he gat him a bump on the head
  'Gainst a butcher's stall, as he staggered by.
  Brief, one might question far and nigh
For a better fellow the cup to trowl.
  Let him in, if you hear him the wicket try:
Good Master Cotard, honest soul.

Envoi

He scarce could spit, he was always so dry,
  And ever "My throat's like a red-hot coal!"
Parched up with thirst, he was wont to cry;
  Good Master Cotard, honest soul.

CXVI

Item, henceforth young Merle shall still
  Manage my change (for evermo'
God wot, it is against my will
  With change I intermeddle) so
  Full change he give to high and low,
Three crowns six half-crowns, and two small
  Angels one great one; for, you know,
A lover should be liberal.

CXVII

Item, I've seen with my own eyes
  That my poor orphans, all the three,
Are grown in age, and wit likewise.
  No sheepsheads are they, I can see;
  From here to Salins none there be
That better bear them at the schools:
  Now by the Confraternity,
Lads of this fashion are no fools.

CXVIII

I will that they to college go;
  Whither? To Master Pierre Richer.
Donatus is too hard, I trow:
  Thereat I will not have them stay.
  I'd rather they should learn to say
An Ave Mary and there stand,
  Without more letters; for alway
Scholars have not the upper hand.

CXIX

Let them learn this and there leave off;
  I do forbid them to proceed:
Meseems it is too hard and tough
  For boys to understand the Creed.
  I halve my long gray tabard wede
And will one half thereof to sell
  And buy them pancakes: for indeed
Children did ever love cates well.

CXX

I will that they well grounded be
  In manners, though it cost them dear:
Close hoods shall they wear, all the three,
  And go with thumbs in girdle-gear,
  Humble to all that come them near,
Saying, "Eh, what? . . . Don't mention it!"
  So folks shall say, when they appear,
"These lads are gently bred," to wit.

CXXI

Item, unto my clerklings lean,—
  To whom my titles and degree
(Seeing them fair and well beseen
  And straight as reeds) I gave in fee.

And also, without price and free,
I did my rent and charge assign,
　　To levy on the pillory,
As safe and sure as if 'twere mine:

CXXII

(Though they be young and of good cheer,
　　On that they nothing me displease:
Come twenty, thirty, forty year,
　　They will be other, so God please.
Ill doth he that maltreateth these,
Since fair they are and in their prime:
　　Fools only will them beat and pheeze;
For younglings grow to men in time,)—

CXXIII

The purses of the Clerks Eighteen
　　They'll have, although my back I break:
They're not like dormice, that grow lean
　　With three months' sleep before they wake.
Ill fares he that his sleep doth take
In youth, when rise and work should he,
　　So that he needs must watch and wake
In age, when he should sleeping be.

CXXIV

Thereof unto the Almoner
　　Letters to like effect I write.
If they to pray for me demur,
　　Let pull their ears for such despite.
Folk often marvel all their might
Why by these twain such store set I;
　　But, fast or feastdays, honour bright,
I never came their mothers nigh.

CXXV

To Michault Culdou I bespeak,
  As also to Charlot Taranne,
One hundred sols. Let neither seek
    Whence; 'twill be manna to each **man**:
    Also my boots of leather tan,
Both soles and uppers, sundry pair;
    So they forgather not with Jehanne
Nor any other like to her.

CXXVI

Unto the Seigneur de Grigny,
  To whom I left Bicêtre of **yore**,
I give the castle of Billy;
    Provided window, gate and door
    He 'stablish as they were before,
That so in good repair it be.
    Let him make money evermore;
For coin I lack and none has he.

CXXVII

To Thibault de la Garde, no less, . . .
  (Thibault? I lie: his name is John)
What can I spare, without distress?
    I've lost enough this year bygone:
    May God provide him! . . . and so **on.**
What if I left him the Canteen?
    No: Genevoys's the elder one
And has more nose to dip therein.

CXXVIII

Item, I give to Basanier,
  The judge's clerk and notary
A frail of cloves, which levied may
  On Master Jehan de Rueil be:

Mautainct and Rosnel the like fee
Shall have, which them I trust will stir
    To serve with courage brisk and free
The Lord who serves Saint Christopher;

CXXIX

On whom the Ballad following
    For his fair lady I bestow: . . .
If love to us no such prize fling,
    I marvel not; for, whiles ago,
    He bore her off from high and low,
At that tourney King René made:
    Hector or Troilus ne'er, I trow,
So much performed, so little said.

BALLAD THAT VILLON GAVE TO A NEWLY MARRIED GENTLEMAN TO SEND TO HIS LAY BY HIM CONQUERED AT THE SWORD'S POINT

I

The falcon claps his wings at break of day,
    For noble usance, ay, and lustihead;
Frolics for glee and strikes and rends his prey;
    Stoops to his mate and does of her his need.
    So now to-you-ward doth desire me lead
Of that all lovers long for joyously;
    Know, Love hath so ordained it in his rede;
And to this end we twain together be.

II

Queen of my heart, unquestioned and alway,
    Till death consume me, thou shalt be indeed.
Clary, that purgest my chagrins, sweet bay,
    That still as champion for my right dost plead,

Reason ordains that I should ne'er be freed
(And therewithal my pleasure doth agree)
From thy sweet service, while the years
          succeed;
And to this end we twain together be.

III

And what is more, when dule doth me essay,
  Through Fate that oftime lowers, with all
          speed
Thy dulcet looks her malice do away,
  As wind disperses smoke from hill and mead.
  In no wise, sweetest, do I lose the seed
Sown in thy field, when the fruit likeneth me;
  God wills me delve and fatten it and weed;
And to this end we twain together be.

Envoi

Princess, I pray, to my discourse give heed:
  My heart shall not dissever aye from thee
Nor thine from me, if it aright I read:
  And to this end we twain together be.

CXXX

Item, I give Jehan Perdryer nought,
  And to his brother Frank the same;
Though still to help me they have wrought
  And make me sharer in their game;
    (Tongues have they, sharp and fierce as
        flame:)
And, too, my gossip Frank, of yore,
  Without command or prayer, my name
At Bourges commended passing sore.

CXXXI

Let them in Taillevent go see
  The chapters that of frying treat,
If they can find my recipe
  For dressing up this kind of meat:
  'Twas Saint Macaire, I once did meet,
Cooking a devil, skin and all,
  That so the roast should smell more sweet,
Gave me this Recipe, that I call.

BALLAD OF SLANDEROUS TONGUES

I

With orpiment, with arsenic red and white
  And boiling lead, for fitter fricassee
Quicklime, saltpetre, soot and pitch unite
  And in this mixture, tempered well with ley
  Of Jewess' excrement, to think the bree;
In water that has lazars' legs made clean,
Wherein old boots and hosen steeped have been;
  In aspics' blood, in deadly drugs and tried,
In badgers', wolves' and foxes' gall and spleen,
  Let all these sharp and poisonous tongues be fried.

II

In brain of cat that water doth affright,
  Black and so old that not a tooth has she;
In foam and slaver from a mad dog's bite,
  Worthless for age, worn out and rickety;
  In froth of broken-winded mule, that ye
Have cut up small with shears; in water green
With festering slime, wherein there may be seen
  Serpents and rats that there have lived and died,
Lizards, toads, frogs and such like beasts obscene,
  Let all these sharp and poisonous tongues be fried.

III

In sublimates, unsafe for mortal wight
  To touch, that in a live snake's navel be;
In blood that, drying, when the moon's at height,
  In barbers' bowls, now green as leeks, we see,
  Now black, and in those tubs unsavourly,
Where soak the foul clouts of the midwife quean;
In bloody flux and cancerous pus venene;
  In baths where whores themselves have purified,
(No apple-squire but knows the thing I mean,)
  Let all these sharp and poisonous tongues be fried.

ENVOI

Prince, all these dainties look you strain and screen,
  If sieve nor bag you have nor yet tameen,
Through shitten hosen, with the breech uptied;
  But in swine's droppings, first, for greater teen,
  Let all these sharp and poisonous tongues be fried.

CXXXII

To Andry Courault, next, give I
  The Counterblast to Franc-Gontier;
As for the Tyrant, set on high,
  I've nought, indeed, to him to say:
  Wisdom forbids that in affray
With mighty men poor folk should strive,
  Lest they spread nets across the way,
To catch the vauntards in alive.

CXXXIII

I fear not Gontier, that no man
  Has nor is better off than I:
But now strife is betwixt us twain;
  For he exalteth poverty:

Good luck he deemeth it, perdie,
Winter and summer to be poor.
Myself, I hold it misery.
Who's wrong? Be you judge, I conjure.

BALLAD ENTITLED THE COUNTER BLAST TO FRANC-GONTIER

I

Athwart a hole in the arras, t'other day,
I saw a fat priest lie on a down bed,
Hard by a fire; and by his side there lay
    Dame Sydonie, full comely, white and red:
    By night and day a goodly life they led.
I watched them laugh and kiss and play, drink
        high
Of spicèd hypocras; then, putting by
    Their clothes, I saw them one another seize,
To take their bodies' pleasure. Thence knew I
There is no treasure but to have one's ease.

II

If, with his mistress Helen, Franc-Gontier
    Had all their life this goodly fashion sped,
With cloves of garlic, rank of smell alway,
    They had no need to rub their oaten bread:
    For all their curds (sans malice be it said)
No jot I care, nor all their cakes of rye.
If they delight beneath the rose to lie,
    What say you? Must we couch afield like
        these?
Like you not better bed and chair there nigh?
There is no treasure but to have one's ease.

III

They eat coarse bread of barley, sooth to say,
  And drink but water from the heavens shed:
Not all the birds that singen all the way
  From here to Babylon could me persuade
    To spend one day so harboured and so fed.
For God's sake let Franc-Gontier none deny
To play with Helen 'neath the open sky!
  Why should it irk me, if they love the leas?
But, vaunt who will the joys of husbandry,
    There is no treasure but to have one's ease.

Envoi

Prince, be you judge betwixt us all: for my
  Poor heart I mind me (so it none displease)
Whilst yet a child, I heard folk testify,
    There is no treasure but to have one's ease.

CXXXIV

Item, since Madame de Bruyères
  Her bible knows, to publish it
(Barring the Gospels) unto her
  And to her damsels I commit,
    To bring each glib-tongued wanton chit
To book; but be the preachment not
  Within the churchyards; far more fit
'Twere in the net-market, God wot.

BALLAD OF THE WOMEN OF PARIS

I

Though folk deem women young and old
  Of Venice and Genoa well eno'
Favoured with speech, both glib and bold,
  To carry messages to and fro;

Savoyards, Florentines less or more,
Romans and Lombards though folk renown,
I, at my peril, I say no;
There's no right speech out of Paris town.

II

The Naples women (so we are told)
Can school all comers in speech and show;
Prussians and Germans were still extolled
For pleasant prattle of friend and foe;
But hail they from Athens or Grand Cairo,
Castile or Hungary, black or brown,
Greeks or Egyptians, high or low,
There's no right speech out of Paris town.

III

Switzers nor Bretons know how to scold,
Nor Provence nor Gascony women: lo!
Two fishfags in Paris the bridge that hold
Would slang them dumb in a minute or so.
Picardy, England, Lorraine, (heigho!
Enough of places have I set down?)
Valenciennes, Calais, wherever you go,
There's no right speech out of Paris town.

ENVOI

Prince, to the Paris ladies, I trow,
For pleasant parlance I yield the crown.
They may talk of Italians; but this I know,
There's no right speech out of Paris town.

CXXXV

Look at them there, by twos and threes
Upon their gowns' hem seated low,
In churches and in nunneries:
Speak not, but softly near them go

And speedily you'll come to know
Such judgments as Macrobius ne'er
   Did give. Whate'er you catch, I trow,
'Twill all some flower of wisdom bear.

CXXXVI

Item, unto Mount Martyr hill
   (Old past the memory of man)
Let them adjoin (it is my will)
   The knoll called Mount Valerian:
   I give it for a quarter's span
The indulgences from Rome I brought;
   Whence shall the convent, where no man
Might come, of many now be sought.

CXXXVII

Item, to serving men and maids
   Of good hostels (in no despite),
Pheasants, tarts, custards and croustades
   And high carousal at midnight:
   Seven pints or eight, the matter's slight,
Whilst sound asleep are lord and dame:
   Thereafter, putting out the light,
Commend them to the asses game.

CXXXVIII

Item, to honest wenches who
   Have fathers, mothers, aunts . . . 'Fore God!
I've nothing left to give to you:
   All on the servants I've bestowed.
   Poor silly wantons, they had showed
Themselves with little satisfied!
   Some scraps might well have gone their road
Of all the convents cast aside.

CXXXIX

Cistercians and Celestines,
    Though they be railed off from the rest,
They eat rich meats and drink sweet wines,
    Whereof poor whores know not the zest:
    As Jehanne and Perrette can attest
And Isabeau that says "Is't not?"
    Since they therefor are so distrest,
One scarce wer? damn'd for it, God wot.

CXL

Item, to sturdy stout Margot,
    Of face and favour fair and feat,
A pious creature, too, eno',—
    I' faith, by God Almighty be't,
    I love her well, the proper peat,
As she (sweet chuck) loves me indeed:
    If any chance with her to meet,
Let him this Ballad to her read.

BALLAD OF VILLON AND MUCKLE MEG

I

Because I love and serve a whore sans glose,
    Think not therefore or knave or fool am I:
She hath in her such goods as no man knows.
    For love of her, target and dirk I ply:
When clients come, I hend a pot therenigh
And get me gone for wine, without word said:
Before them water, fruit, bread, cheese, I spread.
    If they pay well, I bid them "Well, God aid!
Come here again, when you of lust are led,
    In this the brothel where we ply our trade."

II

But surely before long an ill wind blows
When, coinless, Margot comes by me to lie.
I hate the sight of her, catch up her hose,
  Her gown, her surcoat and her girdle-tie,
  Swearing to pawn them, meat and drink to buy.
She grips me by the throat and cuffs my head,
Cries "Antichrist!" and swears by Jesus dead,
  It shall not be: till I, to quell the jade,
A potsherd seize and I score her nose with red,
  In this the brothel where we ply our trade.

III

Then she, peace made, to show we're no more foes,
  A hugeous crack of wind at me lets fly
And laughing sets her fist against my nose,
  Bids me "Go to" and claps me on the thigh;
  Then, drunk, like logs we sleep till, by and by,
Awaking, when her womb is hungered,
To spare the child beneath her girdlestead,
  She mounts on me, flat as a pancake laid.
With wantoning she wears me to the thread,
  In this the brothel where we ply our trade.

Envoi

Hail, rain, freeze, ready baked I hold my bread:
  Well worth a lecher with a wanton wed!
Whether's the worse. They differ not a shred.
  Ill cat to ill rat; each for each was made.
We flee from honour; it from us hath fled:
Lewdness we love, that stands us well in stead,
  In this the brothel where we ply our trade.

CXLI

Item, to Marion (Statue hight)
And to tall Jehanne of Brittany,
I give to keep a school by night,
    Where masters taught of scholars be:
    A thing you everywhere may see,
Except in Mehun gaol alone.
    Wherefore I say, Out on the fee!
Since that the trick is so well known.

CXLII

Item, to Noël! Well-beseen
No other gift I do ordain
Than both hands full of osiers green,
    Out of my garden freshly ta'en:
    (One should to chastisement be fain;
In sooth it is fair almsgiving:)
    Eleven score strokes laid on amain,
Of Master Hal's administ'ring.

CXLIII

Item, the Hospitals unto
    What to bequeath I hardly know:
Here jests are neither right nor due,
    For sick poor folk have ills eno':
    Let each man's leavings to them go.
The Mendicants have had my goose:
    Nought but the bones they'll get, I trow;
The poor can seldom pick and choose.

CXLIV

I give my barber, (an he list)—
    By name that Colin Galerne hight,
Near Angelot's the Herbalist,—
    A lump of ice: let him apply't

Upon his paunch and hold it tight,
So he may freeze as seems him meet:
If thus o' winter deal the wight,
He'll not complain of summer heat.

CXLV

Item, I leave the Foundlings nought:
But to the Lostlings comfort's due,
Who should, if anywhere, be sought
Where lodges Marion the Statue.
A lesson of my sort to you
I'll read: 'twill soon be overpast.
Turn not, I pray, deaf ears thereto,
But listen sadly: 'tis the last.

SEEMLY LESSON OF VILLON TO THE GOOD-FOR-NOUGHTS

I

Fair sons, you're wasting, ere you're old,
The fairest rose to you that fell.
You, that like the birdlime take and hold,
When to Montpippeau or Ruel
(My clerks) you wander, keep you well:
For of the tricks that there be played,
Thinking to 'scape a second spell,
Colin of Cayeulx lost his head.

II

No trifling game is this to play,
Where one stakes soul and body too:
If losers, no remorse can stay
A shameful death from ending you;
And even the winner, for his due,
Hath not a Dido to his wife.
Foolish and lewd I hold him who
Doth for so little risk his life.

III

Now all of you to me attend:
  Even a load of wine, folk say,
When drinking at last comes to an end,
  By fire in winter, in woods in May.
  If you have money, it doth not stay,
But this way and that it wastes amain:
  What does it profit you, anyway?
Ill-gotten good is nobody's gain?

BALLAD OF GOOD DOCTRINE TO THOSE OF ILL LIFE

I

Peddle indulgences, as you may:
  Cog the dice for your cheating throws:
Try if counterfeit coin will pay,
  At risk of roasting at last, like those
  That deal in treason. Lie and glose,
Rob and ravish: what profit it?
  Who gets the purchase, do you suppose?
Taverns and wenches, every whit.

II

Rhyme, rail, wrestle, and cymbals play:
  Flute and fool it in mummers' shows:
Along with the strolling players stray
  From town to city, without repose;
  Act mysteries, farces, imbroglios:
Win money at gleek or a lucky hit
  At the pins: like water, away it flows;
Taverns and wenches, every whit.

III

Turn from your evil courses I pray,
That smell so foul in a decent nose:
Earn your bread in some honest way.
If you have no letters, nor verse nor prose,
Plough or groom horses, beat hemp or toze,
Enough shall you have if you think but fit:
But cast not your wage to each wind that
blows;
Taverns and wenches, every whit.

ENVOI

Doublets, pourpoints and silken hose,
Gowns and linen, woven or knit,
Ere your wede's worn, away it goes;
Taverns and wenches, every whit.

CXLVI

Companions in debauchery,
Ill souls and bodies well bestead,
Beware of that ill sun (look ye)
That tans a man when he is dead:
'Tis a foul death to die, I dread.
Keep yourselves from it, so you may;
And be this still rememberèd,
That all of you must die some day.

CXLVII

Item, I give the Fifteen-score—
(Three hundred just as well 'tmight be)—
For that by them I set great store,
(Paris, nor Provins ones, for me)—
My goggles (sans the case, perdie)
So in the churchyards where they serve,
They may the bad to sever see
From honest folk that well deserve.

CXLVIII

Here * silence doth forever reign:
  Nothing it profiteth the dead
On beds of satin to have lain
    And drunk from gold the vine-juice red
    And lived in glee and lustihead.
Soon all such joys must be resigned:
    All pass away, and in their stead
Only the sin remains behind.

CXLIX

When I consider all the heads
    That in these charnels gathered be,
Those that are sleeping in these beds
    May have (for aught that I can see)
    Been mighty lords of high degree,
Bishops and dames,—or else poor churls:
    There is no difference to me
'Twixt watercarriers' bones and earls.

CL

These ladies all, that in their day
    Each against each did bend and bow,
Whereof did some the sceptre sway,
    Of others feared and courted,—now
    Here are they sleeping all a-row,
Heaped up together anydele,
    Their crowns and honours all laid low.
Masters or clerks, there's no appeal.

CLI

Now are they dead, God have their sprights!
    As for their bodies, they are clay:
Once they were ladies, lords and knights,
    That on soft beds of satin lay

----

* *i. e.,* in the churchyards.

And fed on dainties every day.
Their bones are mouldered into dust,
    They reck not now of laugh or play:
Christ will assoilzie them, I trust.

CLII

I make this ditty for the dead:
    The which I do communicate
To Courts and Pleas, ill doers' dread,
    That unjust avarice do hate;
    That for the welfare of the state
Do work their bones and bodies dry:
    God and St. Dominick abate
Their sins unto them when they die.

CLIII

Item, Jacques Cardon nought of me
    (For nought I have for him) shall get,
—Not that he'd throw't away, perdie—
    Except this roundel; if 'twere set
    To some such tune as "Marionette,"
Composed for Marion Slow-to-come,
    Or "Hold your door open, Guillemette,"
It might belike the vogue become.

ROUNDEL

On my release *from prison strait,*
    Where I have left my life well-nigh,
    If Fate still look at me awry,
Judge if she be inveterate!
Reason meseemeth, past debate,
    Her malice she should mollify
            On my release.

Full of unreason is this Fate,
　Which willeth but that I should die:
　God grant that in His house on high
My soul be ravished from her hate,
　　On my release.

CLIV

This gift shall Lomer have of me,
　—As sure as I'm a fairy's son,—
That he shall "well-belovèd" be,
　But wench or woman love he none
　Nor lose his head for any one,
And that an hundred times a night
　The trick for nought of him be done,
In spite of Holger the good knight.

CLV

To lovers sick and sorrowful,
　(As well as Alain Chartier's Lay,)
At bedhead, a benature-full
　Of tears I give, and eke a spray
　Of eglatere or flowering May,
(To sprinkle with) in time of green;
　Provided they a *Psalter* say.
To save poor Villon's soul from teen.

CLVI

To Master James, that day and night
　Himself at hoarding wealth doth kill,
I give as many girls to plight
　(But none to marry) as he will.
　For whom doth he his coffers fill?
For those that are his kin, alack!
　That which the sows' was, I hold ill
Should to the porkers not go back.

CLVII

Unto the Seneschal I bequeath,—
  (Who once from debt did me release)
Besides the quality of Smith,—
    The right of shoeing ducks and geese.
    I send him all these fooleries,
To help him pass away the time,
  Or make him spillets if he please:
One wearies of the best of rhyme.

CLVIII

The Captain of the Watch, also—
  Two proper youths to serve as page;
Marquet the Stout and Philippot,
    Who for the most part of their age
    Have served (whence are they the more sage)
The Blacksmiths' Provost. Wellaway!
    If they should chance to lose their wage,
They must go shoeless many a day.

CLIX

Item, to Chappelain let there pass
  My simple-tonsure chapelry,
Charged but with saying a low mass:
    There little letters needed be.
    My cure of souls he should of me
Have had; but no one to confess
  (To go by what he says) cares he,
Save chambermaids and mistresses.

CLX

Since my intent he well doth know,
  To Jehan de Calais—(worthy wight!
Who saw me thirty years ago
    And hath not since on me set sight,

Indeed, nor knoweth how I hight)—
If in this Testament befall
  Or hitch or doubt, I give full right
To solve and mend them, one and all.

CLXI

To glose upon it and comment,
  Define, eliminate, prescribe,
Diminish aught or aught augment,
  To cancel it or it transcribe
  With his own hand, although no scribe
He be; such sense as he thinks fit,
  At pleasure, good or bad, ascribe
Thereto: I sanction all of it.

CLXII

And if, perchance, some legatee,
  Without my knowledge, should be dead,
It shall at the discretion be
  Of Jehan de Calais aforesaid
  To see my will interpreted.
And otherwise the gift apply
  Nor take it for himself instead:
I charge him on his soul thereby.

CLXIII

Item, my body, I ordain,
  Shall at St. Avoye buried be:
And that my friends may there again
  My image and presentment see,
  Let one the semblant limn of me
In ink, if that be not too dear.
  No other monument, perdie:
'Twould overload the floor, I fear.

CLXIV

Item, I will that over it
   That which ensues, without word more,
In letters large enough to be writ:
   If ink fail (as I said before),
   Let them the words with charcoal score,
So they do not the plaster drag:
   'Twill serve to keep my name in store,
As that of a good crack-brained wag.

Epitaph

CLXV

HERE LIES AND SLUMBERS IN THIS PLACE
   ONE WHOM LOVE WREAKED HIS IRE UPON:
A SCHOLAR, POOR OF GOODS AND GRACE,
   THAT HIGHT OF OLD FRANÇOIS VILLON:
   ACRE OR FURROW HAD HE NONE.
'TIS KNOWN HIS ALL HE GAVE AWAY;
   BREAD, TABLES, TRESSELS, ALL ARE GONE.
GALLANTS, OF HIM THIS ROUNDEL SAY.

ROUNDEL

Æternam Requiem dona,
   Lord God, and everlasting light,
   To him who never had, poor wight,
Platter, or aught thereon to lay!
Hair, eyebrows, beard all fallen away,
   Like a peeled turnip was his plight.
Æternam Requiem dona.

Exile compelled him many a day
   And death at last his breech did smite,
   Though, "I appeal," with all his might
The man in good plain speech did say.
Æternam Requiem dona.

CLXVI

Item, I will they toll for me
The "Belfry" Bell, that is so great
Of voice, that all astonied be
When he is tolled, early or late.
Many a good city, of old date,
He saved, as every one doth know;
Thunder or war, all ills abate
When through the land his voices go.

CLXVII

Four loaves the ringers' wage shall be:
If that too little, six: (that is
What rich folk wont to give for fee:)
But they St. Stephen's loaves, ywis,
Shall be. Let Vollant share in this;
A man that earns his living hard:
'Twill furnish forth a week of his.
The other one? Jehan de la Garde.

CLXVIII

Item, to carry out this all,
As my executors I name
Men who are good to deal withal
And never shirk an honest claim:
They're no great vauntards, all the same,
Though they've good cause for it, perdie;
They shall fulfill my thought and aim:
Write, I will name six names to thee.

CLXIX

First, Master Martin de Bellefaye,
The King's Lieutenant-criminel.
Who shall be next? Whom shall I say?
It shall be Messire Colombel:

If, as I think, it like him well,
He'll undertake this charge for me.
    The third one? Michel Jouvenel:
I give the office to these three.

CLXX

Natheless, in case they should excuse
    Themselves therefrom, for fear of fees,
Or altogether should refuse,
    I name as their successors these,
    Good men and true in their degrees:
Philip Brunel, the noble squire,
    For next, his neighbour (an he please),
Master Jacques Raguyer, I desire.

CLXXI

Master Jacques James shall be the third:
    Three men of worth and good renown,
That for believers in God's Word
    And right God-fearing souls are known:
    Far rather would they spend their own
Than not my full intent fulfil
    No auditor on them shall frown:
They shall do all at their own will.

CLXXII

The Register of Wills from me
    Shall have nor quid nor quod, I trow:
But every penny of his fee
    To Tricot, the young priest, shall go;
    At whose expense gladly eno'
I'd drink, though it my nightcap cost:
    If but he knew the dice to throw,
Of Perrette's Den I'd make him host.

CLXXIII

Guillaume du Ru, for funeral,
   Shall see the chapel duly lit;
And as to who shall bear the pall,
   Let my executors order it.
   And now, my body every whit
(Groin, eyebrows, hair and beard and all)
   Being racked with pain, the time seems fit
To cry folk mercy, great and small.

BALLAD CRYING ALL FOLK MERCY

I

Frères, be they white or be they grey;
   Nuns, mumpers, chanters awry that tread
And clink their pattens on each highway;
   Lackeys and handmaids, apparellèd
   In tight-fitting surcoats, white and red;
Gallants, whose boots o'er their ankles fall,
   That vaunt and ruffle it unadread;
I cry folk mercy, one and all.

II

Wantons who all their charms display,
   That so more custom to them be led,
Brawlers and jugglers and tumblers gay;
   Clowns with their apes and carpet spread;
   Players that whistle for lustihead,
As they trudge it 'twixt village and town and hall;
   Gentle and simple, living and dead,—
I cry folk mercy, one and all.

III

Save only the treacherous beasts of prey,
   That garred me batten on prison bread
And water, many a night and day.
   I fear them not now, no, not a shred;

And gladly (but that I lie a-bed
And have small stomach for strife or brawl)
  I'd have my wreak of them. Now, instead,
I cry folk mercy, one and all.

ENVOI

So but the knaves be ribroastéd
  And basted well with an oaken maul
Or some stout horsewhip weighted with lead,
  I cry folk mercy, one and all.

BALLAD, BY WAY OF ENDING

I

Here is ended (both great and small)
  Poor Villon's Testament! When he is dead,
Come, I pray, to his funeral,
  Whilst the bell tinkles overhead.
  Come in cramozin garmented;
For to Love martyr did he die.
  Thereof he swore on his manlihead,
Whenas he felt his end draw nigh.

II

For me, I warrant it true in all;
  For of his love, in shameful stead,
He was beaten off, like a bandy-ball.
  From here to Roussillon as he fled,
There's ne'er a bramble but tore some **shred**
Of hose or jerkin from hip or thigh;
  So, without leasing, Villon said,
Whenas he felt his end draw nigh.

III

In such ill places his life did fall,
  He had but a rag when he was sped:
And (yet more luckless) when death did call,
  *Love's prickle galled him; its wounds still **bled***
In him.   His heart was heavy as lead
And salt tears stood in his dying eye:
  At his despair we were wonderèd,
Whenas he felt his end draw nigh.

Envoi

Prince, that art gent as a yearling gled,
  Hear what he did with his latest sigh:
*He drank a long draught of the vine-juice **red**,*
  Whenas he felt his end draw nigh.

**Here Endeth the Greater Testament of
Master Francois Villon**

_____

DIVERS POEMS

BALLAD OF VILLON IN PRISON

I

Have pity, friends, have pity now, I pray,
  If it so please you, at the least, on me!
I lie in fosse, not under holm or may
  In this duresse, wherein, alas! I dree
  Ill fate, as God did thereanent decree.
Lasses and lovers, younglings manifold,
Dancers and mountebanks, alert and bold,
  Nimble as squirrel from a crossbow shot
Singers, that troll as clear as bells of gold,—
  Will you all leave poor Villon here to rot?

II

Clerks, that go caroling the livelong day,
  Scant-pursed, but glad and frank and full of glee;
Wandering at will along the broad highway,
  Harebrained, perchance, but wit-whole too, perdie:
  Lo! now, I die, whilst that you absent be,
Song-singers, when poor Villon's days are told,
You will sing psalms for him and candles hold;
  Here light nor air nor levin enters not,
Where ramparts thick are round about him rolled.
  Will you all leave poor Villon here to rot?

269

III

Consider but his piteous array,
  High and fair lords, of suit and service free,
That nor to king nor kaiser homage pay,
  But straight from God in heaven hold your fee!
  Come fast or feast, all days alike fasts he,
Whence are his teeth like rakes' teeth to behold:
No table hath he but the sheer black mould
  After dry bread (not manchets), pot on pot
They empty down his throat of water cold:
  Will you all leave poor Villon here to rot?

Envoi

Princes and lords aforesaid, young and old,
Get me the King his letters sealed and scrolled
  And draw me from this dungeon: for, God wot,
Even swine, when one squeaks in the butcher's fold,
Flock around their fellow and do squeak and scold.
  Will you all leave poor Villon here to rot?

THE QUATRAIN THAT VILLON MADE WHEN HE WAS DOOMED TO DIE

François am I,—woe worth it me!
At Paris born, near Pontoise citie,
Whose neck, in the bight of a rope of three,
Must prove how heavy my buttocks be.

Variant of the Foregoing Epitaph

François am I,—woe worth it me!
  —Corbier my surname is aright:
Native of Auvers, near Pontoise citie;
  Of folk for sobriquet Villon hight.

But for the gallant appeal I made,
My neck, in the bight of a rope of three,
    Had known ere this what my buttocks weighed.
    The game scarce seemed to me worth to be played.

THE EPITAPH IN BALLAD FORM THAT VILLON MADE FOR HIMSELF AND HIS COMPANIONS, EXPECTING NO BETTER THAN TO BE HANGED IN THEIR COMPANY

I

BROTHERS, that after us on life remain,
  Harden your hearts against us not as stone;
For, if to pity us poor wights you're fain,
  God shall the rather grant you benison.
  You see us six, the gibbet hereupon:

As for the flesh that we too well have fed,
'Tis all devoured and rotted, shred by shred.
  Let none make merry of our piteous case,
Whose crumbling bones the life long since hath fled:
  The rather pray, God grant us of His grace!

II

Yea, we conjure you, look not with disdain,
  Brothers, on us, though we to death were done
By justice. Well you know, the saving grain
  Of sense springs not in every mother's son:
  Commend us, therefore, now we're dead and gone,
To Christ, the Son of Mary's maidenhead,
That he leave not His grace on us to shed
  And save us from the nether torture-place.
Let no one harry us: forsooth, we're sped:
  The rather pray, God grant us of His grace!

III

We are whiles scoured and soddened of the rain
  And whiles burnt up and blackened of the sun:
Corbies and pyets have our eyes out-ta'en
  And plucked our beard and hair out, one by one.
  Whether by night or day, rest have we none:
Now here, now there, as the wind shifts its stead,
We swing and creak and rattle overhead,
  No thimble dinted like our bird-pecked face.
Brothers, have heed and shun the life we led:
  The rather pray, God grant us of His grace!

ENVOI

Prince Jesus, over all empoweréd,
Let us not fall into the Place of Dread,
  But all our reckoning with the Fiend efface.
Folk, mock us not that are forspent and dead;
  The rather pray, God grant us of His grace!

THE REQUEST OF VILLON PRESENTED TO THE HIGH COURT OF PARLIAMENT IN BALLAD FORM

I

ALL my five senses, in your several place,
  Hearing and seeing, taste and touch and smell,
Every my member branded with disgrace,—
  Each on this fashion do ye speak and tell:
  "Most Sovereign Court, by whom we here befell,
Thou that deliveredst us from sore dismays,
The tongue sufficeth not thy name to blaze
  Forth in such strain of honour as it should:
Wherefore to thee our voices all we raise,
  Sister of angels, mother of the good!"

II

Heart, cleave in sunder, or in any case
  Be not more hardened and impermeable
Than was the black rock in the desert-space,
    Which with sweet water for the Jews did swell;
    Melt into tears and mercy call, as well
Befits a lowly heart that humbly prays:
Give to the Court, the kingdom's glory, praise,—
    The Frenchman's stay, the help of strangerhood,
Born of high heaven amidst the empyreal rays:
    Sister of angels, mother of the good!

III

And you, my teeth, your sockets leave apace;
    Come forward, all, and loudlier than bell,
Organ or clarion, render thanks for grace
    And every thought of chewing now repel.
    Bethink you, I was doomed to death and hell,
Heart, spleen and liver palsied with affrays:
And you, my body, (else you were more base
    Than bear or swine that in the dunghill brood,)
Extol the Court, ere worser hap amaze;
    Sister of angels, mother of the good!

ENVOI

Prince, of thy grace deny me not three days
To bid my friends adieu and go my ways:
    Without them, I've nor money, clothes nor food.
Triumphant Court, be't as thy suppliant says;
    Sister of angels, mother of the good!

BALLAD OF VILLON'S APPEAL

I

GARNIER, how like you my appeal?
  Did I wisely, or did I ill?
Each beast looks to his own skin's weal:
  If any bind him, to keep or kill,
  He does himself free to the best of his skill.
When, then, sans reason, to me was sung
  This pleasant psalm of a sentence, still
Was it a time to hold my tongue?

II

Were I of Capet's race somedele
  (Whose kin were butchers on Montmartre hill)
They had not bound me with iron and steel
  Nor forced me to swizzle more than my fill:
  (You know the trick of it, will or nill?)
But, when of malice prepense and wrong,
  They doomed me to swallow this bitter pill.
Was it a time to hold my tongue?

III

Think you that under my cap I feel
  Not reason nor ableness there until,
Sufficient to say, "I do appeal"?
  Enough was left me (as warrant I will)
  To keep me from holding my clapper still,
When jargon, that meant "You shall be hung"
  They read to me from the notary's bill:
Was it a time to hold my tongue?

ENVOI

Prince, had I had the pip in my bill,
  Long before this I should have swung,
A scarecrow hard by Montfaucon mill!
  Was it a time to hold my tongue?

BALLAD OF PROVERBS

I

GOATS scratch until they spoil their bed:
  Pitcher to well too oft we send:
The iron's heated till it's red
  And hammered till in twain it rend:
  The tree grows as the twig we bend:
Men journey till they disappear
  Even from the memory of a friend:
We shout out "Noël" till it's here.

II

Some mock until their hearts do bleed:
  Some are so frank that they offend:
Some waste until they come to need:
  A promised gift is ill to spend:
  Some love God till from church they trend:
Wind shifts until to North it veer:
  Till forced to borrow do we lend:
We shout out "Noël" till it's here.

III

Dogs fawn on us till them we feed:
  Song's sung until by heart it's kenned:
Fruit's kept until it rot to seed:
  The leaguered place falls in the end:
  Folk linger till the occasion wend:
Haste oft throws all things out of gear:
  One clips until the grasp's o'erstrained:
We shout out "Noël" till it's here.

ENVOI

Prince, fools live so long that they mend:
  They go so far that they draw near:
They're cozened till they apprehend:
  We shout out "Noël" till it's here.

BALLAD OF THINGS KNOWN AND UNKNOWN

I

FLIES in the milk I know full well:
  I know men by the clothes they wear:
I know the walnut by the shell:
  I know the foul sky from the fair:
  I know the pear-tree by the pear:
I know the worker from the drone
  And eke the good wheat from the tare:
I know all save myself alone.

II

I know the pourpoint by the fell
  And by his gown I know the frère:
Master by varlet I can spell:
  Nuns by the veils that hide their hair:
  I know the sharper and his snare
And fools that fat on cates have grown:
  Wines by the cask I can compare:
I know all save myself alone.

III

I know how horse from mule to tell:
  I know the load that each can bear:
I know both Beatrice and Bell:
  I know the hazards, odd and pair:
  I know of visions in the air:
I know the power of Peter's throne
  And how misled Bohemians were:
I know all save myself alone.

ENVOI

Prince, I know all things: fat and spare:
  Ruddy and pale, to me are known:
And Death that endeth all our care:
  I know all save myself alone.

BALLAD OF POOR CHIMNEYSWEEPS

I

MEN talk of those the fields that till;
   Of those that sift out chaff from corn;
Of him that has, will he or nill,
   A wife that scoldeth night and morn,—
   As folk hard driven and forlorn:
Of men that often use the sea;
Of monks that of poor convents be;
   Of those behind the ass that go:
But, when all things consider we,
   Poor chimneysweeps have toil eno'.

II

To govern boys and girls with skill,
   God wot, 's no labour lightly borne:
Nor to serve ladies at Love's will;
   Or do knight suit at sound of horn,
   Helmet and harness always worn,
And follow arms courageously:
To joust and tilt with spears, perdie,
   And quintain play, is hard, I know;
But, when all things consider we,
   Poor chimneysweeps have toil eno'.

III

God wot, they suffer little ill
   By whom wheat's reaped and meadows shorn;
Or those that thresh grain for the mill
   Or plead the Parliament beforne;
   To borrow money's little scorn;
Tinkers and carters have to dree
But little hardship, seemeth me;
   Nor does Lent irk us much, I trow:
But, when all things consider we,
   Poor chimneysweeps have toil eno'.

          [ENVOI *deest.*]

BALLAD OF FORTUNE

I

I of old time by makers Fortune hight—
  Whom, François, thou dost rail at and decry,—
Far better men than thou, poor nameless wight,
  I grind into the dust with poverty
  And gar them delve i' the quarries till they die:
Wherefore complainest thou? If thou live ill,
Thou art not singular: so, peace, be still.
  Think but how many mighty men of yore
I've laid stark dead to stiffen in their gore,
By whom thou'rt but a scullion knave, perdie.
  Content thee, then, and chide thy fate no more;
I rede thee, Villon, take it all in gree.

II

Oft have I girded me to wreak my spite
  Upon great kings: lo, in the days gone by,
Priam I slew; and all his warlike might
  Availed him nought, towers, walls nor ramparts
    high.
  'Gainst Hannibal no less did I apply,
Who was attaint in Carthage by my skill:
And Scipio Africanus did I kill:
  Great Cæsar to the Senate I gave o'er
  And wrecked stout Pompey upon Egypt shore:
Jason I drowned by tempest on the sea
  And burned both Rome and Romans heretofore:
I rede thee, Villon, take it all in gree.

III

Nay, Alexander, that renownèd knight,
  Who longed to reach the backward of the sky
And shed much blood, with poison did I blight;
  I made Arphaxad on the field to lie,

Dead, by his royal standard. Thus did I
Full many a time and yet more will fulfil:
Nor time nor reason can awry my will.
    Huge Holophernes, too, that did adore
    Strange gods, whom Judith with his sword of war
Slew as he slept; and Absalom, as he
    Fled, by the love-locks hanged I that he wore.
I rede thee, Villon, take it all in gree.

ENVOI

Poor François, set my rede in thy heart's core:
If I could aught without God's leave or lore,
    I'd leave no rag to one of all that be;
For each ill done I'd compass half a score:
    I rede thee, Villon, take it all in gree.

BALLAD AGAINST THOSE WHO MISSAY
OF FRANCE

I

LET him meet beasts that breathe out fiery rain,
    Even as did Jason hard by Colchis town;
Or seven years changed into a beast remain,
    Nebuchadnezzar-like, to earth bowed down;
Or suffer else such teen and mickle bale
As Helen's rape on Trojans did entail;
    Or in Hell's marshes fallen let him fare
    Like Tantalus and Proserpine or bear
A grievouser than Job his sufferance,
    Prisoned and pent in Dædalus his snare,—
Who would wish ill unto the realm of France.

II

Four months within a marish let him plain,
    Bittern-like, with the mud against his crown;
Or sell him to the Ottoman, to chain
    And harness like an ox, the scurvy clown!

Or thirty years, like Maudlin, without veil
Or vesture, let him his misdeeds bewail;
   Or with Narcissus death by drowning share;
   Or die like Absalom, hanged by the hair;
Or Simon Magus, by his charms' mischance;
   Or Judas, mad with horror and despair,—
Who would wish ill unto the realm of France.

III

If but Octavian's time might come again,
   His molten gold should down his throat be thrown,
Or 'twixt two millstones he should grind for grain,
   As did St. Victor; or I'd have him drown
Far out to sea, where help and breath should fail,
Like Jonah in the belly of the whale;
   Let him be doomed the sunlight to forswear,
   Juno her goods and Venus debonair,
And be of Mars oppressed to utterance,—
   As was Antiochus the king, whilere,—
Who would wish ill unto the realm of France.

ENVOI

Prince, may winds bear him to the wastes of air
Or to the mid-sea woods and sink him there:
   Be all his hopes changed to desesperance;
For he deserves not any fortune fair
   Who would wish ill unto the realm of France.

BALLAD OF THE DEBATE OF THE HEART AND BODY OF VILLON

I

WHAT is't I hear?—'Tis I, thy heart; 'tis I
   That hold but by a thread for frailty,
I have nor force nor substance, all drained dry,
   Since thee thus lonely and forlorn I see,

Like a poor cur, curled up all shiveringly.
How comes it thus?—Of thine unwise liesse.—
What irks it thee?—*I* suffer the distress.
    Leave me in peace.—Why?—I will cast about.—
When will that be?—When I'm past childishness.—
I say no more.—And I can do without.

II

What deemest thou?—To mend before I die.—
    At thirty years?—'Tis a mule's age, perdie.—
Is't childhood?—Nay.—'Tis madness, then, doth ply
    And grip thee?—Where?—By the nape.—Seemeth
        me
Nothing I know?—Yes, flies in milk, maybe:
Thou canst tell black from white yet at a press.—
Is't all?—What words can *all* thy faults express?—
    If't's not enough, we'll have another bout.—
Thou'rt lost.—I'll make a fight for't none the less.—
I say no more.—And I can do without.

III

Dule have I, pain and misery thou thereby:
    If thou wert some poor idiot, happily
Thou mightst have some excuse thy heart anigh.
    Lo, foul and fair are all alike to thee.
    Or harder is thy head than stone by sea
Or more than honour likes thee this duresse.
Canst thou say aught in answer? Come, confess.—
    I shall be quit on't when I die, no doubt.
    God! what a comfort 'gainst a present stress!
I say no more.—And I can do without.

IV

Whence comes this evil?—Surely, from on high:
    When Saturn made me up my fardel, he
Put all these ills in.—'Tis a foolish lie:
    Thou art Fate's master, yet its slave wilt be

Thereof see Solomon his homily;
The wise, he says, no planets can oppress:
They and their influence own his mightiness.—
   Nay, as they've made me, so shall it fall out.—
What sayst thou?—'Tis the faith that I Profess.-
   I say no more.—And I can do without.

ENVOI

Wilt thou live long?—So God vouchsafe me, yes.—
Then must thou—What?—Repent; forswear idlesse
And study—What?—The lore of righteousness.—
   I'll not forget.—Forsake the motley rout
And to amendment straightway thee address:
Delay not till thou come to hopelessness.
   I say no more.—And I can do without.

BALLAD
WRITTEN BY VILLON UPON A SUBJECT
PROPOSED BY CHARLES DUC D'ORLEANS

I

I DIE of thirst, although the spring's at hand;
   Hot as a fire, my teeth with cold do shake:
In my own town, I'm in a foreign land;
   Hard by a burning brazier do I quake;
   Clad like a king, yet naked as a snake.
I laugh through tears, expect sans hope soe'er
And comfort take amiddleward despair;
   Glad, though I joy in nought beneath the sun,
Potent am I, and yet as weak as air;
   Well entertained, rebuffed of every one.

II

Nought's dim to me save what I understand;
   Uncertain things alone for sure I take;
I doubt but facts that all unquestioned stand;
   I'm only wise by chance for a whim's sake;

"Give you good-night!" I say, whenas I wake;
Lying at my length, of falling I beware;
I've goods enough, yet not a crown to spare!
  Leave off a loser, though I still have won;
Await bequests, although to none I'm heir;
  Well entertained, rebuffed of every one.

III

I care for nought, yet all my life I've planned
  Goods to acquire, although I've none at stake;
They speak me fairest, by whom most I'm banned,
  And truest, who most mock of me do make:
  He is my friend, who causes me mistake
Black ravens for white swans and foul for fair;
Who doth me hurt, I hold him debonair;
  'Twixt truth and lying difference see I none;
Nought I conceive, yet all in mind I bear;
  Well entertained, rebuffed of every one.

Envoi

Most clement Prince, I'd have you be aware
That I'm like all and yet apart and rare;
  Much understand, yet wit and knowledge shun:
To have my wage again is all my care;
  Well entertained, rebuffed of every one.

BALLAD OF VILLON'S REQUEST TO THE DUC DE BOURBON

I

Gracious my lord and prince of mickle dread,
  Flower of the Lily, Royal progeny,
François Villon, whom dule and teen have led
  To the blind strokes of Fate to bend the knee,
Sues by this humble writing unto thee,

That thou wilt of thy grace to him make loan.
Before all courts his debit he will own:
  Doubt not but he thy right will satisfy,
With interest thereunder due and grown:
  Nothing but waiting shalt thou lose thereby.

II

Of no prince has thy creature borrowéd,
  Save of thyself, a single penny fee:
The six poor crowns were wholly spent in bread,
  That whiles thy favour did advance to me.
  All shall be paid together, I agree,
And that right soon, ere many days be flown;
For if in Patay wood are acorns known
  Or chestnuts thereabouts folk sell and buy
In season thou shalt have again thine own:
  Nothing but waiting shalt thou lose thereby.

III

If I could sell my youth and lustihead
  Unto the Lombards, usurers that be,
Lack-gold has brought me to such piteous stead,
  I do believe I should the venture dree.
  In purse or belt no money can I see:
I wonder what it is, by God His throne!
For unto me, save it be wood or stone,
  No cross at all appears,—I do not lie:
But, if the true cross once to me be shown,
  Nothing but waiting shalt thou lose thereby.

ENVOI

Prince of the Lys, that lov'st good deeds alone,
Think'st thou it has not cost me many a groan
  That I can not to my intent draw nigh?
Give ear, if it so please thee, to my moan:
  Nothing but waiting shalt thou lose thereby.

SUNDRY POEMS
ATTRIBUTED TO VILLON

HERE FOLLOW SUNDRY POEMS COMMONLY
ATTRIBUTED TO MASTER FRANÇOIS
VILLON

ROUNDEL

Farewell, I say, with tearful eye.
  Farewell, the dearest sweet to see!
  Farewell, o'er all the kindest she!
Farewell, with heavy heart say I.
Farewell, my love, my soul, good-bye!
  My poor heart needs must part from thee:
Farewell, I say, with tearful eye.

Farewell, by whose default I die
  Deaths more than told of tongue can be:
  Farewell, of all the world to me
Whom most I blame and hold most high!
  Farewell, I say, with tearful eye.

A MERRY BALLAD OF VINTNERS

I

By dint of dart, by push of sharpened spear,
  By sweep of scythe or thump of spike-set mace,
By poleaxe, steel-tipped arrow-head or shear
  Of double-handed sword or well-ground ace,

By dig of dirk or tuck with double face,
Let them be done to death; or let them light
On some ill stead, where brigands lurk by night,
    That they the hearts from out their breasts may
        tear,
  Cut off their heads, then drag them by the hair
And cast them on the dunghill to the swine,
    That sows and porkers on their flesh may fare,
The vintners that put water in our wine.

II

Let Turkish quarrels run them through the rear
  And rapiers keen their guts and vitals lace;
Singe their perukes with Greek fire, ay, and sear
    Their brains with levins; string them brace by
        brace
    Up to the gibbet; or for greater grace,
Let gout and dropsy slay the knaves outright:
Or else let drive into each felon wight
    Irons red-heated in the furnace-flare:
    Let half a score of hangmen flay them bare;
And on the morrow, seethed in oil or brine,
    Let four great horses rend them then and there,
The vintners that put water in our wine.

III

Let some great gunshot blow their heads off sheer;
  Let thunders catch them in the market-place;
Let rend their limbs and cast them far and near,
    For dogs to batten on their bodies base;
    Or let the lightning-stroke their sight efface.
Frost, hail and snow let still upon them bite;
Strip off their clothes and leave them naked quite,
    For rain to drench them in the open air;
    Lard them with knives and poniards and then bear
Their carrion forth and soak it in the Rhine;
    Break all their bones with mauls and do not spare
The vintners that put water in our wine.

Envoi

Prince, may God curse their vitals! is my prayer;
  And may they burst with venom all, in fine,
These traitorous thieves, accursèd and unfair,
  The vintners that put water in our wine.

BALLAD OF THE TREE OF LOVE

I

I have within my heart of hearts a tree,
  A plant of Love, fast rooted therewithin,
That bears no fruit, save only misery;
  Hardship its leaves and trouble its flowers bin.
  But, since to set it there Love did begin,
It hath so mightily struck root and spread
That, for its shadow, all my cheer is fled
  And all my joys do wither and decay:
Yet win I not, of all my lustihead,
  Other to plant or tear the old away.

II

Year after year, its branches watered be
  With tears as bitter and as salt as sin;
And yet its fruits no fairer are to see
  Nor any comfort therefrom can I win:
  Yet pluck I them among the leavis thin;
My heart thereon full bitterly is fed,
That better had lain fallow, ay, or dead,
  Than to bear fruits of poison and dismay:
But Love his law allows me not instead
  Other to plant or tear the old away.

III

If, in this time of May, when wood and lea
  Are broidered all with leaves and blossoms sheen,
Love would vouchsafe this succour unto me,—
    To prune away the boughs that lie between,
    That so the sun among the buds be seen,
And imp thereon some graft of goodlihead,—
Full many a pleasant burgeon would it shed,
  Whence joy should issue, lovelier than the day;
And no more where despair solicitèd
  Other to plant or tear the old away.

Envoi

Dear my Princess, my chiefest hope and dread,
Whom my heart serves in penitential stead,
  The woes that harrow it do thou allay
And suffer not thy constant thought be led
  Other to plant or tear the old away.

BALLAD OF LADIES' LOVE

No. 1

I

WELL enough favoured and with substance still
  Some little stored, chance brought me 'neath love's
    spell
And day and night, until I had my will,
  I pined in languor unendurable:
  I loved a damsel more than I can tell;
But, with good luck and rose-nobles a score,
I had what men of maids have had before.
  Then, in myself considering, I did say:
"Love sets by pleasant speech but little store;
  The wealthy gallant always gains the day."

II

So chanced in that, whilst coin my purse did fill,
  The world went merry as a marriage bell
And I was all in all with her, until,
  Without word said, my wanton's loose eyes fell
  Upon a graybeard, rich but foul as hell:
A man more hideous never woman bore.
But what of that? He had his will and more;
  And I, confounded, stricken with dismay,
Upon this text went glosing passing sore:
  "The wealthy gallant always gains the day."

III

Now she did wrong; for never had she ill
  Or spite of me: I cherished her so well
That, had she asked me for the moon, my skill
  I had essayed to storm heaven's citadel.
  Yet, of sheer vice, her body did she sell
Unto the service of that satyr hoar:
The which I seeing, of my clerkly lore
  I made and sent to her a piteous lay:
And she: "Lack-gold undid thee": words but four.
  The wealthy gallant always gains the day.

ENVOI

Fair Prince, more skilled than any one of yore
In pleasant speech, look thou have coin galore
  Within thy pouch: as Meung that clerk so gay
And wise, hath told us, in the amorous war
  The wealthy gallant always gains the day.

BALLAD OF LADIES' LOVE

No. 2

I

WHOSO in love would bear the bell,
  Needs must he prank him gallantly,
Swagger and ruffle it, bold and snell,
  And when to his lady's sight comes he,
  Don cloth of gold and embroidery;
For ladies liken a goodly show.
  This should serve well; but, by Marie,
Not all can nick it that will, heigho!

II

Once on a season in love I fell
  With a lady gracious and sweet to see,
Who spoke me fair, that she liked me well
  And gladly would hearken to my plea,
  But first I must give to her for fee
Fifty gold crowns, nor less nor mo'.
  Fifty gold crowns?—O' right good gree!
Not all can nick it that will, heigho!

III

To bed I went with the damsel
  And there four times right merrily
I did to her what I may not tell
  In less than an hour and a half, perdie.
  Then with a failing voice said she,
"Once more, I prithee! my heart is woe."
  Once more, quotha, sweetheart? Ah me,
Not all can nick it that will, heigho!

Envoi

Great God of love, I crave of thee,
If ever again I lay her low,
Ne'er let my lance untempered ᴏᴇ.
Not all can nick it that will, heigho!

HERE ENDETH THE ʙOOK OF THE ʏOEMS
OF MASTER FRANÇOIS VILLON

MISCELLANEOUS TRANSLATIONS

THREE TRANSLATIONS BY
DANTE GABRIEL ROSSETTI

I

THE BALLAD OF DEAD LADIES

TELL me now in what hidden way is
   Lady Flora the lovely Roman?
Where's Hipparchia, and where is Thaïs,
   Neither of them the fairer woman?
   Where is Echo, beheld of no man,
Only heard on river and mere,—
   She whose beauty was more than human? . . .
But where are the snows of yester-year?

Where's Héloise, the learned nun,
   For whose sake Abeillard, I ween,
, Lost manhood and put priesthood on?
   (From Love he won such dule and teen!)
   And where, I pray you, is the Queen
Who willed that Buridan should steer
   Sewed in a sack's mouth down the Seine? . . .
But where are the snows of yester-year?

White Queen Blanche, like a queen of lilies,
   With a voice like any mermaiden,—
Bertha Broadfoot, Beatrice, Alice,
   And Ermengarde the lady of Maine,—
   And that good Joan whom Englishmen
At Rouen doomed and burned her there,—
   Mother of God, where are they then? . . .
But where are the snows of yester-year?

Nay, never ask this week, fair lord,
  Where they are gone, nor yet this year,
Save with this much for an overword,—
  But where are the snows of yester-year?

II

TO DEATH OF HIS LADY

DEATH, of thee do I make my moan,
  Who hadst my lady away from me,
  Nor wilt assuage thine enmity
Till with her life thou hast mine own;
For since that hour my strength has flown.
  Lo! what wrong was her life to thee,
                    Death?

Two we were, and the heart was one;
  Which now being dead, dead I must be,
  Or seem alive as lifelessly
As in the choir the painted stone,
                    Death!

III

HIS MOTHER'S SERVICE TO OUR LADY

LADY of Heaven and earth, and therewithal
  Crowned Empress of the nether clefts of Hell,—
I, thy poor Christian, on thy name do call,
  Commending me to thee, with thee to dwell,
  Albeit in nought I be commendable.
But all mine undeserving may not mar
Such mercies as thy sovereign mercies are;
  Without the which (as true words testify)
No soul can reach thy Heaven so fair and far.
  Even in this faith I choose to live and die.

Unto thy Son say thou that I am His,
  And to me graceless make Him gracious.
Sad Mary of Egypt lacked not of that bliss,
  Nor yet the sorrowful clerk Theophilus,
  Whose bitter sins were set aside even thus
Though to the Fiend his bounden service was.
Oh help me, lest in vain for me should pass
  (Sweet Virgin that shalt have no loss thereby!)
The blessed Host and sacring of the Mass.
  Even in this faith I choose to live and die.

A pitiful poor woman, shrunk and old,
  I am, and nothing learn'd in letter-lore.
Within my parish-cloister I behold
  A painted Heaven where harps and lutes adore,
  And eke an Hell whose damned folk seethe full sore:
One bringeth fear, the other joy to me.
That joy, great Goddess, make thou mine to be,—
  Thou of whom all must ask it even as I;
And that which faith desires, that let it see.
  For in this faith I choose to live and die.

O excellent Virgin Princess! thou didst bear
  King Jesus, the most excellent comforter,
Who even of this our weakness craved a share
  And for our sake stooped to us from on high,
Offering to death His young life sweet and fair.
Such as He is, Our Lord, I Him declare,
  And in this faith I choose to live and die.

TEN TRANSLATIONS BY ALGERNON CHARLES SWINBURNE

I

THE COMPLAINT OF THE FAIR ARMOURESS

I

MESEEMETH I heard cry and groan
  That sweet who was the armourer's maid;
For her young years she made sore moan,
  And right upon this wise she said;
"Ah fierce old age with foul bald head,
To spoil fair things thou art over fain;
  Who holdeth me? who? would God I were dead!
Would God I were well dead and slain!

II

"Lo, thou hast broken the sweet yoke
  That my high beauty held above
All priests and clerks and merchant-folk;
  There was not one but for my love
  Would give me gold and gold enough,
Though sorrow his very heart had riven,
  To win from me such wage thereof
As now no thief would take if given.

III

"I was right chary of the same,
  God wot it was my great folly,
For love of one sly knave of them,
  Good store of that same sweet had he;

For all my subtle wiles, perdie,
God wot I loved him well enow;
  Right evilly handled me,
But he loved well my gold, I trow.

IV

"Though I gat bruises green and black,
  I loved him never the less a jot;
Though he bound burdens on my back,
  If he said, 'Kiss me, and heed it not,'
  Right little pain I felt, God wot,
When that foul thief's mouth, found so sweet,
  Kissed me—Much good thereof I got!
I keep the sin and the shame of it.

V

"And he died thirty year agone.
  I am old now, no sweet thing to see;
By God, though, when I think thereon,
  And of that good glad time, woe's me,
  And stare upon my changed body
Stark naked, that has been so sweet,
  Lean, wizen, like a small dry tree,
I am nigh mad with the pain of it.

VI

"Where is my faultless forehead's white,
  The lifted eyebrows, soft gold hair,
Eyes wide apart and keen of sight,
  With subtle skill in the amorous air;
  The straight nose, great nor small, but fair,
The small carved ears of shapeliest growth,
  Chin dimpling, colour good to wear,
And sweet red splendid kissing mouth?

VII

"The shapely slender shoulders small,
　Long arms, hands wrought in glorious wise,
Round little breasts, the hips withal
　High, full of flesh, not scant of size,
　Fit for all amorous masteries;

*　　　*　　　*　　　*　　　*
　*　　*　　*　　*　　　*
*　　　*　　　*　　　*　　　*

VIII

"A writhled forehead, hair gone grey,
　Fallen eyebrows, eyes gone blind and red,
Their laughs and looks all fled away,
　Yea, all that smote men's hearts are fled;
　The bowed nose, fallen from goodlihead;
Foul flapping ears like water-flags;
　Peaked chin, and cheeks all waste and dead,
And lips that are two skinny rags:

IX

"Thus endeth all the beauty of us.
　The arms made short, the hands made lean,
The shoulders bowed and ruinous,
　The breasts, alack! all fallen in;
The flanks too, like the breasts, grown thin:
*　　*　　*　　*　　*
　For the lank thighs, no thighs but skin,
They are specked with spots like sausage-meat.

X

"So we make moan for the old sweet days,
　Poor old light women, two or three
Squatting above the straw-fire's blaze,
　The bosom crushed against the knee,

Like fagots on a heap we be,
Round fires soon lit, soon quenched and done;
And we were once so sweet, even we!
Thus fareth many and many an one."

II

A DOUBLE BALLAD OF GOOD COUNSEL

Now take your fill of love and glee,
        And after balls and banquets hie;
In the end ye'll get no good for fee,
        But just heads broken by and by;
        Light loves make beasts of men that sigh;
They changed the faith of Solomon,
        And left not Samson lights to spy;
Good luck has he that deals with none!

Sweet Orpheus, lord of minstrelsy,
        For this with flute and pipe came nigh
The danger of the dog's heads three
        That ravening at hell's door doth lie;
        Fain was Narcissus, fair and shy,
For love's love lightly lost and won,
        In a deep well to drown and die;
Good luck has he that deals with none!

Sardana, flower of chivalry,
        Who conquered Crete with horn and cry,
For this was fain a maid to be
        And learn with girls the thread to ply;
        King David, wise in prophecy,
Forgot the fear of God for one
        Seen washing either shapely thigh;
Good luck has he that deals with none!

For this did Amnon, craftily
        Feigning to eat of cakes of rye,
Deflower his sister fair to see,
        Which was foul incest; and hereby

Was Herod moved, it is no lie,
To lop the head of Baptist John
For dance and jig and psaltery;
Good luck has he that deals with none!

Next of myself I tell, poor me,
How thrashed like clothes at wash was I
Stark naked, I must needs agree;
Who made me eat so sour a pie
But Katherine of Vaucelles? thereby
Noé took third part of that fun;
Such wedding-gloves are ill to buy;
Good luck has he that deals with none!

But for that young man fair and free
To pass those young maids lightly by,
Nay, would you burn him quick, not he;
Like broom-horsed witches though he fry,
They are sweet as civet in his eye;
But trust them, and you're fooled anon;
For white or brown, and low or high,
Good luck has he that deals with none!

III

FRAGMENT ON DEATH

AND Paris be it or Helen dying,
Who dies soever, dies with pain.
He that lacks breath and wind for sighing,
His gall bursts on his heart; and then
He sweats, God knows what sweat! again,
No man may ease him of his grief;
Child, brother, sister, none were fain
To bail him thence for his relief.

Death makes him shudder, swoon, wax pale,
    Nose bend, veins stretch, and breath surrender,
Neck swell, flesh soften, joints that fail
    Crack their strained nerves and arteries slender.
    O woman's body found so tender,
Smooth, sweet, so precious in men's eyes,
    Must thou too bear such count to render
Yes; or pass quick into the skies.

IV

BALLAD OF THE LORDS OF OLD TIME

(AFTER THE FORMER ARGUMENT)

WHAT more? Where is the third Calixt,
    Last of that name now dead and gone,
Who held four years the Papalist?
    Alfonso king of Aragon,
    The gracious lord, duke of Bourbon,
And Arthur, duke of old Britaine?
    And Charles the Seventh, that worthy one?
Even with the good knight Charlemain.

The Scot too, king of mount and mist,
    With half his face vermilion,
Men tell us, like an amethyst
    From brow to chin that blazed and shone;
    The Cypriote king of old renown,
Alas! and that good king of Spain,
    Whose name I cannot think upon?
Even with the good knight Charlemain.

No more to say of them I list;
    'Tis all but vain, all dead and done;
For death may no man born resist,
    Nor make appeal when death comes on.

I make yet one more question;
Where's Lancelot, king of far Bohain?
    Where's he whose grandson called him son?
Even with the good knight Charlemain.

Where is Guesclin, the good Breton?
    The lord of the eastern mountain-chain,
And the good late duke of Alençon?
    Even with good knight Charlemain.

V

BALLAD OF THE WOMEN OF PARIS

ALBEIT the Venice girls get praise
    For their sweet speech and tender air,
And though the old women have wise ways
    Of chaffering for amorous ware,
    Yet at my peril dare I swear,
Search Rome, where God's grace mainly tarries,
    Florence and Savoy, everywhere,
There's no good girl's lip out of Paris.

The Naples women, as folk prattle,
    Are sweetly spoken and subtle enough:
German girls are good at tattle,
    And Prussians make their boast thereof;
    Take Egypt for the next remove,
Or that waste land the Tartar harries,
    Spain or Greece, for the matter of love,
There's no good girl's lip out of Paris.

Breton and Swiss know nought of the matter,
    Gascony girls or girls of Toulouse;
Two fishwomen with a half-hour's chatter
    Would shut them up by threes and twos;
    Calais, Lorraine, and all their crews,
(Names enow the mad song marries)
    England and Picardy, search them and choose,
There's no good girl's lip out of Paris.

Prince, give praise to our French ladies
  For the sweet sound their speaking carries;
'Twixt Rome and Cadiz many a maid is,
  But no good girl's lip out of Paris.

VI

BALLAD WRITTEN FOR A BRIDEGROOM

WHICH VILLON GAVE TO A GENTLEMAN NEWLY MAR-
RIED TO SEND TO HIS WIFE WHOM HE HAD
WON WITH THE SWORD

AT daybreak, when the falcon claps his wings,
  No whit for grief, but noble heart and high
With loud glad noise he stirs himself and springs,
  And takes his meat and toward his lure draws nigh;
  Such good I wish you! Yea, and heartily
I am fired with hope of true love's meed to get;
  Know that Love writes it in his book; for why,
This is the end for which we twain are met.

Mine own heart's lady with no gainsayings
  You shall be always wholly till I die;
And in my right against all bitter things
  Sweet laurel with fresh rose its force shall try;
  Seeing reason wills not that I cast love by
(Nor here with reason shall I chide or fret)
  Nor cease to serve, but serve more constantly;
This is the end for which we twain are met.

And, which is more, when grief about me clings
  Through Fortune's fit or fume of jealousy,
Your sweet kind eye beats down her threatenings
  As wind doth smoke; such power sits in your eye.
  Thus in your field my seed of harvestry
Thrives, for the fruit is like me that I set;
  God bids me tend it with good husbandry;
This is the end for which we twain are met.

Princess, give ear to this my summary;
    That heart of mine your heart's love should forget,
Shall never be: like trust in you put I:
    This is the end for which we twain are met.

VII

BALLAD AGAINST THE ENEMIES OF FRANCE

MAY he fall in with beasts that scatter fire,
    Like Jason, when he sought the fleece of gold,
Or change from man to beast three years entire,
    As King Nebuchadnezzar did of old;
Or else have times as shameful and as bad
As Trojan folk for ravished Helen had;
Or gulfed with Proserpine and Tantalus
Let hell's deep fen devour him dolorous,
    With worse to bear than Job's worst sufferance,
Bound in his prison-maze with Dædalus,
    Who could wish evil to the state of France!

May he four months, like bitterns in the mire,
    Howl with head downmost in the lake-springs
        cold
Or to bear harness like strong bulls for hire
    To the Great Turk for money down be sold;
Or thirty years like Magdalen live sad,
With neither wool nor web of linen clad;
Drown like Narciss', or swing down pendulous
Like Absalom with locks luxurious,
    Or liker Judas fallen to reprobance;
Or find such death as Simon sorcerous,
    Who could wish evil to the state of France!

May the old times come of fierce Octavian's ire,
    And in his belly molten coin be told;
May he like Victor in the mill expire,
    Crushed between moving millstones on him rolled,

Or in deep sea drenched breathless, more adrad
Than in the whale's bulk Jonas, when God bade:
From Phœbus' light, from Juno's treasure-house
Driven, and from joys of Venus amorous,
    And cursed of God most high to the utterance,
As was the Syrian king Antiochus,
    Who could wish evil to the state of France!

ENVOY

Prince, may the bright-winged brood of Æolus
To sea-king Glaucus' wild wood cavernous
    Bear him bereft of peace and hope's least glance,
For worthless is he to get good of us,
    Who could wish evil to the state of France!

VIII

THE DISPUTE OF THE HEART AND BODY
OF FRANCOIS VILLON

WHO is this I hear?—Lo, this is I, thine heart,
    That holds on merely now by a slender string.
Strength fails me, shape and sense are rent apart,
    The blood in me is turned to a bitter thing,
    Seeing thee skulk here like a dog shivering.—
Yea, and for what?—For that thy sense found
        sweet.—
What irks it thee?—I feel the sting of it.—
    Leave me at peace.—Why?—Nay now, leave me
        at peace;
I will repent when I grow ripe in wit.—
    I say no more.—I care not though thou cease.—

What art thou, trow?—A man worth praise perfay.—
    This is thy thirtieth year of wayfaring.—
'Tis a mule's age.—Art thou a boy still?—Nay.—
    Is it hot lust that spurs thee with its sting,

Grasping thy throat? Know'st thou not any-
    thing?—
Yea, black and white, when milk is specked with flies,
I can make out.—No more?—Nay, in no wise.
Shall I begin again the count of these?—
Thou art undone.—I will make shift to rise.—
    I say no more.—I care not though thou cease.—

I have the sorrow of it, and thou the smart.
  Wert thou a poor mad fool or weak of wit,
Then might'st thou plead this pretext with thine heart;
  But if thou know not good from evil a whit
  Either thy head is hard as stone to hit,
Or shame, not honour, gives thee most content.
What canst thou answer to this argument?—
  When I am dead I shall be well at ease.—
God! what good luck!—Thou art over eloquent.—
    I say no more.—I care not though thou cease.—

Whence is this ill?—From sorrow and not from sin.
  When Saturn packed my wallet up for me
I well believe he put these ills therein.—
  Fool, wilt thou make thy servant lord of thee?
  Hear now the wise king's counsel; thus saith he;
All power upon the stars a wise man hath;
There is no planet that shall do him scathe.—
  Nay, as they made me I grow and I decrease.—
What say'st thou?—Truly this is all my faith.—
    I say no more.—I care not though thou cease.—

Wouldst thou live still?—God help me that I may!—
Then thou must—What? turn penitent and pray?—
Read always—What?—Grave words and good to say;
  Leave off the ways of fools, lest they displease.—
Good; I will do it.—Wilt thou remember?—Yea.—
Abide not till there come an evil day.
    I say no more.—I care not though thou cease.

IX

EPISTLE IN FORM OF A BALLAD TO HIS FRIENDS

HAVE pity, pity, friends, have pity on me,
  Thus much at least, may it please you, of your
    grace!
I lie not under hazel or hawthorn-tree
  Down in this dungeon ditch, mine exile's place
  By leave of God and fortune's foul disgrace.
Girls, lovers, glad young folk and newly wed,
Jumpers and jugglers, tumbling heel o'er head,
  Swift as a dart, and sharp as needle-ware,
Throats clear as bells that ring the kine to shed,
  Your poor old friend, what, will you leave him
    there?

Singers that sing at pleasure, lawlessly,
  Light, laughing, gay of word and deed, that race
And run like folk light-witted as ye be
  And have in hand nor current coin nor base,
  Ye wait too long, for now he's dying apace.
Rhymers of lays and roundels sung and read,
Ye'll brew him broth too late when he lies dead.
  Nor wind nor lightning, sunbeam nor fresh air,
May pierce the thick wall's bound where lies his bed;
  Your poor old friend, what, will you leave him there?

O noble folk from tithes and taxes free,
  Come and behold him in this piteous case,
Ye that nor king nor emperor holds in fee,
  But only God in heaven; behold his face
  Who needs must fast, Sundays and holidays,

Which makes his teeth like rakes; and when he hath
  fed
With never a cake for banquet but dry bread,
Must drench his bowels with much cold watery fare,
With board nor stool, but low on earth instead;
Your poor old friend, what, will you leave him there?

Princes afore-named, old and young foresaid,
Get me the king's seal and my pardon sped,
  And hoist me in some basket up with care:
So swine will help each other ill bested,
For where one squeaks they run in heaps ahead.
  Your poor old friend, what, will you leave him
    there?

X

THE EPITAPH IN FORM OF A BALLAD

WHICH VILLON MADE FOR HIMSELF AND HIS COM-
  RADES, EXPECTING TO BE HANGED ALONG WITH
  THEM

MEN, brother men, that after us yet live,
  Let not your hearts too hard against us be;
For if some pity of us poor men ye give,
  The sooner God shall take of you pity.
  Here are we five or six strung up, you see,
And here the flesh that all too well we fed
Bit by bit eaten and rotten, rent and shred,
  And we the bones grow dust and ash withal;
Let no man laugh at us discomforted,
  But pray to God that he forgive us all.

If we call on you, brothers, to forgive,
  Ye should not hold our prayer in scorn, though we
Were slain by law; ye know that all alive
  Have not wit alway to walk righteously;

Make therefore intercession heartily
With him that of a virgin's womb was bred,
That his grace be not as a dry well-head
    For us, nor let hell's thunder on us fall;
We are dead, let no man harry or vex us dead,
    But pray to God that he forgive us all.

The rain has washed and laundered us all five,
    And the sun dried and blackened; yea, perdie,
Ravens and pies with beaks that rend and rive
    Have dug our eyes out, and plucked off for fee
    Our beards and eyebrows; never we are free,
Not once, to rest; but here and there still sped,
Drive at its wild will by the wind's change led,
    More pecked of birds than fruits on garden-wall;
Men, for God's love, let no gibe here be said,
    But pray to God that he forgive us all.

Prince Jesus, that of all art lord and head,
Keep us, that hell be not our bitter bed;
    We have nought to do in such a master's hall.
Be not ye therefore of our fellowhead,
    But pray to God that he forgive us all.

FROM VILLON

By ARTHUR SYMONS [1]

No, I am not, as others are,
Child of the angels, with a wreath
Of planets or of any star.
My father's dead, and lies beneath
The churchyard stone: God rest his breath!
I know that my poor old mother
(And she too knows) must come to death,
And that her son must follow her.

I know that rich and poor and all,
Foolish and wise, and priest and lay,
Mean folk and noble, great and small,
High and low, fair and foul, and they
That wear rich clothing on the way,
Being of whatever stock or stem,
And are coiffed newly every day,
Death shall take every one of them.

Paris and Helen are both dead.
Whoever dies, dies with much pain;
For when his wind and breath are sped
His gall breaks on his heart, and then
He sweats, God knows that sweat of men!
Then shall he pray against his doom
Child, brother, sister, all in vain:
None will be surety in his room.

Death makes him tremble and turn pale,
His veins stretch and his nose fall in,
His flesh grow moist and his neck swell,
Joints and nerves lengthen and wax thin;

---

[1] "Knave of Hearts" by Arthur Symons, 1913.

Body of woman, that hath been
Soft, tender, precious, smooth and even,
Most thou be spoiled in bone and skin?
Yes, or else go alive to heaven.

VILLONAUD FOR THIS YULE [1]

By EZRA POUND

Towards the Noël that morte saison
(Christ make the shepherds' homage dear!)
Then when the grey wolves everychone
Drink of the winds their chill small-beer
And lap o' the snows food's gueredon
Then makyth my heart his yule-tide cheer
(Skoal! with the dregs if the clear be gone!)
Wineing the ghosts of yester-year.

Ask ye what ghosts I dream upon?
(What of the magians' scented gear?)
The ghosts of dead loves everyone
That make the stark winds reek with fear
Lest love return with the foison sun
And slay the memories that me cheer
(Such as I drink to mine fashion)
Wineing the ghosts of yester-year.

Where are the joys my heart had won
(Saturn and Mars to Zeus drawn near!) [2]
Where are the lips mine lay upon,
Aye, where are the glances feat and clear
That bade my heart his valour don?
I skoal to the eyes as grey-blown mere
(Who knows whose was that paragon?)
Wineing the ghosts of yester-year.

Prince: ask me not what I have done
Nor what God had that can me cheer
But ye ask first where the winds are gone
Wineing the ghosts of yester-year.

---

[1] From "Personæ" by Ezra Pound, 1909.
[2] Signum Nativitatis.

A VILLONAUD BALLAD OF THE GIBBET [1]

Or the Song of the Sixth Companion

By EZRA POUND

SCENE: "En cest bourdel ou tenoms nostr estat."

It being remembered that there were six of us with Master
Villon, when that expecting presently to be hanged he writ a
ballad whereof ye know:

"Frerés humains qui aprés nous vivez."

Drink ye a skoal for the gallows tree!
François and Margot and thee and me,
Drink we the comrades merrily
That said us, "Till then" for the gallows tree!
    Fat Pierre with the hook gauche-main,
Thomas Larron "Ear-the-less,"
Tybalde and that armouress
Who gave this poignard its premier stain
Pinning the Guise that had been fain
To make him a mate of the "Haulte Noblesse"
And bade her be out with ill address
As a fool that mocketh his drue's disdeign.

    Drink we a skoal for the gallows tree!
François and Margot and thee and me,
Drink we to Marienne Ydole,
That hell brenn not her o'er cruelly.

    Drink we the lusty robbers twain,
Black is the pitch o' their wedding dress. [2]

---

[1] From "Personæ" by Ezra Pound, 1909.
[2] Certain gibbeted corpses used to be coated with tar as a
preservative; thus one scarecrow served as warning for considerable time. See Hugo, "L'Homme qui Rit."

Lips shrunk back for the wind's caress
As lips shrink back when we feel the strain
Of love that loveth in hell's disdeign
And sense the teeth through the lips that press
'Gainst our lips for the soul's distress
That striveth to ours across the pain.
Drink we skoal to the gallows tree!
François and Margot and thee and me,
For Jehan and Raoul de Vallerie
Whose frames have the night and its winds in fee.

Maturin, Guillaume, Jacques d'Allmain,
Culdou lacking a coat to bless
One lean moiety of his nakedness
That plundered St. Hubert back o' the fane:
Aie! the lean bare tree is widowed again
For Michault le Borgne that would confess
In "faith and troth" to a traitoress,
"Which of his brothers had he slain?"

But drink we skoal to the gallows tree!
François and Margot and thee and me:

These that we loved shall God love less
And smite alway at their faibleness?

Skoal!! to the Gallows! and then pray we:
God damn his hell out speedily
And bring their souls to his "Haulte Citee."

The end of this volume